Inclusive Lesson Plans Throughout the Year

Laverne Warner, Sharon Lynch, Diana Nabors and
Cynthia Simpson

Dedication

This book is dedicated to the community of learners at Sam Houston State University and the children who have taught us so much over the years.

Table of Contents

Chapter 3—Winter Themes

Chapter 5—Summer Themes

JUST FOR FUN

GAMES AND SPORTS

LET'S PRETEND

Introduction

Good teachers plan. Just as architects use blueprints, doctors and dentists use x-rays, and pilots use flight plans, effective teachers organize for instruction. They think about what they want to teach, how they want to teach it, and when they will teach it. Implementing effective instruction requires forethought, time, and knowledge of children.

Inclusive Lesson Plans Throughout the Year is designed for both veteran and novice teachers who have a classroom with a child (or children) with special needs, or who have a classroom of typically developing children. This resource provides appropriate lesson plans that are useful to both novice and veteran teachers. This book will help new teachers develop plans, and provide veteran teachers with new ideas and approaches to add spark their classroom teaching.

Generally, early childhood teachers develop lesson plans using topics that relate to the month or season of the year. These topics focus on things that children encounter in their daily lives and that they find interesting. For example, studying the changes in trees and leaves in fall develops the children's curiosity about their environment. Making Valentine's cards in February relates to typical activities on Valentine's Day, thus enhancing children's social knowledge. Learning about snow is best achieved when the first snowfall occurs. Having a lesson plan ready facilitates teachers' abilities to teach children about seasonal and everyday phenomena.

What Is Lesson Planning?

What does lesson planning mean? Basically, six components are essential for each lesson plan.
1. Objective(s) (what you want to teach)
2. Materials needed for the lesson
3. The lesson activity (or activities)
4. Review of the content (sometimes referred to as closure)
5. Assessment strategy (to determine what children learned from the lesson)
6. Curriculum extensions (multiple extensions of a lesson that connect the concept to other curricular areas)

Planning ensures that each component is included in the lesson. Writing objectives for every lesson shows teachers' understanding that good planning yields results. When a lesson is well planned with a specific objective (or objectives) in mind, then teachers are better able to demonstrate observable outcomes. In addition, if lessons aren't going well, teachers can notice the problems and adjust accordingly. They might modify the activity, spontaneously choose another activity, or they might abandon the lesson, choosing to teach it at a later date. Planning follow-up activities in various centers is also easier if the learning objective(s) is clear.

Assessment strategies are a direct effort to determine children's knowledge and skill acquisition. In an era of accountability, all interested parties, including teachers and parents, want to know what children are learning.

Lesson plans are the foundation that keeps the day running smoothly from beginning to end. Teachers find planning helps keep children on task and motivated to learn. Once a concept has been introduced, teachers can determine whether children have acquired the knowledge and plan for additional exposure to the concept if necessary. Teachers are better able to communicate to parents the content children have received and provide feedback to them about whether children are learning the information.

Teachers also discover that planning ahead makes it more possible to meet the needs of all children. This book recognizes that all children learn in a variety of ways. No one lesson fits all children. If a child has autism, for example, modifications are needed to meet her or his needs. If teachers plan ahead, they can include lesson adaptations for every child in the group. *Inclusive Lesson Plans Throughout the Year* provides recommended modifications and accommodations that help teachers plan for all the children in the classroom.

Good teachers plan; great teachers plan and reflect. After the lesson is taught, a great teacher asks, "What went well? How can I improve this lesson? Did I meet Oralio's needs today? And Taylor's? What will I do differently next time I use this lesson?" If plans aren't working, then teachers need to develop alternative strategies to meet the needs of the children they serve.

Inclusive Lesson Plans Throughout the Year will be one of the resources you use to prepare lessons for your preschool classroom. No one resource is ever completely adequate for any classroom, but we are hopeful that what you find in this book will improve the quality of teaching in your classroom.

1 Lesson Planning

for Inclusive Early Childhood Classrooms

Planning for Children's Needs

The phrase "developmentally appropriate practice" means that the teaching strategies used and classroom activities planned for young children match their developmental needs and characteristics. Children should have experiences that allow them to feel competent as learners, and, at the same time, that are challenging enough to ensure that they are learning.

Planning to meet children's needs means that you, as the teacher or caregiver, know your children. If you are working in a kindergarten setting, you know that most five-year-olds are curious, active, social, spontaneous, and egocentric. When you plan for kindergartners, organize activities that will keep them busy, spark their creative and cognitive minds, and provide social experiences. Beyond that, you need to know individual children. For example, Martin is five, but he may be shy, reserved, quiet, intelligent, and methodic in his approach to learning, quite unlike his peers. As Martin's teacher, you plan activities to entice him and enhance his capacity for learning. As you plan for children, look at all aspects of children's development, taking into account individual differences.

Planning for children's needs also means focusing on all developmental domains, including physical (movement and physical activity), social and emotional (interactions with others), intellectual or cognitive (being challenged to learn), and creative (self-expression).

As you plan for children's learning, consider all aspects of children's development, including:
- providing activities that promote success in the classroom;
- encouraging important social and emotional skills essential to lifelong physical and mental health;
- developing age-appropriate expressive experiences; and
- allowing exploration and discovery to ensure that learning is meaningful and relevant.

Create diverse lesson plans that meet many of the children's needs, interests, and abilities. While listening to a book may not hold the interests of all of the children, reading about alligators (or any other animal that the children are interested in), then crawling like alligators, snapping mouths like alligators, and pretending to sleep or swim like alligators keeps the lesson alive and the children engaged. As an observant teacher, you know what children need and you plan accordingly.

Best Practices in Inclusive Early Childhood Classrooms

The principles that guide best practices include:

- developing topics of study that are relevant to the children you teach;
- allowing children as much choice as possible;
- limiting large-group experiences;
- providing activities that meet children's developmental needs;
- using centers and center play for child-directed play and instructional purposes;
- developing hands-on activities that allow children to work directly with objects and materials in their environment;
- utilizing individualized instruction as often as possible; and
- planning activities that offer multi-level challenges for children.

The guidelines suggest that every classroom varies in its approach to what constitutes "best practices." A teacher's class in urban Detroit is likely to be different in cultural makeup from a class of children in Del Rio, Texas. Appropriate classroom strategies begin with the children in the classroom and match the guidelines in diverse ways. Strategies for use in a classroom are detailed below.

Center Choices

Children need opportunities to make choices every day. Decision-making skills are developed as children decide which center to visit. Learning to select activities and staying with a choice offer important lessons.

Instructional Centers

While centers provide opportunities for child-directed play, some may be designed for specific instructional purposes. For example, a Writing Center allows children to explore and experiment with print. A Literacy Center shows how print is formed. Asking children to dictate their stories as you (or other helpers in the classroom) write them stresses the importance of being able to use and read print.

Discovery Centers

Set up special tables in the classroom to display materials related to a topic of study that children might otherwise overlook. For example, placing an Ant Farm and books about ants on a special table allows children to observe and find out about ants on their own, hence the name Discovery Center!

Group (or Circle) Times

Limit large group time. Presenting lessons early in the morning when children are fresh allows them to absorb information more easily. Keeping activities within lessons short (about 20 minutes) and to the point helps children gain maximum knowledge in a minimum of time. Overall, lessons should take no longer than 20 or 30 minutes. Vary activities within the lesson to accommodate children's needs across developmental domains.

Hands-On Experiences

Focus on hands-on activities that allow children to safely touch, taste, smell, and look closely at objects that are topics of classroom discussion. For example, if earthworms are the topic, try to bring earthworms to class. If feather pillows are a topic of discussion, bring in feather pillows for children to touch and smell. Cutting open and tasting a watermelon is far more engaging for children than simply looking at a picture of a watermelon. Hands-on experiences offer powerful learning opportunities.

Projects

Projects typically require several days or even weeks to complete; they accompany and relate to a topic and to children's interests. Examples include building a fire truck during a transportation theme, constructing a farm in the sandbox when learning about farm animals, making pretend musical instruments when talking about music and musicians, or acting out nursery rhymes.

Word Walls

Word Walls are permanent collections of words that are meaningful to children. Word Walls may be on chalkboards, on charts, or on large pieces of paper. As themes are introduced to children, write down words that accompany the themes to help children understand that print has meaning and that print is predictable. The words are pronounced the same way each time one sees them. Pairing pictures with words on the Word Wall helps children associate print with concepts.

Big Books

Big books are oversized children's books designed for use with groups of children. The pages and pictures are large, and the print is large. When you use big books, run your hands under the print to help children see specific words and understand that print has meaning. On pages 335-336 of the Appendix is a list of big book titles; some of these books are mentioned in specific lesson plans.

Individualized Instruction

Working one-on-one with children in various centers is the best way to approach and support their learning. Individualized instruction is as simple as helping a child put a puzzle together or sitting nearby and responding to children's questions on how to write certain letters. In inclusive classrooms, the need for individualized instruction is critical.

Planning the Classroom Environment

The classroom is children's home away from home as well as their learning environment. The classroom must be warm and inviting and packed with opportunities for the children to learn new concepts and practice developing ones. Set up classrooms that:

- are visually appealing,
- offer choices to all children,
- have logically arranged centers, and
- offer safe places to learn.

Visual Appeal

Every classroom should be an appealing work environment for you and an enticing learning environment for children. Rugs and mats add warmth to tile floors. Use natural light from windows as much as possible, and reduce the use of overhead lights (often fluorescent lighting). (You may need to change the light bulbs in your classroom if the glare interferes with children's learning.) The full spectrum of natural light and colors will add a warm, healthy glow to your classroom. Add decorations, including children's work and charts, around the classroom for display and to reinforce skills. Remember to place these displays at the children's eye level.

Walk around your classroom on your knees to see what the children see. You may be surprised to find that they have a different view of the room. You also want the room to be pleasant to other adults. When you put up material for adults, hang it at a level appropriate for them. Hanging things from the ceiling can be eye-appealing to children as they scan the total environment, but it is out of their line of sight as they work. Hang appropriate items from the ceiling, such as an art project of birds; rules, directions, or reinforcement items are not appropriate to hang from the ceiling.

Offer a Choice to All Children

In planning the layout of the classroom, it is important to designate places for large group activities, small group activities, and individual activities. The area for large group gatherings may include a cart or shelf. This is where you can keep your daily and weekly plans, folders for observational notes, and materials for that day's group lesson. The children will sit on the floor in this large group area, so displays and charts should be at their seated eye level. The space should be large enough for each child in the group to stand or sit without touching or bumping other children. A child's "bubble space" is the size of a small, invisible bubble that surrounds the child when seated cross-legged on the floor, making an "elbows in" circle around his or her body. When playing movement games, this "bubble space" expands to the size of full-arm circles around the child's body. To create a large enough space in the classroom for large group activities, visualize the number of children and their "bubble space" areas. Keep this large group area free of tables, chairs, open shelves, and anything else that may hinder children from participating in group activities.

Small group areas can be situated within activity centers or in portions of the large group area. Organize activity centers so the children will have a choice of activities. The total number of places in the activity centers should be at least one and one-half times the number of children in the classroom. For example, if there are 16 children in your class, plan to have at least 24 total places among the small group activities for children to select from. Each center should have a posted number of how many participants are allowed in that center, determined by the type of activity. For example, the space in the block area may allow for four to six children, where the Listening Center may only allow for two to four children. Arrange all materials in activity centers so they are easily accessible to all of the children, including children who are limited in physical abilities by either range of motion or size. Include all necessary materials in that center so the children do not need to leave the center to get what they need. Shelves and trays allow for easy access, neat organization, and simple cleanup of the materials.

Children need time to learn with others as well as time to learn alone. Many children can work together in an activity center, but some children may wish to have a space away from others to work on a project, read a book, or just think. It is important to plan for individual space for children. To meet the needs of the children in your classroom, you may need to set up both a quiet area with pillows to comfort a child and a table/chair area where a child can work on a difficult problem or puzzle. Not only is it important to provide individual learning areas, it is also important to provide an individual "home base" area for each child, a place where each child has his or her own space, whether a particular seat or rug on the floor or a cubby with a hook for his or her exclusive use. This gives each child ownership of a small place in the classroom, a physical spot that shows the child belongs in the class.

Arrangement of Centers

When children are fully engaged in play, some centers are louder than others. It is wise to separate the noisier centers, such as Home Living and Blocks, from the quieter centers, such as the Listening Center, which could be interrupted by the noise coming from the Block Center. Create a wave of sound in the classroom by placing noisier centers next to moderately noisy centers, which, in turn, are next to quiet centers. Then continue around the room with moderately noisy centers, then back to noisier centers. Locate messy centers that need water for cleanup near a classroom sink. Centers that need electricity, such as the Listening Center, should be near an electrical outlet to avoid stretching electrical cords across the room. During the course of the year, there will be changes to your centers. Add or remove materials from various centers as children grow in knowledge and experience. Some centers are specific to a particular topic or theme and are only set up in the classroom during the time of study.

Planning your classroom environment provides you and the children with an inviting place for learning. As you plan your classroom, lay out the centers on paper, prior to moving furniture. Don't be surprised if you need to shift some centers around once you have seen the centers come alive with children and learning opportunities.

Safety

Safety is always an important consideration in the early childhood classroom. In order to ensure a safe classroom, examine class materials and furniture every day. Remove any broken materials until they are repaired or replaced. Teaching children how to use materials properly in activity centers will reduce the likelihood of broken materials and help to ensure that no harm will come to them. But accidents do happen. Observation and monitoring keep children safe.

Maintaining visual contact with children is a must for assuring their safety, assessing their learning, and using inquiry to develop their learning. Low shelving and dividers between activity centers allow you to monitor all areas of the classroom wherever you are located.

Traffic flow in the classroom is another important consideration. Wide open spaces invite large, active movements; smaller areas invite more careful and planned movement. Placing the large group area on one side or corner of a classroom reduces the likelihood that children will run, hop, and dance their way to another center. Areas between activity centers must be free of items that may be accidentally stepped on or tripped over. This includes the arms, legs, and hands of other children. In each activity center, it is best to have the children engage in activities in a way that keeps their bodies and the materials they are using from spilling over into traffic areas. Define activity areas by placing colored tape on the floor or rugs in the activity center.

Including All Children: Modifications and Accommodations

Every child with a disability has the right to accommodations and modifications in order to succeed. For children with disabilities to be successful both socially and academically, they may require specific accommodations to lessons and instruction, as well as specific adaptations to the physical environment.

The Individuals with Disabilities Education Act (IDEA) identifies and defines disabilities that establish eligibility for special education services. The law states that children with disabilities should be served in the environment that is most like that of their non-disabled peers (least restrictive environment). This environment is often referred to as an inclusive setting.

For effective inclusion, you must be flexible, adaptable, and supportive of all children. You must be willing to make adaptations to the structure of the classroom and to your instructional style to ensure you are engaging children with disabilities and their non-disabled peers equally (SPeNCE, 2001). This section provides general guidelines and specific examples of instructional modifications and classroom accommodations.

General Characteristics of Children with Specific Disabilities

Children with specific disabilities are often lumped into one "disability category" without consideration of the type of disability that child may have. Children with special needs who are more commonly placed in inclusive early childhood classrooms are often put in the broad category of "higher-incidence" disabilities. Such disabilities include speech and language impairments, specific learning disabilities, emotional disturbance, and mental retardation. The degree of severity of each disability may vary from mild to more severe in nature. Children with low-incidence disabilities such as visual impairments, hearing impairments, orthopedic impairments, autism, other health impairments, and severe multiple impairments are less frequently placed in child care settings. However, in recent years, the number of children with lower-incidence disabilities in early childhood classrooms has been rising.

Although 13 disabilities are addressed in IDEA 2004, the following disability categories are more closely linked to the structure of this book. Although **Learning Disabilities** is a category identified in IDEA, it is not addressed in the accommodation sections of each lesson plan. For preschoolers, learning disabilities, when diagnosed, typically fall in the areas of listening comprehension and oral expression. Each chapter addresses accommodations for speech and language impairments.

In recent years, the number of children diagnosed with **Autism** has increased, and, thus, more children with autism are being enrolled in early childhood classrooms. Autism is classified as a developmental disability, generally becoming evident before the age of three. Children with autism typically have difficulty in communication and social interactions. They frequently demonstrate repetitive motor behaviors such as rocking or hand waving.

Children with **Speech and Language Disorders** are commonly cared for in inclusive classrooms. Children with such impairments tend to have problems in communication and in oral motor functions. Children with speech and language disorders may have impairments related specifically to the proper enunciation of specific sounds (articulation disorders) or language impairments that involve syntax or semantic errors in speech. Language disorders may also involve delayed language or limited vocabulary.

A Hearing Impairment, as referred to in this book, is an impairment in hearing that negatively affects a child's educational performance. This impairment is not so severe that a child could not hear speech and environmental sounds in the classroom when wearing a hearing aid. If the child cannot hear speech or environmental sounds, even with the help of a hearing aid, the child would be identified as deaf.

Another sensory impairment addressed within the accommodation section of the lesson plans is **Visual Impairment.** Children with visual impairments are identified as those children who, even with correction (such as glasses or contacts), experience limited vision that adversely affects their educational experience.

The National Dissemination Center for Children with Disabilities (NICHCY) defines **Mental Retardation** as "when a person has certain limitations in mental functioning and in skills such as communicating, taking care of him or herself, and social skills. These limitations will cause a child to learn and develop more slowly than a typical child. Children with mental retardation may take longer to learn to speak, walk, and take care of their personal needs such as dressing or eating." Mental retardation may or may not coexist with other specific disabilities such as speech and language Impairment, hearing impairment, or other health impairments. This book uses the term **Cognitive and/or Developmental Delays** rather than mental retardation because many early education programs do not diagnose mental retardation at young ages.

Emotional Disturbance is another disability identified under IDEA. Children identified with an emotional disturbance show one of the following problems for an extended period of time:

- a difficulty learning that is not due to lack of intelligence, problems with vision or hearing, or health problems;
- difficulty getting along with peers or teachers;
- inappropriate types of behavior or feelings under normal circumstances;
- an overall mood of unhappiness or depression that is not due to temporary problems in the home or in development; and
- a tendency to develop physical symptoms (for example, stomachaches or headaches) or fears associated with personal or school problems.

To be diagnosed as emotionally disturbed, a child demonstrates symptoms far beyond typical childhood behavior when experiencing a traumatic life event. Emotional disturbance is usually not the result of a single cause. It is often associated with a variety of factors, such as problems in the home, difficulty in school with developmental skills such as language and later academic skills, a family history of emotional problems, and environmental stressors. A psychologist diagnoses this disability. Although emotional disturbance is occasionally diagnosed in preschoolers, it is identified most often in the upper-elementary and middle school years.

Other Health Impairments refers to significant limitations in strength, vitality, or alertness that affect a child's learning. This disability can be the result of asthma, heart problems, diabetes, or other health issues, and includes children diagnosed with **Attention Deficit Hyperactivity Disorder** (ADHD). ADHD is diagnosed by a physician or psychologist, and includes children with serious problems with overactivity or attention, or both.

Children with **Orthopedic Impairments** have physical disabilities such as a loss of limb, cerebral palsy, or amputation that negatively affects their educational experience. Many children with specific Orthopedic Impairments use wheelchairs or other assistive devices for mobility.

The last specific disability is **Multiple Disabilities.** A child with multiple disabilities possesses a combination of specific disabilities; for example, an orthopedic disability and mental retardation.

For additional information, the National Dissemination Center for Children with Disabilities—a leading source of information and resources for parents, caregivers, educators, and other professionals in the field of special education—provides a complete resource list and fact sheet on each of the above mentioned disabilities. Fact sheets, parent resources, and teaching tips are available on its website (www.nichcy.org/resources).

Accommodations or Modifications

Accommodations or modifications for children with special needs usually focus on three primary areas: the curriculum, the method or delivery of instruction, and the physical environment. Within these areas, the eight where modifications are most frequently made in the classroom are as follows:

- environmental support—altering the physical environment to increase participation,
- materials adaptation—modifying materials to promote independence,
- activity simplification—breaking down a complicated task into smaller parts or steps,
- child preferences—capitalizing on a child's favorite activity,
- special equipment—using adaptive devices to facilitate participation,
- adult support—employing direct adult intervention to support the child's efforts,
- peer support—having classmates help children learn by modeling and assistance, and
- invisible support—arranging naturally occurring events to assist inclusion (Sandall et al, in press).

The terms *modifying* and *accommodating* are two separate concepts. To *accommodate* instruction, you might provide a new way for a child to access information, or change how the child demonstrates mastery of a skill. Accommodating instruction, however, does not mean providing a substantial change in the level, content, or assessment criteria. This accommodation could be thought of as a support to enable the child to utilize the same learning material as the other children. For example, an accommodation for a child with a language impairment might entail assessing her learning by having her choose a picture to represent a concept (such as which ball is blue), rather than saying it verbally. The child is still expected to learn the concept, although she is not required to say it out loud.

A *modification* would entail changing the criteria on an assessment task. For instance, instead of assessing a child's ability to recite the numbers 1–10, the child might be expected to recite the numbers 1–5. A modification would allow a change in what a child is expected to learn.

Deciding which accommodations or modifications to use will depend on the instructional objective and the individual needs of the child. In public school settings, the Individual Education Plan (IEP) team determines which accommodations and adaptations are appropriate based on a variety of data. Examples of accommodations and modifications to the classroom environment, curriculum content, and method of instruction and assessment can be found in Tables 1–3.

Accommodations and modifications are types of adaptations that are made to the environment, curriculum, instruction, or assessment practices in order for children with disabilities to be successful learners and to participate actively with other children in the classroom and in all-school activities (Peak Parent Center, 2003). However, these adaptations alone cannot ensure the success of children with disabilities in inclusive settings. It is necessary to provide a variety of measures, including promoting interaction among children with and without disabilities. Also important is the evaluation of your own beliefs and attitudes toward inclusion (SPeNCE, 2001). Successful inclusion is guided by your willingness to accept change and provide accommodations within the daily routine.

Table 1

Examples of Accommodations/Modifications to the Classroom Environment

Altering seating arrangements to meet the needs of the child, such as near the teacher, near a peer buddy, near a quiet space, and so on	All identified disabilities
Rearranging the physical arrangement of classroom furniture to meet children's needs	All identified disabilities
Providing space for movement within the classroom setting	Orthopedic Impairment
Limiting clutter on walls as a means to reduce distractions	Autism, Other Health Impairment (ADHD)
Designating quiet areas in the room	Autism, Emotional Disturbance
Providing carpet squares for young children to sit on Adapting writing utensils/building up pencils/pens/paintbrushes	Autism Orthopedic Impairment
Providing soft music or "white noise"	All identified disabilities, except Autism, if used for sensory stimulation
Reducing noise level in room	Visual Impairment, Hearing Impairment
Changing amount of lighting/brightening or dimming	Visual Impairment, Autism
Adapting furniture, such as lowering chairs, securing desks	Orthopedic Impairment
Creating slant boards throughout room for writing support and painting	Orthopedic Impairment
Using pegs to adapt handles on puzzles, doors, shelving, coat racks, and backpack areas	Orthopedic Impairment, Cognitive and/or Developmental Delay

Table 2 **Examples of Accommodations/ Modifications to Curriculum Content**	
Using real objects instead of pictures for math-based activities involving counting aloud or with fingers	Cognitive and/or Developmental Delay
Reducing number of steps involved in completing a specific task	Cognitive and/or Developmental Delay
Accepting answers of general concepts vs. specific concepts	Autism, Cognitive and/or Developmental Delay
Assigning child a peer buddy for activity support	Cognitive and/or Developmental Delay, Emotional Disturbance

Table 3 **Examples of Accommodations/Modifications to the Mode of Instruction and Evaluation**	
Providing one-to-one instruction	All identified disabilities
Avoiding speaking with your back to the child	Hearing Impairments
Providing daily structure	Autism, Emotional Disturbance, Cognitive and/or Developmental Delay
Using short sentences and simple directions	Cognitive and/or Developmental Delay, Autism
Modifying pace of instruction	Cognitive and/or Developmental Delay
Prefacing activity with introduction/ sequence of events	Visual Impairments
Varying method of instruction, such as small groups, large groups, and independent activities	Cognitive and/or Developmental Delay
Providing more frequent questioning and feedback	Autism, Cognitive and/or Developmental Delay
Providing sample of end product	Cognitive and/or Developmental Delay, Autism
Incorporating sign language into daily activities, such as Circle Time, small group activities, and large group instruction	Hearing Impairments
Providing more frequent opportunities for language usage	Speech and Language Impairment

Table 3 (continued)
Examples of Accommodations/Modifications to the Mode of Instruction and Evaluation

Encouraging and reinforcing positive behavior	All identified disabilities with emphasis on Emotional Disturbance
Increasing size of font on visual presentations (utilization of Big Books)	Visual Impairments
Extending "wait time" for child's responses	Autism, Cognitive and/or Developmental Delay, Speech and Language Impairment
Allowing additional time to complete tasks and activities	Cognitive and/or Developmental Delay, Emotional Disturbance
Incorporating switches or other assistive technology devices	Orthopedic Impairments, Multiple Disabilities
Adapting evaluation to include portfolios or video/audio recordings	Visual Impairments
Using activity and self-monitoring checklists with Visual Impairments	Autism, Cognitive and/or Developmental Delay
Providing opportunities to redirect child's behavior as needed, with constant feedback	Emotional Disturbance, Cognitive and/or Developmental Delay
Supporting activities with sensory materials	Visual Impairments
Using bookstands to hold materials in place	Orthopedic Impairments
Using real objects instead of pictures whenever possible	All children benefit from this form of instruction including children with and without disabilities

Writing Instructional Objectives

In this age of accountability, instructional objectives are an important aspect of educational programs. Writing instructional objectives helps you manage your time and the children's time wisely.

Use these steps for developing instructional objectives:

1. Decide exactly what you want to teach.
2. Write what you want to teach in observable and measurable terms.
3. Divide the skills that you want to teach into several smaller parts, if necessary.

What to Teach

Effective educational programs begin with effective curriculum development. If your center or school has an adopted curriculum, it may have a list of overall goals targeted for young children. While the goals listed in the curriculum are appropriate for the children, they often are broad rather than specific. Instructional objectives should help you determine what you want to teach as well as the concepts children should learn. For example, the curriculum may have as a goal, "The child will develop an awareness of shapes." This valid and age-appropriate aim requires work before it takes the form of an instructional objective. You must decide exactly what you want to teach in relationship to the goal. Which shapes do you want children to recognize? How will they show you that they recognize the shapes? Do you expect them to name each shape? How will they describe the shapes? Consider questions such as these when you determine instructional objectives.

Stating the Objective Behaviorally

When you state the objective behaviorally, describe a behavior or action that is observable and measurable. For example, if you expect children to recognize shapes, they must do this through some specific action, such as pointing to named shapes (circle, square, triangle), naming shapes (circle, square, triangle), or verbally describing shapes (the round one, the one with three sides). If you expect children to know letters of the alphabet, they must demonstrate this knowledge in a manner such as pointing to named letters or naming the letters presented.

Some words are associated with visible and measurable objectives, while other words are vague and non-explicit. The chart below gives examples of clear vs. vague vocabulary:

Vague	Clear
Knows colors	Points to named primary colors
Recognizes shapes	Names circle, square, triangle
Appreciates	Tells three good things about…
Participates	Sings songs with the group; follows directions given in a group; uses three-word sentences related to ongoing activity
Attends to	Looks at speaker during group activity
Learns	Verbally answers three questions about…; tells three characteristics of…
Enjoys	Demonstrates positive facial expression

Instructional Objective to Activities

When teaching, start from the instructional objective and use developmentally appropriate activities to teach the specific objective. For example, you can start from the objective "The child will use a complete sentence to describe one characteristic of a shape (circle, square, triangle)." It could be an art activity where children decorate masks with various pre-cut shapes. When the children share their masks with the class, they can describe the masks. You can scaffold the children's descriptions so the children describe the shapes they used on their masks.

Another example is illustrated in the table below that shows how one developmentally appropriate skill can be addressed during several ongoing activities. When you know the concepts and skills that you want to teach, you can weave them throughout your daily schedule.

One Objective	Many Activities
The child will verbally use the terms "big" and "little" to describe sizes.	Chooses car (big/little) to play with during centers
	Describes turtles as big/little during a unit on turtles
	Chooses the ball (big/little) to play with during outdoor play
	Chooses the mat (big/little) to sit on during Circle Time

Activity to Instructional Objectives

Whether you are an experienced teacher or a beginning teacher, whether you know several activities that children enjoy, you may not have analyzed the activities for their suitability in exploring the skills they incorporate. When you analyze an activity, you may find several opportunities to address instructional objectives related to the school curriculum.

The table below shows how one activity involves multiple objectives. When you plan your daily schedule and are aware of concepts and skills that need to be addressed, you can maximize the children's opportunities to learn.

One Activity	Many Objectives
Painting on an easel (select paint color of choice).	The child will name primary colors
	The child will use the words big/little to describe objects (choose a paintbrush).
	The child will use pincer grasp to pick up objects.
	The child will paint/draw/color, keeping within the boundaries of the page.

Things to Remember

The following guidelines should help you in developing instructional objectives:

- Instructional objectives should be observable and measurable.
- Instructional objectives can be broken down into smaller units, as needed.
- Instructional objectives can use a variety of activities to teach skills.
- Activities can be analyzed to determine the skills that they incorporate.
- In this age of accountability, it is vital to understand what you are teaching.

Planning for Curriculum Connections

Planned lessons may highlight a single curriculum area, such as science or math, and still cover additional curricular areas. During the planning phase, assess what you know about the children and their knowledge base. This will include assessing what the children have previously learned or experienced on the topic at hand, what the children want to know about the topic, and what additional knowledge is important for the children to experience. This three-tiered process will help to make an activity relevant and purposeful. Connection to other curricular areas will allow the children to practice the new concept and to view it in other ways.

For instance, a child who sees a few raindrops on a window may know that these droplets can be measured and counted. He can count the droplets. He can reproduce the location of the drops on a piece of paper. The child may even describe the droplets using size and positional relationships: "The big one is above the two little ones." The observation, recording, and discussion demonstrate the child's ability to use the scientific process to organize and make meaning in his environment.

In a well-planned classroom, you can increase the educational opportunities provided by the raindrop with an oral language discussion about raindrops or by singing a song, such as "Pitter, Patter." The Literacy Center may offer books about rain, water, and storms. In the Science Center, there may be eyedroppers, colored water, jar lids, and measuring beakers. In the Art Center, colored water, straws, and art paper give children the opportunity to create designs with water droplets. These fun, varied activities bring a single educational topic into many different curricular areas.

A well-designed classroom will allow for multiple extensions of a lesson, providing various forms that illustrate meaningful connections between the concept and the curricular areas. Content areas such as Math, Science, Language and Literacy, Social Studies, Art, Music, and Dramatic Play often include learning that overlaps multiple areas. For example, even though counting from 1–10 seems to be a math concept, blending such an exercise with manipulative ladybugs adds the science-based component of observation. Children can count the dots on the back of a ladybug using one-to-one correspondence. They can also read a story about the protective coloration of the ladybug. This can be infused with songs about ladybugs and physical movement activities as children observe and catch ladybugs on the playground.

Teaching through the unit themes in this book allows children to learn concepts in various curricular areas. Each unit in the book provides different ways to approach children's developmental domains in a variety of curricular areas.

Assessment and Evaluation of Young Children

The National Association for the Education of Young Children (NAEYC) promotes and provides resources on developmentally appropriate practices—including assessment of young children—to teachers. Understanding that young children are in a rapid period of growth and development and are easily distracted makes it clear that assessment of young children can pose unique problems (Katz, 1997), including short attention spans, inability to establish rapport with unfamiliar adults, separation from parents or primary caregivers, inconsistency in responses, insufficient expressive language, heightened stress during the assessment process, and lack of sensitivity toward cultural differences. Such factors suggest that traditional standardized assessment practices acceptable for older children may hold little value in the assessment of young children.

Recognizing the problems associated with assessing young children and acting proactively, many teachers and caregivers have turned toward alternative means in assessing young children. Portfolio assessment is one form of alternative assessment emerging in the field of education. Regardless of which type of assessment process you choose to implement in your classroom, you should use ongoing assessment, multiple methods of assessment, and common sense when analyzing results of the assessment data obtained from young children.

Purpose of Assessment

As you select the type of assessment processes to be used in your classroom, first examine the main purposes for which the assessment data will be used. These may include:

- for instructional planning,
- to ensure teaching effectiveness,
- to communicate and provide feedback to families,
- to establish eligibility for special education services,
- to guide curriculum and instruction decisions,
- for placement or promotion purposes, and
- to monitor the progress of a child in meeting standards or guidelines.

Principles and Guidelines in Assessing Young Children

After determining the need for assessment and the purpose of the assessment results, begin to set up the assessment process of your choice. Adhere to general principles and guidelines to assure that the assessment process is valid and reliable. Bates and Barratt (2000) offer six general principles for screening and assessment.

1. Assessment should be conducted only if such assessment will benefit the child.
2. Assessment should be reliable, valid, fair, and tailored to a specific purpose.
3. Method and content of data collection should be age-appropriate.
4. Assessment should be linguistically appropriate.

5. Parents should be a valued source of information.
6. Policies should recognize that the relationship of results obtained by the assessment of young children to later performance increases with the child's age.

In conducting any assessment, it is your responsibility to remain fair and impartial. This can be achieved by being as objective as possible, avoiding labeling or categorizing children, accurately collecting and recording information, and taking time to reflect on assessment procedures and instructional practices.

Authentic Assessment

The use of authentic assessment with young children has increased in the past decade with the recognition that the formal, standardized assessment measures used for older children often fail to accurately evaluate what learning has taken place with young children. Authentic assessment can provide reliable and usable information. To evaluate what a person has learned, the assessment used should provide a collective picture of an individual child's strengths and weaknesses. Authentic assessment processes used with young children present them with real-world situations and challenges that require them to apply their knowledge and skills in responding to tasks in meaningful, real-life contexts.

Portfolio Assessment

The use of portfolios has increased as teachers have become more involved in designing curriculum and assessing children. Portfolio assessment is defined as a purposeful collection of children's work samples that displays progress of predetermined outcomes and achievements in one or more developmental domains. Together with the child, you systematically collect the work sampling over time. This "snapshot" of a child's classroom-based performance can be integrated into existing curriculum, allowing the portfolio to be seen as a supplement to curriculum rather than as a separate assessment measurement.

"Collect, Select, and Reflect" has been loosely used as a starting point for entering into the portfolio process. As the statement implies, you and the children begin to collect children's work samples throughout the year. The materials selected should align with the purpose of the assessment process.

Sample Items for Children's Portfolios	
Paintings	Drawings
Writing Samples	Photographs/Videos/Audio tapes
Dictated Stories	Checklists
Children's Journals	Parent Comments/Interviews
Children's Reflections	Anecdotal Records
Teacher Comments	Documentation of Peer Interactions

Strong samples of work provide an accurate, "authentic" picture of the needs of the individual child and can provide a mechanism to evaluate how the curriculum used will meet (or has met) those needs. This especially holds true when assessing children with identified or possible disabilities.

Once the collection process is under way, you and the child should collaboratively select items to be placed into the portfolio (a container that can be placed within reach of the children and can hold an ample amount of materials). These items must match the purpose of the assessment. For instance, if the purpose of assessment is evaluating the effectiveness of the literacy program, writing samples and dictated stories are valuable selection pieces. During a conference with the child, offer feedback on the progress he or she is making. The child can self-reflect on the pieces while you write down that child's reflection for future evaluation. Take time to share your reflections of the selected pieces by identifying children's strengths, interests, and needs. Such information can help you to evaluate the design of the curriculum and to determine what you need to do to meet the needs of the children in your classroom.

Understanding and Assessing the Progress of a Child with a Disability

Every child who enters the classroom brings with him or her a wealth of prior knowledge and experiences as well as differing abilities. Evaluating the progress of children is as valid for a child with a disability as it is for a child without a disability. The use of portfolio assessments will strengthen the documentation needed to identify the child as needing additional support or to document the progress in which the child is progressing towards his or her Individual Education Plan (IEP) or Individual Family Service Plan (IFSP). Researchers have found that information gathered in portfolios leads to more specific and helpful recommendations in improving instructional programs as compared to norm-referenced assessment data results (Rueda & Garcia, 1997).

Children with disabilities are typically given standardized assessment measures to determine progress and establish eligibility. This limited approach often overlooks the fact that children with disabilities, as well as all young children, tire easily, become easily distracted, and are frequently inconsistent in responses. This is especially evident when assessing a child with sensory impairments. To avoid inaccurate assessment results, use a wide range of assessment techniques and verify assessment results with multiple sources.

Portfolio assessment, as well as other authentic assessment practices, provides ongoing assessment materials to assist in placement and instructional decisions. The portfolio also demonstrates the strengths and progress the child is making. Parents of children have the opportunity to see aspects of their child's life that take place at school. Social and emotional development, cognitive development, physical development, and self-help skills can be accurately and materially represented in the portfolio.

Assessment and evaluation of young children is not without controversy in the field of early childhood education, but it is a vital tool. Identifying and utilizing non-traditional forms of assessment such as portfolio assessment enables you to obtain information about the children in your classroom. This information strengthens curriculum, meets the academic needs of children, and provides children with ownership over the learning and evaluation process.

How to Use This Book

We hope you find *Inclusive Lesson Plans Throughout the Year* useful in your classroom. Children will enjoy and benefit from the learner-centered experiences in the lesson plans, and the accompanying accommodations and modifications. The following are tips for successfully incorporating the lesson plans in this book as you plan for children's learning:

1. Because you know your children better than we do, use these lesson plans as guides for your classroom. Using your own questions, choosing your own activities from the suggestions in this book, and adapting specific ideas to your children's needs is the best plan of action. Our hope is that you will find our ideas useful for developing optimal learning experiences for your children.

2. As you begin any lesson, familiarize yourself with the plan prior to starting activities. Putting your nose in this book while working with children will not facilitate their learning. They may become bored or disinterested if you are not sharing information with them confidently. Make eye contact with your group, and you will find that activities generate spontaneity and enjoyment for the children.

3. Use our lessons in relationship to what you know about your children. Not all recommendations in our plans will be appropriate for every group of young children. If your children do not sit still for any length of time, you may need to divide the lessons into two or three sessions to introduce concepts to smaller groups of children. Continuing to follow a lesson plan when children are obviously not interested causes stress for everyone.

4. Not all lessons are relevant for your children. A study of seashore life may not be appropriate in Oklahoma, for example. If this is the case, skip the lesson or develop one of your own that you know will help your children feel successful.

5. Throughout the book, we have suggested time frames for each of the lessons. These are approximations; children's responses to lessons will determine the time needed to teach the lesson. Some topics will create interest and passionate discussions among children, while others will be less attractive to them. Be willing to adapt to their needs.

6. Occasionally lessons may need to be abandoned: for instance, when children do not respond as you had hoped. If this happens, prepare the lesson again another day, or consider finding another approach to sharing the lesson concepts with the children.

7. On other occasions, responses from children will change the direction of the lesson plan. This is called a "teachable moment," and following the children's lead will yield more learning on their part. As you are reading a book, for example, children might become excited about the spider they see on a page, and you will spend time

discussing the habits of spiders rather than continuing to read the book. As Bev Bos suggests, "Life is a conversation," and allowing children an opportunity to talk about what they want to talk about is important to their cognitive development. Take advantage of "teachable moments." They are the heart of teaching children.

8. Throughout this book, we have suggested children's books for some of the lessons. If you do not have a particular book, substitute with another appropriate title. Teaching children requires flexibility on the part of the teacher.

9. Most importantly, demonstrate your enjoyment of learning when you are working with children. If you do not enjoy learning, then children will not understand that learning is worthwhile. Your attitude is key in the development of learning in children.

Lesson Components Defined

Use the following information about each of the elements in the lesson plans in *Inclusive Lesson Plans Throughout the Year,* to plan for teaching and interacting with children.

Title
The title describes the content of the lesson as it relates to the unit theme.

Objectives
Objectives are designed to show teachers what children will learn as a result of the lesson.

Time
Time frames will vary based on children's interest levels and their ability to stay focused on lesson content.

Materials
A list of materials needed to teach each lesson accompanies the plan.

Preparation
This describes anything that needs to be done prior to beginning the lesson.

Lesson
Each lesson will have an activity or activities to teach the defined objectives while the children are gathered in a group time, often referred to as Group or Circle Time. Use the activities as written, add your own activities, or delete activities you think are inappropriate for the children in your class. Lessons include questions and suggestions for comments as the lesson is presented.

Review
Reviewing the content at the end of the lesson is often called closure. The purpose of closure is to help children remember the content of the lesson.

Assessment Strategies

The assessment strategies in the lesson plans are to help you find out what the children learned by participating in the lesson. With young children, assessment is almost always done on an individual basis.

Accommodations/Modifications

This component is the backbone of *Inclusive Lesson Plans Throughout the Year.* Knowing how to modify lessons for individual learners in the classroom helps teachers reach all children.

Curriculum Connections

Curriculum connections are activities that reinforce and extend the learning of the original lesson. Connecting the content in various centers or with follow-up activities ensures that children are developing concepts that enhance their learning.

References

Bates, L. & Barratt, M. Ph.D. November, 2000. Institute for Children, Youth, & Families, 27 Kellogg Center, Michigan State University, East Lansing, MI 48824, with Consortium for Applied Research on Child Abuse & Neglect (ARCAN) and Michigan Children's Trust Fund. http://www.icyf.msu.edu/publicats/z5dissem/assess-p.html

Katz, L.G. 1997. *A developmental approach to assessment of young children.* ERIC Clearinghouse on elementary and Early Childhood Education. Champaign, IL: ERIC Digest. ED407172.

Mastropieri, M. & Scruggs, T. 2004. *The inclusive classroom: Strategies for effective instruction.* Upper Saddle River, NJ: Prentice Hall.

Peak Parent Center: Accommodations and Modifications Fact Sheet. 2003. Retrieved on April 20, 2004, from http:www.peakparent.org/pdf/fact_sheets/accommodations.pdf

Prater, M. 2000. She will succeed: Strategies for successful inclusive classrooms. *Teaching Exceptional Children.* Vol. 35 (5), pp.58-64.

Rueda, R. & Garcia, E. 1997. Do portfolios make a difference for diverse students? The influence of type of data on making instructional decisions. *Learning Disabilities Research and Practice,* 12(2), 114-122

Sandall, S. R., Joseph, G., Chou, H., Schwartz, I. S., Horn, E., Lieber, J., Odom, S. L., & Wolery, R. (in press). Talking to practitioners: Focus group report on curriculum modifications in inclusive preschool classrooms. *Journal of Early Intervention.*

SPeNSE Fact Sheet: Study of Personnel Needs in Special Education. 2001. Retrieved April 23, 2004, from http:www.spense.org/results.html.

2 Fall Themes

I Am Special

Time

20–30 minutes

Materials

- Competed sheet (see page 38)
- Grocery bag containing items packed by the selected child (with help from her family)

Objectives

Children will:

1. Share information that they think is special about themselves.
2. Use oral language to describe items they have brought to share with the class.
3. Answer questions.

Preparation

A few days before the lesson, select one child and give her the "I Am Special" sheet along with an instruction sheet to take home. Include on the instruction sheet any information that might help the family and child complete the questionnaire, as well as a request for the child to gather three to five items that are special to her and to place them in a grocery bag.

Note: Repeat this activity throughout the year, focusing on one child at a time, until all the children have had a turn.

Lesson

- As the children gather on the rug for Group or Circle Time, ask the selected child to come to the front with her bag of items and her completed "I Am Special" sheet.
- Read the first part of the sentence and ask her to complete it. (My name is _____. In my family there are _____ people, and so on.)
- Invite the child to tell the rest of the children about herself.
- Encourage the children to ask her questions.
- Then ask the child to present the items she has brought in the grocery bag and tell the class why each item is special to her.

Ask the child to display the items that she brought to class for continued discussion during the day.

Assessment Strategy

Observe the language the child uses to tell you about herself. Chart or note if the child is able to use complete sentences, to find descriptive words to tell you about herself, and to answer questions pertaining to the information presented. Place the questionnaire in the child's portfolio as an example of self-expression.

Accommodations/Modifications

Autism—Use Picture Communication Symbols or clip art to provide pictorial cues for the child during the group discussion.

Speech or Language Impairments—Pre-plan with the child by selecting specific words that can be used in response to questions.

Hearing Impairments—Present information visually when possible. As you hold up specific items, point to the child who is speaking.

Visual Impairments—Allow children to touch the items brought to the class. Supervise them as needed. Modeling an activity for a child with visual impairments must include touching the items.

Cognitive and/or Developmental Delays—Allow other adults or other children to assist the child by giving the child any needed clarification of information. Rephrase the information as necessary for the child to understand.

Emotional Disturbance—Allow the child to sit in close proximity to the adults for behavior management.

Other Health Impairments/Attention Deficit Hyperactivity Disorder—Assist the child in attending to the task using verbal cuing and signals. This includes pointing and assisting the child to focus on the child who is speaking, along with pointing and holding up the items the child is presenting.

Orthopedic Impairments—Provide a tray to hold the items from the bag, or assign a class peer to assist the child in retrieving items from the bag if necessary.

Curriculum Connections

- **Art**—Encourage each child to draw pictures of herself and her friend and place the pictures in a class book.
- **Language and Literacy**—Add the "I Am Special" sheets (see page 38) to a class book with illustrations for individual reading.
- **Math**—Work with the children to complete a graph of family members, pets, and/or favorite foods. Discuss the concepts of more, less, and the same.
- **Social Studies**—Help the children to create a map of places where they were born or have visited. If appropriate, mark locations on the map using a child's name or a photograph.

I Am Special

My name is

I am   years old.

In my family, there are   people.

I have   pets.

Share something about your pets.

My favorite food is

My least favorite food is

For fun, I like to

I also like to

because

Something special about me is

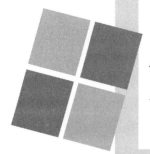

What I Like

Time

- Group time:
  20–30 minutes
- Individual time:
  20–30 minutes

Materials

- Paper
- Stapler
- Chart paper
- Marker
- Post-it notes

Objectives

Children will:

1. Discuss things they like.
2. Read the "I Like" poem orally.
3. Make a personal poem book.

Preparation

Make a mini-book for each child by taking a single sheet of paper, folding it into quarters, and stapling it on the last fold to form the binding. Cut the first fold so that there are six pages: the cover, the back, and four writing pages. Write the "I Like" poem (below) on a piece of chart paper and hang it in the classroom near the rug. During the day, prior to the lesson, share with the children different things that you like and ask them what they like. "I like the way Marie is sitting." "I like apples. I have one for lunch today." "Marie, what color would you like to use on your paper?" "What do you like to do after school?"

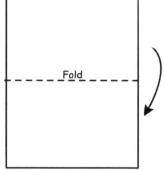

Fold

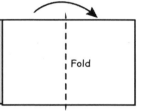

Fold

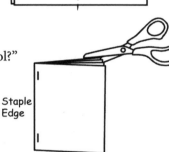

Staple Edge

I Like
I like cats.
Eating spaghetti is so cool.
I like swimming in the pool,
But I don't like spiders.

Lesson

- Gather the children together on the rug. Read "I Like" to the children, and then ask them to read it with you.
- Ask the children what they like. Write down each like on a Post-it note and place the notes on a wall, chart paper, or board.
- Then ask the class what they do not like. Write down each dislike on a Post-it note and place it on the wall, chart paper, or board.
- Suggest that the children replace some of the likes and dislikes posted on the board with those in the poem to create different poems. Using Post-it notes will allow you to place and replace different words in the poem.

What I Like

- Talk with the children about their likes and dislikes. Point out that different people have different likes and dislikes. Help the children understand that some children like items that others dislike.
- Pass out the individual mini-books so each child can create his own "I Like" poem book.
- Ask the children to draw items they like on the first three pages (following the cover page) and something they dislike on the last page.
- You or a classroom volunteer can write the poem in each child's book.

Cover: I Like
Page 1: I like _____.
Page 2: I like _____.
Page 3: I like _____.
Page 4: But I don't like _____.

Accommodations/Modifications

Autism—Use cue cards and clip art to assist the child in responding during the group discussion. Have small clip art pictures available for him to insert into his booklet.

Speech or Language Impairments—Use pictures or clip art to assist the child in selecting likes and dislikes.

Hearing Impairments—Pointing to the words in the poem as you read it aloud will help the child say the next word, even if he cannot read the chart. Pictures on the Post-it notes will also assist with comprehension of the children's likes and dislikes.

Visual Impairments—Have the child move or sit where he can easily see the chart poem and the Post-it notes as they are placed into the poem. Reading the Post-it notes aloud also adds in comprehension.

Cognitive and/or Developmental Delays—Give the child three choices for likes and dislikes to help him choose items for discussion.

Emotional Disturbance—Before the lesson, preteach differences in likes and dislikes. This will assist in the reactions if a child does not like his selected item or dislikes another child's item.

Review

Place the children's mini-books in the literacy center for individual review throughout the year. Choose a different book to read during story-reading times throughout the year.

Assessment Strategy

Have each child read his book to you. Assess emergent reading and writing skills. Can he hold the book and turn the pages one at a time? Does he focus on the print to make meaning of the page? Does he use the picture clues to read his book?

Other Health Impairments/Attention Deficit Hyperactive Disorder—Help the child attend to the task using verbal cuing and signals. Hand motions and "do-it" signals will assist the child in focusing and completing his book. Do-it signals are brief statements for beginning work such as:

Begin here
Turn the page
Write your name

Orthopedic Impairments—Help the child with drawing and writing by using specialized utensils and hand-over-hand assistance in gripping the Post-it notes.

Curriculum Connections

- **Art**—Encourage the children to draw different pictures to represent their likes and dislikes.
- **Language and Literacy**—Provide additional blank books in the literacy center for children's writings.
- **Math**—Chart the items that the children like and dislike. Compare graphic representations using more, less, and the same.
- **Music**—Recite the poem as a chant to practice rhythm.

ALL ABOUT ME

Body Tracings

Time
- 5 separate 20–minute sessions
- The children will complete this in a series of settings (total time 1–1½ hours)

Materials
- Pictures of teacher (3–5) Blank paper doll cutout
- Butcher paper pieces of 3'–5' in length (1 per child)
- Unbreakable mirror
- Scissors
- Crayons and markers
- Construction paper
- White paper or butcher paper scraps
- Glue
- Wire and clothespins for display

Objectives

Children will:
1. Complete life-size representations of their bodies.
2. Compare and contrast their features with those of their classmates.
3. Practice fine motor skills of coloring and cutting.

Lesson

Session 1
- Provide 3–5 recent photographs of yourself for the children to see.
- Talk with the children about photographs and pictorial representations. Talk about eye color, hair color and style, and clothing.
- Show the children a small paper doll cutout. Ask them to describe how they might make the small paper doll look like one or more of the children in the class.
- Focus the discussion on clothing, design, hair color and style, eye color, and other visual attributes.

Session 2
- One at a time, have the children lie down on a piece of butcher paper and trace the child's body shape on the paper.
- Help each child cut on the traced line to make a life-size paper representation.

Sessions 3–5
- Ask each child to add details to her body, such as clothing and features, such as face, hands, skin, as well as personal features of eye color and hair. Use additional paper for detailed representation. Encourage the children to use a mirror to explore their features.
- Display the children's representations by hanging them on a clothesline between sessions until they are completed. This will allow children to view other children's representations as they complete their own.
- Develop class discussions of size, colors, and physical features to help children complete their representations.

Review

Listen to the children as they discuss their body representations with peers and as they are viewed around the room. Notice the children who add features to their bodies as they gain new insights by viewing other children's representations.

Assessment Strategy

Listen to each child individually as she discusses with peers and with you her unique personal characteristics.

Accommodations/ Modifications

Autism—Provide photographs of the child to use when pointing to body characteristics. Use the photos to help the child replicate her likeness.

Speech or Language Impairments—Increase vocabulary of body parts and physical descriptions by having the child repeat the selected characteristics you name as you point to them on your body.

Hearing Impairments—Use physical gestures and point to specific physical characteristics to help the child understand the conversation. Directions during the coloring of the body tracings can include specifically addressing the child's clothing and physical features. An unbreakable mirror will be especially useful.

Visual Impairments—When you show photos of yourself to the class, allow the child to hold and closely examine the photos.

Cognitive and/or Developmental Delays—Extend time needed to complete the task, using verbal cuing as well as signals and eye contact to keep the child engaged.

Emotional Disturbance—Use photos to help the child see herself and her physical characteristics. Give the child enough space to move around her body representation with ease.

Other Health Impairments/Attention Deficit Hyperactive Disorder—Use close proximity and vocal cuing to assist the child in focusing on her task. Clear directions about specific characteristic representations will assist in breaking down the project into manageable parts.

Orthopedic Impairments—Make materials accessible at the child's body level. When the child is coloring, use large body supports and assists so she can maneuver around the large paper tracing.

Curriculum Connections

- **Art**—Provide opportunities for the children to continue adding to their visual representations by cutting, coloring, and drawing.
- **Language and Literacy**—Provide opportunities for group oral language and discussion of personal traits, including likenesses and differences.
- **Math**—Provide times for individual groups of children to graph and group the categorized features of their classmates, observing likenesses and differences. Provide Unifix blocks or inch cubes to allow the children to measure the size of each body and to order them by height or length.
- **Science**—Help the children observe and discuss their body features, individual traits, and differences.
- **Social Studies**—Provide opportunities to discuss individual differences and to celebrate self-awareness.

Family Members

Time
20–30 minutes

Materials
- Chart paper
- Marker
- Paper
- Crayons
- Hearts to place on chart
- Glue

Objectives
Children will:
1. Describe their family members.
2. Draw representations of their family members.
3. Chart the number of members in their families.

Preparation
Using chart paper, create a class chart or graph that has one column for each child in the class.

CLASS CHART

CHILD'S NAME	
JEREMY	
TABATHA	
KEITH	
ELIZABETH	
MARCUS	
EDDIE	

Lesson
- Gather the children together to talk about families, including all the members of each child's family.
- Have the children draw pictures of their families on sheets of paper.
- While the children are drawing their families, visit with each child and write the name of each member of the child's family on an individual heart. Invite children to include pets, non-relatives who live in their homes, and extended family.
- Provide every child a heart for each of their family members, including themselves.

Review

Post the graph of families in the classroom for children to review during independent time.

Assessment Strategy

Question each child individually about the number of family members in various families.

- When the children are finished with their family drawings, ask them to glue their hearts in their family column.
- Once the chart is completed, ask the children who has the largest family, the smallest family, and which families have the same number of members.
- Tell the children that all families spread love among all members.

Accommodations/Modifications

Autism—Use picture cues to associate each family heart with the appropriate member of the child's family.

Speech or Language Impairments—Help the child with family vocabulary. Define concepts that may be unfamiliar to the child.

Hearing Impairments—Use hand gestures and face the child when giving directions and during discussions.

Visual Impairments—Help the child locate the correct box on the grid for placement of his family hearts. Use gestures and verbal cues to help him focus.

Cognitive and/or Developmental Delays—Discuss each family member with the child to help him in organization skills. Verbal cues to indicate when to proceed to the next step may be necessary.

Emotional Disturbance—Provide warnings before transitions to assist in completing the first part of the activity and moving on to the next.

Other Health Impairments/Attention Deficit Hyperactive Disorder—Have the child count and name family members. Assist him in gathering the correct number of hearts to correspond to each family member. Use verbal cues to assist the child in focusing.

Orthopedic Impairments—Have the materials accessible at the child's body level. Assist the child by moving the chart to him rather than placing the hearts for him. Position the child within easy reach of materials for drawing the family picture.

Curriculum Extensions

- **Art**—Provide additional paper and other art materials for children to draw more pictures of their families.
- **Language and Literacy**—Engage the children in a discussion about family size.
- **Math**—Use paper cutouts of families to group different family sizes.
- **Social Studies**—Provide photos of adults and children for the children to use as they create various families.

Name Recognition

Time

15–20 minutes

Materials

- Chart of class names written in different colors
- Markers
- Name cards written in black on index cards
- File box for name cards

Objectives

Children will:

1. Match the written representations of their first name.
2. Identify the written representation of their first name from other names.
3. Identify the written representation of other classmate's names.

Preparation

Make a chart of children's names using different colors to help children identify their name and the names of their friends. Post the chart of names in the classroom. Using a black marker, write each child's name on a separate index card.

Lesson

- Read each name and then ask all the children to repeat the name aloud.
- Give each child her name card with her name written in black ink.
- Ask each child to match her name card to the chart of names.
- After practice with matching, place all name cards in a file box so children can match and choose their name and read the names of their friends.

Accommodations/Modifications

Autism—Use hand-over-hand assistance for matching the child's name on the chart. Dual choice responses will allow for success.

Hearing Impairments—Point to names on the chart while showing the child her name card.

Review

Allow children to use the name cards to match the names that are posted throughout the classroom.

Assessment Strategy

Observe each child matching her name.

Visual Impairments—Allow the child to match the names with the chart at her eye level.

Cognitive and/or Developmental Delays—Show the name card, say the name, ask the child to repeat the name, and then point to the name on the chart. Directional clues and dual choice questions will help the child locate her name.

Emotional Disturbance—Break down the task into five names at a time.

Other Health Impairments/Attention Deficit Hyperactive Disorder—Allow peer assistance in matching the names. If the child is in a group, have her sit close to the adult.

Orthopedic Impairments—Make the materials accessible at the child's body level. Move the chart to the child's level or allow her to use a pointer to show where her name is on the chart.

Curriculum Connections

- **Art**—Encourage the children to identify the color of their names on the chart. Using multiple colors, suggest that the children trace or color in the letters in their names.
- **Language and Literacy**—Ask the children to find environmental print that looks similar to their name and then describe the differences in their name and the environmental print.
- **Math**—Have the children count and record the number of letters in their names. Using one inch for each letter on one-inch graph paper, ask the children to write and rewrite their names.

ALL ABOUT ME

Name Copy

Time

10 minutes

Materials

- Name cards written in black (use the cards created for Name Recognition, see page 46)
- Blank, unlined paper
- Mailing labels
- Pencils
- Markers

Objectives

Children will:

1. Identify the written representation of their first names.
2. Practice copying the written representation of their first names.

Lesson

- Talk with the children about the importance of names. Remind the children that the best way to get someone's attention is to call that person by his or her name. Point out that their belongings (lunch kit, backpack, and jacket) may have their names written on them to show whom the items belong to.
- Tell the children that writing their names on artwork and class work identifies who drew or made each piece.
- Have the children find their name cards from the file box. Assist children who have trouble by reminding them of the first letters in their names.
- Using a pencil or marker, ask the children to copy their names on unlined sheets of paper or sheets of mailing labels. Assist and praise children as they complete this task.
- Young children will initially copy the "picture" of their name. As preschoolers develop their literacy skills, it is normal to see letters written backwards and in incorrect order.
- If the children have written their names on mailing labels, let them use these labels to tag their artwork or any other work they have created.

Accommodations/Modifications

Autism—Provide tracing paper to allow the child to trace the letters in his name from the name card before he tries to write it by copying the letters. Place the child's picture on the card to make it easier for him to select the card. This can be removed as the child becomes more familiar with his written name.

Visual Impairments—Writing the child's name in block lettering with a thick black marker on white cardstock helps the child see the letters of his name.

Keep the file box in the writing center. Initially, write each name in a different color so the children can readily identify their names. As the children become more skilled at identifying their names, write them in a single color to encourage finer discrimination skills.

Assessment Strategy

Collect and evaluate the writing samples. During the year, add selections of name writing samples to the child's portfolio to show his growth in fine motor development as well as ability to write his name.

Cognitive and/or Developmental Delays—Provide the child with tracing paper to trace the letters in his name from his name card with a marker before trying to copy each letter. Place the child's picture on the card to help him select his card. Remove the photo as the child becomes more familiar with his written name.

Emotional Disturbance—Provide extra sheets of paper to allow the child to repeat writing his name, so he can discard the ones he doesn't like.

Other Health Impairments/Attention Deficit Hyperactive Disorder—Use verbal cues to keep the child focused.

Orthopedic Impairments—Be sure the materials are accessible at the child's body level.

Curriculum Connections

- **All areas**—Ask the children to add their names to their artwork or other works samples, allowing them to use their name cards from the file box.
- **Math**—Ask the children to count the letters in their names and then compare the numbers of letters in their names to the numbers of letters in their classmates' names.

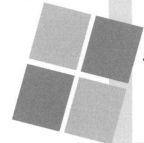

Being Healthy

Time

30–45 minutes

Materials

- Ball, jump rope, or beanbag
- CD of both lively and quiet music
- Tricycle or wagon
- Book, rest mat, or pillow
- Paper
- Marker and crayons
- Magazines and glue

Objectives

Children will:

1. Identify times of exercise and times of rest.
2. Select healthy choices of exercise.

Lesson

- Gather the children together on the floor. Display a few of the exercise items (ball, rope, beanbag, and cones) and the quiet-time items (book, rest mat, and pillow). Tell the children that you are going to play some music and they must decide which types of music are the best for each activity. Play three or four short segments of music. Ask the children to identify the music as fast or slow.

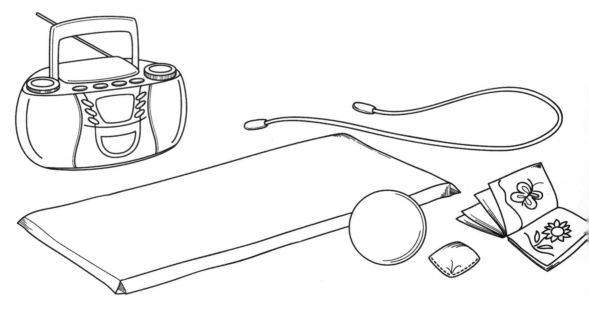

- While the same music is playing a second time, talk with the children about things that they do fast and things that they do slowly. Engage the children in a discussion about how both adults and children do some things fast and some things slowly.
- Talk about the need for quiet, rest times during the school day and at night. Ask the children to identify items among those displayed that are used during rest activities.
- Discuss the need for active play and exercise during the day. Ask the children to identify some of the items displayed that are used during active, exercise times.
- Take the children outside to participate in active exercise for 10–15 minutes while playing fast, energizing music.

Review

Ask the child to describe to you or a classroom volunteer the active and restful activities that she has depicted on the page.

Assessment

Observe what the child says in talking with her classmates about her favorite active and restful activities.

- Return to the classroom and participate in quiet, restful activities for 10–15 minutes while playing slow, soothing music.
- To reinforce or extend the lesson, ask the children to fold a piece of paper in half. On one side, ask the children to draw pictures or glue pictures from magazines of active exercise, and on the other side to draw or glue pictures from magazines of restful activities.

Accommodations/Modifications

Autism—Model the activities for the child and encourage her participation. You may need to shadow the child to elicit her participation.

Speech or Language Impairments—Provide definitions for words that may be unfamiliar to the child. Reinforce correct sentence structure.

Hearing Impairments—Ask questions to make certain that the child understands. Provide peer assistance and gestures as needed.

Visual Impairments—Ask questions to make certain that the child understands. Provide peer assistance and gestures as needed.

Cognitive and/or Developmental Delays—Model activities for the child and encourage participation in both active and restful activities.

Emotional Disturbance—Provide choices of restful and active activities. Talk with the child as she participates.

Other Health Impairments/Attention Deficit Hyperactive Disorder—Provide a choice of activities, both restful and active. Discuss the level of activity to check for comprehension.

Orthopedic Impairments—Model activities and help the child participate in both active and restful activities, as she is able.

Curriculum Connections

- **Art**—Encourage a group of children to prepare poster board collages showing restful and active activities by drawing pictures or gluing pictures cut from magazines on the poster board.
- **Language and Literacy**—Provide paper so children can record activities they participate in during a day. Suggest that they categorize them as active or restful activities.
- **Science**—Place a stethoscope in the Science Center to allow children to listen to differences in their heart rates during restful activities and active activities.

Spreading Germs

Time

20–30 minutes

Materials

- Chart paper and marker or chalkboard and chalk
- Water spray bottle
- Soap
- Water
- *Germs Make Me Sick!* by Melvin Berger

Objectives

Children will:

1. Discuss washing germs off their hands.
2. Participate in an examination of germs on their hands.

Lesson

- Begin the lesson as soon as the children come inside from playing outdoors. Talk with them about how some dirt stays on their hands after playtime.
- Ask the children to look at their hands on both sides to determine if they are clean, mostly clean, a little bit dirty, or very dirty.
- Make a chart on chart paper or the board to write each child's selection.
- Ask the children what they must do to get their hands clean. Talk with them about how long they need to wash with soap. Suggest 30 seconds to one minute. Tell them that it takes about 30 seconds to sing the "Happy Birthday" song. Have the children practice rubbing their hands together and singing "Happy Birthday."
- You may mist each child's hand with water as they rub their hands together singing "Happy Birthday." Talk about the possible "dirt rolls" that appear on their hands as they rub them with the misted water.

CLASS CHART

	CLEAN	MOSTLY CLEAN	A LITTLE BIT DIRTY	VERY DIRTY
Jason				
Micah				
Lucas				
Michelle				
Anna				
Tamika				
Damon				
Marcus				
Shawna				
Oliver				
Rebecca				
Joshua				

Review

Each time the children go to the bathroom, they will scrub their hands with soap while singing "Happy Birthday" two times.

Assessment Strategy

Observe the children throughout the weeks of school as they wash their hands.

- Take the children to the sink area to wash their hands with soap and water, scrubbing for as long as it takes to sing two "Happy Birthday" songs.
- Gather the children and read *Germs Make Me Sick!* by Melvin Berger.
- Talk about the germs that may have been on the children's hands.

Accommodations/Modifications

Autism—Discuss the transfer of germs with the child.

Speech or Language Impairments—Encourage the child to participate in the discussion. Give the child positive feedback when he uses the correct word.

Hearing Impairments—Use gestures to help the child understand the directions.

Visual Impairment—Use gestures to help the child understand the content of the lesson.

Cognitive and/or Developmental Delays—Encourage the child to participate and comment favorably when he adds to the discussion. Ask forced-choice questions to aid in participation.

Emotional Disturbance—Encourage the child to participate and comment favorably when he adds to the discussion. Ask forced-choice questions to aid in participation.

Other Health Impairments/Attention Deficit Hyperactive Disorder—Encourage the child to participate and comment favorably when he adds to the discussion. Ask forced-choice questions to aid in participation.

Orthopedic Impairments—Help the child with hand washing, if necessary.

Curriculum Connections

- **Art**—Suggest that the children trace their hands and then use a light color to add dots of dirt to their handprints.
- **Language and Literacy**—Encourage the children to recite other rhymes and songs as they wash their hands.
- **Social Studies**—Suggest that the children use a timer to observe the teacher or a classmate for two minutes to note the items in the class the teacher or classmate touches. Did the teacher transfer germs to new surfaces?
- **More Social Studies**—Have the children put a small amount of baby powder on their hands and begin to play in centers. After five minutes, ask them to look around the area to notice the things that have baby powder residue on them. Talk about how germs are transferred from one surface to another.

Cover That Sneeze!

Time
20–30 minutes

Materials
- Paper plates
- Scissors
- Balloons
- Crayons
- Small pieces of confetti (lightweight)
- *"Stand Back," Said the Elephant, "I'm Going to Sneeze!"* by Patricia Thomas
- Tissues

Objectives
Children will:
1. Describe the spread of germs from a sneeze.
2. Practice healthy procedures to cover a sneeze.

Preparation
Before the children arrive, prepare a paper plate for each child with a small cross slit cut in the middle to hold a small balloon. Prepare another paper plate with a small cross slit in the middle for a balloon to use as a demonstration. Draw and color a face on the plate using the cross slit as a nose area. Place a small balloon with the open end on the back of the paper plate. Fill the deflated balloon partially with small pieces of lightweight confetti. Set this demonstration plate aside until needed in the lesson.

Confetti-Filled Balloon

Lesson
- Have the children gather on the rug for story time. Read *"Stand Back," Said the Elephant, "I'm Going to Sneeze!"* by Patricia Thomas.
- After reading a page or two, stop the story and pretend that you have a large sneeze. Say, "Ahhh, ahhh, ahhh," and then stop. Ask the children what you need. (A tissue)
- Discuss with the children what happens when someone sneezes and why they must cover a sneeze.

Review

Ask the children to repeat the reasons for covering their sneezes.

Assessment Strategy

Observe whether the children cover their sneezes and whether they remind their peers to cover their sneezes.

- Bring out the paper plate face and again say, "Ahhh, (blow a little into the balloon), ahhh, (blow a little more into the balloon), ahhh chooo (release the balloon)!" The confetti will fly out of the nose drawn on the plate and all over the children.
- Continue talking with the children about sneezing, germs, and why they must cover their sneezes.
- Read the rest of *"Stand Back," Said the Elephant, "I'm Going to Sneeze!"*
- Have children make their own plate faces (consider adding confetti to the balloons the children use for their plate faces).

Accommodations/Modifications

Autism—Discuss and predict what will happen during the sneeze. Release the balloon in a direction away from the child.

Speech or Language Impairments—Encourage the child to take part in the discussion and to use good sentence structure.

Hearing Impairments—Use visual gestures and repeat the highlights of the discussion in a one-on-one situation.

Visual Impairments—Make gestures to direct the child's attention to the spray of germs.

Cognitive and/or Developmental Delays—Discuss and predict what will happen during the sneeze. Release the balloon in a direction away from the child.

Emotional Disturbance—Discuss and predict what will happen during the sneeze. Release the balloon away from the child.

Other Health Impairments/Attention Deficit Hyperactive Disorder—Spray the confetti in a direction away from the child to contain additional excitement.

Orthopedic Impairments—If necessary, give the child a pre-blown balloon to practice filling a balloon with air. Discuss germ transfer with her.

Curriculum Connections

- **Health**—Encourage the children to talk about ways to keep healthy.
- **Language and Literacy**—Have children dictate stories about ways in which germs are transferred from one person to another and ask them to illustrate their stories.
- **Outdoors**—Allow children to use balloons to spray water on a fence during Outdoor Time.

INTRODUCTION TO THE

Five Senses

Time

15–20 minutes

Materials

- Large paper bag
- Popped popcorn
- Chart paper and marker
- Individual cups

Objectives

Children will:

1. Discuss how they learn about their environment.
2. Identify the five senses and how they use those senses to gain information.

Preparation

Inside a large paper bag, place enough popped popcorn to allow each child in the class to have a small cup of popcorn. Keep the small cups out of sight.

Lesson

- Gather the children together in the Group Time area rug facing the large paper bag.
- Tell the children that you have a surprise in the bag, but they must guess what it is in order to receive the surprise.
- Let the children take turns guessing what they think is in the paper bag.
- After each guess, talk about whether the guess is a real possibility. A possible guess is something that might be in the bag. A leaf might be possible; a tree is not possible!
- Accept all guesses and record each guess on chart paper without giving away the surprise.
- Encourage the children to use their senses by allowing some individuals to hold (touch) the bag, shake (hearing) the bag, and sniff (smell) the bag.
- After each child has guessed for a second time, allow two or three children to peek inside the bag and to whisper what they see.
- Then select two or three children to close their eyes and taste the surprise.
- Give each child a small cup of popcorn while discussing how to use the senses to gain information.
- Ask the children which senses they used when they guessed for the second time what was in the bag.

Accommodations/Modifications

Autism—Model the directions. Have the child repeat the directions for what he will do.

Speech or Language Impairments—Model the directions. Have the child repeat the directions for what he will do. Help the child form a question from the statements given.

Hearing Impairments—Use gestures and motions to help the child understand the directions.

Cognitive and/or Developmental Delays—Limit the child's choices in guessing what is in the bag. "How did you know? Did your ears or nose help you choose the answer?"

Emotional Disturbance—Allow the child to discuss his guesses and the reason for his guesses with a peer.

Other Health Impairments/Attention Deficit Hyperactive Disorder—Help the child to attend using close proximity of contact. Allowing the child to whisper the answer to you will keep individuals from yelling out their responses.

Orthopedic Impairments—Provide access to the guessing bag at the child's level of sight and her ability to touch.

Curriculum Connections

- **Language and Literacy**—Use the question "How do you know?" during the lesson. Encourage the children to use one of their senses to answer the question.
- **Science**—Help the children make a chart of items they learn about by using their senses. Under a "nose" picture, list things they smell. Under an "ear" picture, list things they hear, and so on.

Hearing

Time

20 minutes

Materials

- Noisemaker, such as a handheld clicker, rattle, or bells
- Blindfold (optional)

Objectives

Children will:

1. Identify the location of a sound in the room.
2. Use their ears to listen carefully to sounds.

Lesson

- Gather the children on the floor. Have a noisemaker behind your back. As you sit with the children, make a noise with the noisemaker.
- Ask the children what they hear and where the sound is coming from.
- Show the children the noisemaker and demonstrate how it works.
- Have the children sit in a circle in the middle of the rug area. Select one child to sit in the middle and ask her to close or cover her eyes.
- Ask the children to join you as you sing "Listen, Listen, What Do You Hear?" During the song, give the noisemaker to a child seated in outer ring of the circle. Ask her to hold the noisemaker behind her back and shake it one time at the end of the third line in the song.

Listen, Listen, What Do You Hear? by Diana Nabors
(Tune: "Row, Row, Row Your Boat")
Listen, listen, what do you hear?
All around the room,
Listen carefully, listen now. (make the noise)
Tell us where it is.

- Ask the child who had her eyes closed to open her eyes and walk around the inside of the circle to listen as the sound is made one more time. Ask her to point to the child who has the noisemaker.
- Continue, with the child who had the noisemaker closing or covering her eyes and the listener (the child in the middle of the circle with her eyes closed or covered) giving the noisemaker to another child.
- Repeat as many times as needed for most children to have a turn, or until the children are tired of singing and playing.

Review

During transition times, repeat the activity in various locations.

Assessment Strategy

Ask each child questions about the location of sounds.

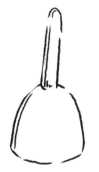

Accommodations/ Modifications

Autism—Give the child verbal cues and make gestures to encourage her participation in group games.

Speech or Language Impairments—Praise the child's verbalizations.

Hearing Impairments—Face the child when talking. Visually cue the child on the direction of the sound.

Visual Impairments—Use language as effectively as possible, especially in giving information and directions. Provide verbal orientation should the child appear momentarily confused.

Cognitive and/or Developmental Delays—Help the child attend to the task using verbal cuing, eye contact, and signals, including waiting until it is her turn. Sit near the child and invite her to tell you her guesses about who is holding the noisemaker to help her participate in the game.

Emotional Disturbance—Help the child attend to the task using verbal cuing, eye contact, and signals, including waiting until it is her turn. Sit near the child and invite her to tell you who is holding the noisemaker to help her participate in the game.

Other Health Impairments/Attention Deficit Hyperactive Disorder—Use carpet squares or small rugs to signify seated spots.

Orthopedic Impairments—Make materials accessible at the child's body level. Seat the child on the same level as other children when playing the game. You or the teaching assistant can maneuver the child when she is participating. Use questioning skills to help her participate.

Curriculum Connections

- **Language and Literacy**—Suggest that the children discuss and describe sounds in the environment, including sounds in stories, poems, songs, as well as daily environment.
- **Music**—Play the listening game like you play Musical Chairs so all the children can listen for sounds in their environment.
- **Science**—Provide times during the day when the children can sit quietly and listen to the environmental sounds around them.

Hearing Shakers

Time

10 minutes

Materials

- 8 small unbreakable jars that are the same or similar (film canisters or baby food jars work well)
- Materials to put into the jars, such as pebbles, small bells, paper clips, marbles

Review

Place the shaker jars in centers to enable the children to repeat the experience.

Assessment Strategy

Note whether each child is able to match the sounds of the jars.

Objectives

Children will:

1. Use their sense of hearing to match the sounds they hear.
2. Match sounds that are alike.

Preparation

If the jars are clear, cover the outside with construction paper or contact paper. Fill two jars with pebbles, two with small bells, two with paper clips, and two with marbles.

Lesson

- Have a small group of children gather at a table with four pairs of small jars.
- Ask the children to shake the jars and listen to the sounds.
- Ask the children to match the jars that make the same sound.

Accommodations/Modifications

Autism—Allow the child individual and peer time to complete the activity.

Speech or Language Impairments—Encourage the child to verbalize what he hears in the shakers.

Hearing Impairments—Allow the child to place the shaker jar close to his ear for maximum discrimination.

Visual Impairments—Help the child locate the shakers by using directional words and placing shakers on a tray.

Cognitive and/or Developmental Delays—Use a limited number of shakers at a time.

Emotional Disturbance—Use a limited number of shakers at a time.

Other Health Impairments/Attention Deficit Hyperactive Disorder—Use a tray to help the child organize the materials.

Orthopedic Impairments—Place the materials at the child's level. If necessary, ask peers to help him shake the jars.

Curriculum Connections

- **Art**—Suggest that the children draw pictures of things they enjoy hearing.
- **Language and Literacy**—Listen to a story about sounds or repeat the children's favorite rhymes.
- **More Language and Literacy**—Talk about other sounds children hear during the day.
- **Math**—Create a graph of loud and soft sounds with the children.

THE FIVE SENSES
Hearing Game

Time

20–30 minutes

Materials

Blindfold/bandana

Review

Place a blindfold in centers so that the children can play this game during center time. Supervise their use of the blindfold.

Assessment Strategy

Assess each child's ability to identify another child's voice correctly.

Objectives

Children will:

1. Identify sounds that they hear.
2. Work cooperatively in a game format.

Lesson

- Sit on the floor in a circle. Choose one child and put a blindfold on this child and ask her to sit in the center of the circle.
- Point to a child seated in the outer ring of the circle and without saying this child's name have him say, "Guess who this is." Ask the blindfolded child to guess whose voice she heard.
- When the blindfolded child guesses correctly, all children in the circle chant, "What a Good Listener He Is!"

What a Good Listener He Is! by Diana Nabors
(Tune: "For He's a Jolly Good Fellow")
Oh, what a good listener he is! Oh, what a good listener he is!
Oh, what a good listener he is! Oh, what a good listener (say child's name) *is!*

- The blindfolded child joins the circle and the child whose name was said becomes the next blindfolded child. Play until all children get a turn.

Accommodations/ Modifications

Autism—Allow the child to close her eyes rather than using a bandana or a blindfold.

Speech or Language Impairments—Use forced-choice questions. "Did you hear a girl or boy?" "Did you hear Juan or Mark?"

Hearing Impairments—Have the child saying "Guess who this is" near this child when it is her turn to guess. Close proximity increases the ability to hear in a group situation.

Cognitive and/or Developmental Delays—Assist with forced-choice questions. "Did you hear a girl or boy?" "Did you hear Juan or Mark?"

Emotional Disturbance—Allow the child to close her eyes rather than being blindfolded. Use forced-choice questions to help the child identify her classmate.

Other Health Impairments/Attention Deficit Hyperactive Disorder—Use carpet squares or rug "spots" to help the child with excessive movement.

Curriculum Connections

- **Art**—Encourage the children to draw items they enjoy hearing.
- **Language and Literacy**—Talk with the children about the things they hear. Record the discussion on chart paper.

Mystery Box

Time

20 minutes

Materials

- Box
- Soft material, such as felt or sheets of soft foam
- Small items collected from the classroom, such as crayons, small blocks, small balls, paintbrushes, books, and so on
- Picture of each item (optional)

Objectives

Children will:

1. Identify items by using their sense of touch.
2. Discuss the way items feel.

Preparation

Make a mystery box by cutting a 6" square hole in a paper box (boxes for copy paper work well) and then decorating it. Cover the hole with felt or soft foam sheets. Cut slits in the felt or foam to allow children to reach inside the box easily and feel the items inside. Cut the hole and covering large enough for children to extract the items as needed.

Lesson

- Gather the children on the floor in front of the mystery box.
- One at a time, ask each child to place one hand inside the mystery box and feel around until he finds an object.
- Ask each child to identify the object using only his sense of touch.
- After the child has identified the object, let him take the item from the box to see if he was correct.
- (Optional: Using picture cards depicting items on the box, ask the child to draw a card from the pile of picture cards and feel inside the box to find the pictured item.)

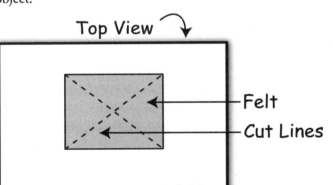

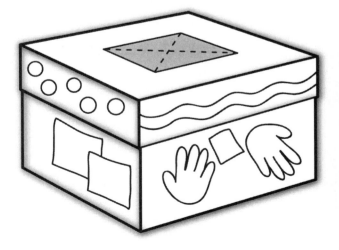

Review

Place the mystery box in centers. Allow the children to place items in the box for their peers to identify through their sense of touch.

Assessment Strategy

Note whether each child can identify the item placed in the mystery box.

Accommodations/ Modifications

Autism—Allow child to observe the lesson if he is tactilely defensive.

Speech or Language Impairments—Help the child find words to describe what he feels in the box.

Hearing Impairments—Use gestures to convey the meaning of the directions.

Cognitive and/or Developmental Delays—Let the child try several times to identify the object, or let him feel for a certain item in the box.

Emotional Disturbance—Allow the child to explore the mystery box individually before using it with the group.

Other Health Impairments/Attention Deficit Hyperactive Disorder—To help him wait his turn, give the child a number card that shows when it is his turn.

Orthopedic Impairments—Help the child place his hand in the box and with your hand guiding his, move items to his hand.

Curriculum Connections

- **Art**—Provide opportunities for the children to draw an unknown item in the mystery box.
- **Connecting with Home**—Invite families to send objects to be placed in the mystery box.
- **Language and Literacy**—Provide ample time to discuss, predict, and draw an item in the mystery box.

Seeing

Time

10–15 minutes

Materials

- Set of large colored pictures from magazines or other sources
- 6" x 6" cards
- Glue
- 6" x 6" pieces of paper
- Scissors

Objectives

Children will:

1. Identify what they see.
2. Identify seeing as a way of gaining information.

Preparation

Select magazine photographs or other pictures. Glue each picture on a separate 6" x 6" card. Create two to four 6" x 6" overlays with different shaped holes in them. (The overlays should look like Swiss cheese!) Stack the overlays over the photograph to allow a gradual revealing of the photograph.

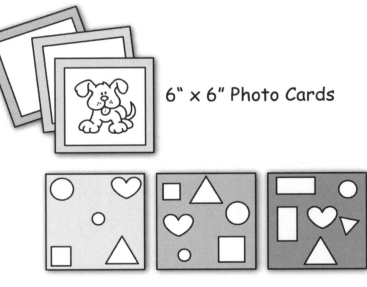

6" x 6" Photo Cards

6" x 6" Overlays

Lesson

- Tell the children they will play a guessing game like Hide and Seek. Tell them this game will be different because it will be with hidden pictures.
- Engage the children in a discussion about using their eyes to find out information.
- Present a Hidden Picture (one picture card covered by two to four overlays).

Review

Place overlays and magazine pictures in centers for the children's use.

- Ask the children to guess what the picture is. Remove one sheet of paper at a time, each time revealing a little more of the picture. Continue to ask the children to guess until all of the overlays are removed.
- Repeat the activity using a new picture behind the overlays.

Accommodations/ Modifications

Autism—Provide time for the child to look at the materials before the lesson begins.

Speech or Language Impairments—Describe what you see and ask the child to describe what she sees. Define any new vocabulary words.

Hearing Impairments—Use gestures to help the child focus on the pictures. Make sure materials are easily visible.

Visual Impairments—Allow the child preferential seating and provide a tripod magnifier or stationary magnifying glass for ease in focusing.

Cognitive and/or Developmental Delays—Extend the questioning wait time. Model language choices to allow the child more accuracy in her guesses.

Emotional Disturbance—Provide assistance with attention. Once the picture is revealed, allow the child a chance to repeat the lesson. Provide translucent paper during Center Time to allow her to see the majority of the hidden picture.

Other Health Impairments/Attention Deficit Hyperactive Disorder—Provide carpet squares for individual space. Provide visual cues and cues using gestures to gain the child's attention.

Orthopedic Impairments—Place the pictures at an easy viewing level.

Curriculum Connections

- **Art**—Provide paper and drawing materials for children to draw their own pictures. Have children cover parts of their pictures so others can use their sense of sight to identify the pictures.
- **More Art**—Provide toilet tissue tubes so the children can make spyglasses to look through as they practice using their sense of sight.
- **Language and Literacy**—Provide copies of Tana Hoban's books *Just Look* and *Look Again!* for children to read and identify the pictures hidden in the book by an overlay template.
- **Science**—Provide a magnifying glass so children can look closely at their environment.
- **More Science**—Provide colored glasses for the children to wear and ask them to describe how the environment looks different through the colored glasses.

Spectacles

Time

20 minutes

Materials

- *Spectacles* by Ellen Raskin
- Poster board
- Scissors
- Colored transparencies or colored translucent file folders (blue, red, yellow, green, orange, purple, gray)
- Stapler or tape

Objectives

Children will:

1. Be able to retell the story *Spectacles* by Ellen Raskin.
2. Describe items they see in the classroom.

Preparation

Prior to the lesson, make looking glasses for each child by cutting two magnifying glass shapes out of poster board. The circular hole should be 5"–7" in diameter. Cut the colored transparencies or colored file folders to fit the hole in each magnifying glass. To create each magnifying glass, place a single sheet of color transparency between the magnifying glass shapes. Staple or tape the magnifying glass shapes together to make colored, handheld looking glasses. (If a visual distortion of the image is desired, brush a thin glaze of equal parts school glue and water on the transparency. Let it dry before assembling the looking glasses.)

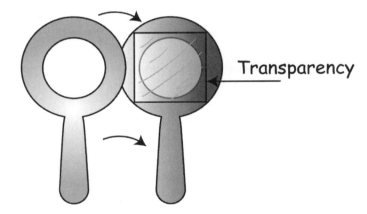

Transparency

Lesson

- Have the children gather on the rug to listen to *Spectacles*.
- Ask the children questions about the story. Focus your questions on why each character in the story saw things differently from the other characters.
- Give each child one of the looking glasses.

Review

Leave colored overlays in the Science Center for use throughout the day.

Assessment Strategy

Question each child individually as to what he sees when looking through distorted lenses.

- Have the children discuss the things that look different when they look through the looking glasses.
- Discuss the distorted images and talk about how people use their sight to gain information.

Accommodations/ Modifications

Autism—Discuss the sense of sight with the child. Talk him through the activity and encourage him to participate.

Speech or Language Impairments—Reinforce correct sentence structure and encourage new vocabulary.

Hearing Impairments—Have the child sit near you while you read the story.

Visual Impairments—Help the child with the visual part of the activity by describing what is seen.

Cognitive and/or Developmental Delays—Help the child describe what he sees with his looking glasses.

Emotional Disturbance—Help the child describe what he sees with his looking glasses.

Other Health Impairments/Attention Deficit Hyperactive Disorder—Help the child describe what he sees with his looking glasses.

Orthopedic Impairments—Have the child sit near the book so he can see the pictures. Using bolsters and wedges will allow the child to participate at the same level as other children.

Curriculum Connections

- **Art**—Have children use tissue paper to create overlapping designs. Brush glue thinned with water over the tissue paper design to seal the artwork.
- **Dramatic Play**—Purchase large oversized sunglasses to add to the Dress-Up Center for the children to use in their play.
- **Science**—Place small cups of colored water, eyedroppers, and clear cups in the Science Center for children to use to make different colored waters.

Binoculars

Time

30–40 minutes

Materials

- Toilet paper tubes
- Rubber bands
- Red and yellow colored cellophane paper pre-cut into 4" squares
- Rubber bands
- Tape or large rubber bands

Objectives

Children will:

1. Share their view of the environment through different lenses.
2. Identify a pair of binoculars when they see them.

Preparation

Make several sets of binoculars by placing the 4" square sheets of cellophane paper on the ends of paper tubes and securing them with rubber bands. Put yellow cellophane on one tube and red cellophane on the other. Use tape or larger rubber bands to secure two tubes—one yellow and one red—to form a set of binoculars.

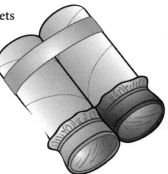

Lesson

- Present one set of the colored binoculars to the children. Talk with them about looking through the binoculars.
- Pass several sets of colored binoculars through the group so every child has a turn looking through them.
- Ask the children to remember the previous lessons about the sense of sight (Seeing and Spectacles).
- Help the children make their own set of binoculars by covering one paper tube with a red cellophane square and one tube with a yellow cellophane square. Have them attach the cellophane to the tube with a rubber band.
- Let the children look around the room with one eye tube and then the other. Engage them in a discussion about how things look with each eye tube.
- Help the children use a large rubber band or tape to hold the two eye tubes together to make binoculars.
- Discuss with the children the difference each color and then both colors make as they view their environment.

Accommodations/Modifications

Autism—Provide opportunities for the child to view her environment using many different colored lenses. Different sunglasses work well for this.

Review

Allow the children to use their binoculars during the day to look at and notice the differences in their environment.

Assessment Strategy

Ask each child to describe what she sees through her binoculars.

Speech or Language Impairments—Help the child with any new vocabulary words. Encourage the child to use descriptive words to describe the colored environment.

Hearing Impairments—Have the child repeat directions for clarity and comprehension.

Visual Impairments—Encourage the child to use the sight she has and to discuss with the other children what she sees.

Cognitive and/or Developmental Delays—Provide opportunities for the child to view her environment using many different colored lenses. Different sunglasses work well for this.

Emotional Disturbance—Provide opportunities for the child to view her environment using different covered overlays. Transparent colored file folders work well for this.

Other Health Impairments/Attention Deficit Hyperactive Disorder—Stay close to the child to help her during the viewing times with the binoculars.

Orthopedic Impairments—Provide materials at the child's level. If needed, ask a peer to help her attach the cellophane with a rubber band.

Curriculum Connections

- **Art**—Have the children draw pictures of their new views of the environment. They can lay colored cellophane over their pictures for visual effects.
- **Language and Literacy**—In a small group or individually, ask the children to dictate a story about their binoculars.
- **Science**—Provide a pair of binoculars for children to use to observe their classroom and the playground.

THE FIVE SENSES
Colored Balls

Time

20 minutes

Materials

Four balls, such as ping-pong balls, juggling balls, rubber balls, or Nerf balls, that are the same, in four different colors—red, yellow, blue, black

Review

Place the balls in the Science Center so the children can continue to explore this activity.

Assessment Strategy

Observe each child's guess. Use questioning skills to note whether each child is able to connect how she uses one or more of her senses to obtain information from the environment.

Objectives

Children will:

1. Select objects using the sense of touch.
2. Discuss the sense of sight.

Lesson

■ Show the children the four colored balls. Select one child to stand with his back to you, holding his hands behind his back and keeping his eyes closed.

■ Select one colored ball, show it to the class, and place it, unseen by the child, into the child's hands.

■ Ask the child to tell the other children the color of the ball he is holding without looking at it. Repeat with other children.

■ Discuss with the children why it is hard to know the color of the ball.

■ Repeat the lesson, this time letting the child keep his eyes open and showing him the ball you are placing into his hands.

■ Continue with other children. Discuss why it is easier to name the color of the ball this time.

Accommodations/Modifications

Autism—Use pictures of the balls to help the child select the ball he is feeling.

Speech or Language Impairments—Give the child forced-choice questions to help him communicate.

Hearing Impairments—Repeat the directions for the child.

Cognitive and/or Developmental Delays—Use gestures to help the child understand the instructions. Allow the child to observe other children guessing before it is his turn. Allow him to repeat directions to help him understand them.

Emotional Disturbance—Discuss "incorrect" answers prior to his turn.

Other Health Impairments/Attention Deficit Hyperactive Disorder—Stay close to the child to help him participate.

Orthopedic Impairments—If the child cannot place his hands behind his back, have him close his eyes or place a scarf or cloth over the ball as he feels it.

Curriculum Connections

■ **Language and Literacy**—Provide opportunities for the children to describe items both seen and unseen.

■ **Outdoors**—Hide balls around the playground for children to search for and find.

■ **Science**—Provide other items in the classroom for the children to touch and describe.

Smelly Paint

Time

15 minutes

Materials

- Jell-O and water, or powdered Jello-O and tempera paint
- Paintbrushes
- Paper

Review

Discuss the smells of the paints with the children and ask them to describe their experiences with "scratch and sniff" items.

Assessment Strategy

Assess each child's use of his sense of smell as he paints. Ask the child what he smells.

Objectives

Children will:

1. Use their sense of smell as they paint.
2. Paint pictures using a variety of scented paints.

Preparation

Make different smelly paints by mixing a packet of Jell-O with 2 ounces of water or add 2 tablespoons of dry Jell-O to tempera paint. Place the smelly paints in the Art Center.

Lesson

- The children at the Art Center can select different prepared Smelly Paints to use as they create their pictures, experiencing the different scents as they paint.
- As the children paint, talk with them about the smells of the Smelly Paints and about different scents and paints.
- Once the paint is dry, the children can scratch the paint and sniff the smell again.

Accommodations/Modifications

Autism—With the child discuss the sense of smell and the scents used.

Speech or Language Impairments—Help the child by preteaching vocabulary relating to scents.

Cognitive and/or Developmental Delays—Discuss the scents used and explain that the paint is still paint and is not edible. Name and discuss each scent and using one's nose to smell.

Emotional Disturbance—Monitor use of paints, assisting as needed. Use eye contact to encourage participation.

Other Health Impairments/Attention Deficit Hyperactive Disorder—Encourage the child to verbalize his thoughts about the scents.

Orthopedic Impairments—Use grips on paintbrushes to help the child hold the paintbrush.

Curriculum Connections

- **Art**—Add food extracts to different paints and art materials.
- **Language and Literacy**—Discuss and write about the power of the sense of smell using class-dictated stories.
- **Science**—Add food extracts to different paints and art materials such as glue and playdough. Discuss the scents.

Matching Smells

Time

15–20 minutes

Materials

- 10 items that have distinct smells, such as minced onions, peanut butter, banana slices, lemon slices, cinnamon sticks or ground cinnamon, black pepper, peppermint extract, vinegar, garlic, perfume
- Small four-ounce paper drinking cups
- Aluminum foil
- Toothpicks
- Pictures of each item with a distinct smell

Objectives

Children will:

1. Use their sense of smell to match scents.
2. Identify scents of familiar items.

Preparation

Before the children arrive, prepare several smelly cup pairs by putting individual items with distinct smells (see list to left) into two cups, and then grouping the like-smelling pairs together. Cover each cup with a piece of aluminum foil and pierce the foil cover five or six times with a toothpick. Draw or cut out magazine pictures of each item in the paper cups.

Put in Cup

Banana Slices

Holes Foil

Lesson

- Gather a small group of children at a table that has various foil-covered cups on it.
- Hand one child two cups with peanut butter and one cup with perfume.
- Ask the child to match the two cups with the same scent.
- Observe while each child takes a turn smelling the cups and matching the cups that are the same until all 20 cups have been matched.
- After the cups are matched, show the children the ten pictures. Ask them to match each picture to the cup with the correct scent.

Accommodations/Modifications

Autism—Limit the number of cups to four pairs. Give the child three cups at a time to match.

Speech or Language Impairments—Reinforce the child's verbalizations of what she smells.

Hearing Impairments—Face the child when you give directions. Allow her to watch peers prior to her turn.

Visual Impairments—Place the cups on a tray to aid in location of pairs.

Cognitive and/or Developmental Delays—Limit the number of cups and pairs.

Emotional Disturbance—Use only pleasant smells. Let the child select the scents to match.

Review

Place the smelling jars in centers so the children can repeat the activity on their own.

Assessment Strategy

Record each child's success in matching the scents.

Other Health Impairments/Attention Deficit Hyperactive Disorder—Limit the number of cups for matching at one time.

Orthopedic Impairments—Help the child move as needed.

Curriculum Connections

- **Art**—Suggest that the children draw a picture of one of the items in a specific "smelly jar."
- **Language and Literacy**—Encourage the children to record, in writing or by drawing, pleasant and unpleasant smells.
- **Math**—Ask the children to categorize scents in their environment. Help them to graph the scents in two categories: pleasant and unpleasant.
- **Science**—Have children use their sense of smell to identify other items, including "What's for Lunch?"
- **More Science**—Provide an opportunity for children to find a hidden scent in the classroom.

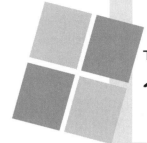

Touch

Time

15–20 minutes

Materials

- Assorted small objects with different textures, such as a sponge, a cotton ball, a small ball, burlap material, sandpaper, a plastic card, and a ball of adhesive putty
- Tray
- Chart paper and marker

Review

Place the items in centers for further investigation by the children.

Assessment Strategy

Ask each child to use words to describe the way an object feels.

Objectives

Children will:

1. Practice using their sense of touch.
2. Discuss the way items feel.

Lesson

- Display the objects on a tray. Sit in a circle with a small group of children. Place the tray in the middle of the circle.
- Ask the children to look at the objects and, without touching any of them, to describe the objects.
- Select a child to pick up a named item and to say one new descriptive word about that item as she picks it up. Write this word on chart paper.
- Discuss with the children the information the child's sense of touch gave her when she picked up the item. Continue with other objects.
- Have the children categorize the items using the descriptors listed on chart paper.

Accommodations/Modifications

Autism—Have the child sit near you to maintain interaction. Allow the child to touch the item and use a forced-choice answer as she describes the item.

Speech or Language Impairments—Assist the child with vocabulary as needed.

Hearing Impairments—Use gestures to help the child understand the directions.

Visual Impairments—Have the child sit near the items.

Cognitive and/or Developmental Delays—Allow the child to practice touching the items and describing them.

Emotional Disturbance—Allow the child to choose the item she wishes to touch. Encourage her to use sentences when describing the objects.

Other Health Impairments/Attention Deficit Hyperactive Disorder—Help the child take turns by using cues and gestures.

Orthopedic Impairments—Place the item in the child's hand and help her manipulate it so she can describe its traits.

Curriculum Connections

- **Art**—In the Art Center, put out items with different textures, such as sandpaper, sand, wire mesh, and feathers, for the children to use to make art products that have tactile sensations.
- **Language and Literacy**—Provide ample time for discussion in small groups or with individuals about the way things feel. Make a list of texture words to include on the classroom Word Wall.

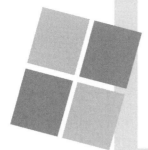

THE FIVE SENSES
Touching Water

Time
10 minutes

Materials
- 2 similar dishpans of water, one with warm water and one with chilled water
- Trays
- Towels

Review
Place ice cubes in one jar and warm or room temperature water in a second jar in the Science Center for the children to feel the difference.

Assessment Strategy
Assess each child's description of the two temperatures of water.

Objectives
Children will:
1. Discuss similarities and differences.
2. Identify differences using the sense of touch.

Lesson
- Place one dishpan on each tray. Place the two trays on a towel side by side on the floor.
- Gather the children on the floor. Ask them to describe what they see in the dishpans. Have them focus on the similarities in the trays of water.
- Ask individual children to dip their fingers or hands into each tray and describe any differences between the two trays of water.
- Allow each child to feel the difference in the water and to describe the differences.

Accommodations/Modifications
Autism—Understand that the child may be defensive about placing his hands in the water.
Speech or Language Impairments—Help the child use complete sentences.
Hearing Impairments—Face the child when talking to him.
Visual Impairments—Help the child place his hands in the water.
Cognitive and/or Developmental Delays—Discuss the water with the child and his feelings about the temperature of the water.
Emotional Disturbance—Explain and discuss with the child the water and the feelings he is having about the temperature of the water.
Other Health Impairments/Attention Deficit Hyperactive Disorder—To avoid spills and splashes, help the child place his hands in the water. Talk the child through the demonstration and his exploration of the water.
Orthopedic Impairments—Help the child place his hands in the water.

Curriculum Connections
- **Bulletin Board**—Take photographs of the children as they conduct experiments with the water. Display them on a bulletin board with the class report (see Language and Literacy).
- **Language and Literacy**—Engage the children in a discussion about the temperature of the water in the two dishpans. Write a class report on chart paper about the children's experiences with the water.
- **Science**—Place three open buckets of water in the Science Center: one with warm water, one with room temperature water, and one with cold water. Have the children place one hand in the warm water and one hand in the cold water for one minute. Then have them place both hands in the room temperature water. Listen to the children's discussion about the temperature changes they feel. Monitor the children at all times.

Tasting and Smelling Lemonade

Time
10–15 minutes

Materials
- 4 small pitchers: 1 with sweetened lemonade, 1 with unsweetened lemonade, 1 with peppermint extract mixed with water, and 1 with water
- Small 2-ounce cups

Objectives
Children will:
1. Discuss the sense of taste and smell.
2. Match similar items.

Preparation
Before Group or Circle Time, fill the four pitchers with the liquids as described in materials.

Lesson
- Gather a small group of children at a table. Place on the table the four small pitchers. Two will contain lemonade and two will contain water.
- Ask the children to use their sense of sight and look at the liquids in the pitchers and match the pitchers that are alike.
- Have the children match the pitchers using their sense of sight.
- Tell the children that while the sense of sight is important, they can also use other senses.
- Explain that the two lemonade pitchers are different. Tell the children that one does not have sugar. Ask the children which sense they would like to use to learn which lemonade has sugar and which does not.
- Encourage children to taste a small amount of each of the two lemonade mixtures to decide which has sugar.
- Review with the children what they know about the senses of sight and taste. Then direct the children to look at the other two pitchers. Tell them that one contains peppermint water and one contains plain water.
- Talk again about the sense of sight. Help the children decide which sense they should use to determine which pitcher has the peppermint water in it. Guide them to use their sense of smell to find out which pitcher contains the peppermint water.
- Continue to talk about the senses, focusing on the importance of using many senses.

Accommodations/Modifications

Review

Place the materials in the Science Center for a week so children can review the experience.

Assessment Strategy

Listen to each child describe her senses of smell and taste. Have her discuss other smells and tastes that she enjoys.

Autism—Provide time for the child to experience the pitchers of water with one-on-one assistance from you or another adult.

Speech or Language Impairments—Provide the children with vocabulary words for the senses that they can use. Help the child by using descriptive words to describe scents and tastes.

Hearing Impairments—Provide visual cues and peer modeling to help the child understand the lesson.

Visual Impairment—Allow the child time to look at the pitchers of water prior to the lesson.

Cognitive and/or Developmental Delays—Provide additional times for the child to replay the lesson and discuss the senses of sight, smell, and taste.

Emotional Disturbance—Encourage discussion by providing opportunities for the child to practice the lesson with the guidance of an adult.

Other Health Impairments/Attention Deficit Hyperactive Disorder—Reinforce the child's ability to wait until she has a turn to match, smell, and taste the liquids in the pitchers.

Orthopedic Impairments—Provide straws for the cups as needed and enough room for the child to maneuver physically in and out of the activity.

Curriculum Connections

- **Language and Literacy**—Provide opportunities for the children to brainstorm descriptive words as they taste and smell. Write their suggestions on the classroom Word Wall.
- **More Language and Literacy**—With small groups of children, make a chart of words that describe their favorite tastes and smells.
- **Science**—Provide other food items for the children to taste and describe. This activity must be supervised to prevent the spread of germs among children and to ensure that children who are allergic to certain foods do not eat them, and to be sure that the foods do not pose a choking hazard.

Tasting Apples

Time
30–45 minutes

Materials
- Four different types of apples, such as Granny Smith, Golden Delicious, Winesap, Fuji, or Gala
- Knife (adult use only)
- Cutting board
- Paper plates
- Napkins
- Paper
- Poster board
- Scissors
- Crayons
- Graph mat or chart to glue apple cutouts
- *The Apple Pie Tree* by Zoe Hall

Objectives
The children will:
1. Identify different tastes.
2. State their taste preferences.

Preparation
Cut up apples to give each child in the class one taste of each of the four types of apples. Place each type of apple on a separate paper plate. Place the remaining apples in a basket. Cut out the shape of an apple from poster board for each child. Make a graph chart with four columns, each one for a different apple.

Lesson
- Gather the children on the rug around a basket filled with a variety of apples. Engage the children in a discussion about the differences they notice in the apples.
- Encourage the children to taste all four types of apples and describe the differences in taste, using terms such as sweet, tart, and sour.
- Give each child an apple cutout and ask them to color the apple.
- Have the children graph their taste preferences by asking each child to put his cutout apple on the graph under the apple that he likes best.
- Ask the children questions to look at the graph to determine which type of apple children enjoyed tasting the most, least, and the same.
- As the children finish tasting the remaining apple slices, read *The Apple Pie Tree* by Zoe Hall.

Review

Place apple cutouts in the Science Center with another basket of apples so the children can discuss their favorite and least favorite apples and give reasons for their selections.

Assessment Strategy

Assess each child's reasoning for his selection. Monitor and reinforce the use of descriptive words.

Accommodations and Modifications

Autism—Encourage the child to taste different apples and to engage in the graphing, assisted by a peer or another adult as needed.

Speech or Language Impairments—Encourage and praise the child for correct sentence structure and word choice. Define new words for the child.

Hearing Impairments—Use cuing and gestures, and face the child during discussions.

Visual Impairments—Provide ample opportunity for the child to look at the apples before cutting and direct his attention to the apple peel to help him select his favorite apple.

Cognitive and/or Developmental Delays—Encourage and dialogue with the child as he tastes and selects his favorite apple.

Emotional Disturbance—Encourage and dialogue with the child as he tastes and selects his favorite apple.

Other Health Impairments/Attention Deficit Hyperactive Disorder—Cue the child and have him sit near you so you can help him take turns in the discussion. Provide opportunities for the child to select his favorite apple.

Orthopedic Impairments—Provide apple slices or small taste bits, depending on the child's level of ability.

Curriculum Connections

- **Book Center**—Place *The Apple Pie Tree* by Zoe Hall in the Book Center for children to enjoy.
- **Math**—Help the children use the apple graph to explore the math concepts of more, how many, less, difference, and equal.
- **Science**—Have the children experiment with placing apple slices on different parts of their tongues. Which areas of the tongue do they use to taste different apple slices?

Senses Center Game

Time

20–30 minutes

Materials

- Chart with 5 columns; the top of each column will have a picture and a corresponding word:
  - Eye–Seeing
  - Nose–Smelling
  - Mouth–Tasting
  - Ear–Hearing
  - Hand–Touching
- 25 picture cards of the following items: light bulb, sun, moon and stars, flashlight, mirror, garbage can, skunk, perfume bottle, flower, smoke, ice cream, candy, apple, hamburger, soda, piano, bell, person yelling, ambulance, music notes, pinecone, pencil, book, ice cube, pool of water

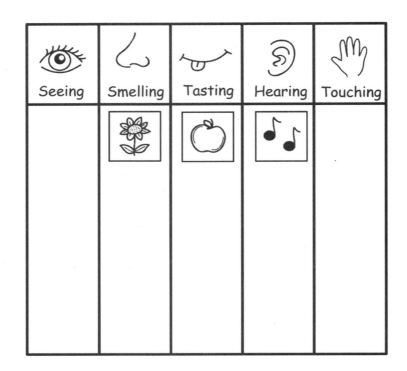

Objectives

Children will:

1. Match the pictures that go with each sense.
2. Discuss the pictured items with their classmates.

Lesson

- Place the chart and the picture cards in centers for the children to use on their own or with others.
- Tell the children to look at the top of each column for a sense that is used to learn about the item on each picture card.
- Have the child or children pick up one of the picture cards and place that picture card under an open space in the column that designates the sense used to learn about the item on the picture card.

Review

Allow the child to repeat the game later in the day or on another day.

Assessment Strategy

Observe whether each child can identify the sense used to identify each of the items on the picture cards.

Accommodations/Modifications

Autism—Help the child focus on the task by handing her one picture card at a time.

Speech or Language Impairments—Ask the child to name each picture card or to complete sentences about the picture card and the sense used to identify the picture on each card. "I can smell the perfume with my nose."

Visual Impairments— Help the child use her sense of sight.

Cognitive and/or Developmental Delays—Limit the number of picture cards.

Emotional Disturbance—Praise the correct placement of cards during the activity.

Other Health Impairments/Attention Deficit Hyperactive Disorder—Limit the number of cards accessible with each turn.

Orthopedic Impairments—Help the child place the cards on the chart by using Velcro strips or felt pieces.

Curriculum Connections

- **Art**—Encourage the children to develop a collage of items for each sense by cutting or tearing pictures of objects from magazines that relate to that sense.
- **Language and Literacy**—Have the children use their drawings to describe a particular sense, including writing or dictating a description of that sense. Combine into a class booklet about the senses.
- **Science**—Encourage children to categorize the picture cards in a variety of ways and to explain their logic for the choices they make.

INTRODUCTION TO

My Body

Time
15 minutes

Materials
- Chuck Murphy's *My First Book of the Body* (or a suitable substitute)
- Classroom skeleton model, (borrow from a high school science lab or purchase a miniature skeleton from a novelty store); or cut pictures from magazines to show various parts of the body

Review
Ask children to point to each body part as you name specific body parts.

Assessment
Ask each child to show you various body parts.

Objectives
Children will:
1. Identify the parts of their bodies.
2. Compare their bodies with the classroom skeleton model.

Lesson
- Gather the children together for Group or Circle Time.
- Show the children *My First Book of the Body,* a book with pop-up flaps, and ask them to guess what the book will be about.
- Read the book and engage the children in a discussion as you show them each flap.
- Ask the children to point to their own body parts as you turn the pages of the book.
- Ask the children to compare their own body parts to the parts of the skeleton model or pictures of parts of the body.

Accommodations/Modifications
Autism—Model pointing to body parts before asking the child to point to his body parts.

Speech or Language Impairments—During the discussion of the book, scaffold the child's language and have him complete sentences as you show the body parts on each flap.

Hearing Impairments—Seat the child across from you as you read the book and present the lesson so he can see your lips as you speak.

Visual Impairments—Describe your actions as you read the book and present the lesson. Allow the child to feel the skeleton, if available, and to describe what he is doing.

Cognitive and/or Developmental Delays—Repeat and review body parts frequently to ensure the child is learning and retaining the information.

Emotional Disturbance—Seat the child next to you and give him positive feedback when he participates and when he uses appropriate behavior.

Other Health Impairment/Attention Deficit Hyperactivity Disorder—Provide mats for the child to sit on during the activity to help him define his boundaries while seated.

Orthopedic Impairment—Assist the child in pointing to body parts, if needed.

Curriculum Extensions
- **Language and Literacy**—Place *My First Book of the Body* by Chuck Murphy in the Book Center for children to enjoy.
- **Math**—Prepare body part puzzles using pictures from magazines. Children can put the puzzles together during Center Time.
- **Science**—Place pictures of skeletons or the skeleton model in a prominent spot in the classroom where children can observe and touch them during the day.

MY BODY

Head

Time

15–20 minutes

Materials

- Photographs of children's heads and infants' heads
- Replica of a skull and/or a miniature brain (optional)

Objectives

Children will

1. Demonstrate their understanding of head and point to where it is on their bodies.
2. Identify heads in pictures.

Lesson

- Point to your head and tell the children that today you are going to talk about heads. Remind them that the head is part of the body. Talk about how animals have heads, too.
- Ask the following questions:
  - "Is everyone's head the same?"
  - "How are heads different?"
  - "What are the features of your head?"
  - "How do your parents' heads look different from your head?" (Mention size, color of hair, and so on)
  - "What about your grandparents' heads? How are they different from your head?" (Mention size, color of hair, and so on)
  - "Let's look at pictures of babies' heads. How are they different from your heads?" (Mentions size, amount of hair, and so on)
- Continue the discussion, asking, "What is inside your head?"

Head

- If possible, show the children the replica of a skull and brain and talk about the importance of each. Tell the children that using the brain is what people use to talk, move, and think.
- Teach the children the following song, which is sung to the tune of "If You're Happy and You Know It."

My Brain by Laverne Warner
Inside my head is a brain,
My brain helps me think every day.
Inside my head is a great big brain,
That helps me do many things.

My brain helps me talk, yes it does.
My brain helps me talk, yes it does.
My brain helps me talk and move and sing;
My brain helps me do many things.

My brain helps me think every day.
Without my brain, I'd be a silly kid;
My brain helps me think every day.
My brain helps me think every day.

- Tell the children that you will place the models of the skull and brain in the Science Center for them to look at later.

Accommodations/Modifications

Autism—Use pictures of the heads of grownups, children, and babies when you ask the child questions about heads. Discuss the ways heads are the same and how they are different using the pictures as reference.

Speech or Language Impairments—Scaffold language when asking questions by having the child complete sentences that you have begun or by asking leading questions. Use pictures when you ask the questions.

Hearing Impairments—Use gestures or signs with the song, and encourage the child to participate using gestures or signs. Seat the child across from you as you introduce the lesson.

Visual Impairments—When talking about heads, have the child point to her head. Describe your actions as you perform them during the lesson.

Review

Ask the children to point to their heads and to tell you that their brains are inside their heads.

Cognitive and/or Developmental Delays—Use short phrases and simple sentences when asking the child questions. Provide cues to help her answer questions; for example, point to the body part to answer the question.

Emotional Disturbance—Seat the child next to you during the lesson.

Other Health Impairment/Attention Deficit Hyperactivity Disorder—Use pictures or objects to promote the child's engagement during the discussion of heads.

Curriculum Connections

- **Art**—Ask children to use clay or playdough to make heads shaped like their own. Encourage them to work on the project for several days using unbreakable hand mirrors to look at their heads and then to use what they see to shape their playdough heads.

Assessment Strategy

Ask individual children to discuss what they know about their heads and what is inside their heads. You can also conduct this assessment in small groups.

- **More Art**—Use a Styrofoam model of a head as a base for gluing on sequins, beads, yarn, ribbon, and other art material. This is a good project for a small group of children who enjoy tactile experiences.
- **Language and Literacy**—Print the song on a poster board or chart paper and place it in the Art Center for children to sing as they make their head sculptures.
- **Listening Center**—Use a cassette recorder to record the song for children to listen to at their leisure.
- **Science**—Invite the children to look at strands of hair with magnifying glasses. This is a good introduction to the lesson on hair.

Ears

Time

15–20 minutes

Materials

- Diagram of the ear canal and eardrum (commercial posters are available or go to www. enchanted learning.com/ subjects/ anatomy/ear/ label/label.shtml for a diagram)
- Drum and drumstick
- Small objects such as paper clips or pennies
- Paper cups with bottoms removed, one for each child
- Megaphone (optional)

Objectives

Children will

1. Be able to point to their ears on their own bodies.
2. Tell that they use ears to hear.

Preparation

Remove the bottoms from the paper cups.

Lesson

- Gather the children together for Group or Circle Time.
- Point to your ears and ask the children to name that part of the body. Tell the children that their ears help them hear, but that the ability to hear also depends on the inner canal and eardrum.
- Show the children the diagram of the ear canal and eardrum. Talk about sounds going into the canal and bumping into the eardrum, causing it to vibrate.
- Place a few small objects on a drum. Demonstrate what happens to the objects when the drum is struck: the drum head vibrates and makes the objects move. Explain to the children that this is exactly how the eardrum works. The vibration on the eardrum travels to the brain and allows us to hear. **Note:** Remind children that they should not place objects in their ear canals because doing so could impair their hearing.
- Show children how to cup their hands around their ears to hear things more effectively.
- Let the children place the paper cups that have had their bottoms removed over their ears to experiment with how they change the way they hear sounds. Show children how sounds can be muffled, too.
- If children are interested, talk about the volume of sound (loud or soft), pleasant or unpleasant sounds, how sounds can be amplified (with microphones or megaphones), and why older people sometimes need hearing aids.
  Note: If your school performs an annual screening for children's hearing, this lesson Is a good springboard for inviting the individual who evaluates the children's hearing to come into the classroom and talk with them.

Accommodations/Modifications

Autism—When talking about sound volume or loudness, demonstrate a loud voice and a quiet voice. Have the child demonstrate loud and quiet voices.

Speech or Language Impairments—Refer to the diagram of the ear as you explain the

Review

As children leave the circle area, ask them to share one thing they learned about their ears.

Assessment Strategy

Use the review as an assessment strategy, or assess individual children's knowledge about ears at another time.

hearing process.

Hearing Impairments—Invite the child to talk about his experience in going to the ear doctor. If the child has a hearing aid, ask him to tell the class about it.

Visual Impairments—Describe your actions as you demonstrate with the drum. Let the child feel the objects as you beat the drum.

Cognitive and/or Developmental Delays—Use short, simple sentences to describe the hearing process. Stress that the function of ears is to hear sounds.

Emotional Disturbance—Seat the child near you during the discussion of ears.

Other Health Impairment/Attention Deficit Hyperactivity Disorder—If the child is becoming restless during the discussion, have the group stand up when you demonstrate loud and quiet sounds, megaphones, and how to use the paper cups.

Orthopedic Impairment—Help the child hold the paper cup to his ear if needed.

Curriculum Connections

■ **Language and Literacy**—Recite the following poem and ask children to fill in the blanks:

When I hear the word "dears," I use my _____.
When I hear the word "clears," I use my _____.
When I hear the word "fears," I use my _____.
When I hear the word "tears," I use my _____.
When I heard the word "rears," I use my _____.
When I heard the word "cheers," I use my _____.

Continue with other rhyming words. Ask the children to suggest their own rhyming words.

■ **Listening Center**—Make a tape cassette of children making sounds for others to listen to and identify.

■ **Science**—Place an assortment of objects, such as spoons, forks, musical instruments, bells, wooden cooking utensils, and so on, in the Science Center. Ask the children to experiment with sounds the objects can make. Ask how they heard the sounds.

■ **Social Studies**—Provide funnels and tubing so children can make a telephone; this experience may need to be done in the Art Center or at the Discovery Center. Ask children to tell you why they can hear through the tubing. (It resembles the ear canal).

Eyes

Time

25–30 minutes

Materials

- Pictures of eyes
- Variety of child-sized glasses
- Sunglasses
- Magnifying glass
- Eye chart (borrow from an optometrist, buy one at a health supply store, or download one from www.i-see.org/eyecharts.html)

Objectives

Children will:

1. Learn that eyes help people see their world.
2. Point to their eyes on their own bodies.

Lesson

- Ask the children to close their eyes and cover them with their hands. Ask, "Why can't you see anything?"
- Now ask the children to remove their hands and to open their eyes. Ask, "Why can you see now?"
- Show children pictures of eyes and talk about the differences among them.
- Explore the different things eyes can with the children, such as wink, blink, look up, look down, and move your eyes all around. Ask the children to try not to blink! Ask if they know the color of their eyes.
- Talk to the children about how important their eyes are for vision. Be sensitive to children who may have poor vision or who need glasses. Talk about children who are born blind or become blind or vision-impaired because of illnesses or accidents.
- Tell the children that most people see better during the daytime when the sun is shining. Point out that lamps, candles, lanterns, and other sources of artificial light enable us to see at night.
- Show the children the collection of glasses and allow them to explore with them. Talk about the effects of the sunglasses and the magnifying glass.
- Ask the children why they need to protect their eyes.
- Tell the children that doctors called optometrists check our eyes to make sure they are in good shape. Show them the eye chart that is in most doctors' offices.

Accommodations/Modifications

Autism—Have the child imitate specific eye actions, such as winking, blinking, and so on.

Speech or Language Impairments—As you explain concepts (for example, eyes, eye chart, glasses, candles, lamps), refer to the objects and to pictures of them.

Hearing Impairments—Seat the child across from you so she can see your lips as you speak.

Visual Impairments—Ask the child to tell the class what it is like to go to the eye doctor. If the child uses glasses or visual aids, ask her to tell her classmates how they help her to see.

Cognitive and/or Developmental Delays—The child should learn two things from this lesson: that eyes are used to see and the location of her eyes. Provide many opportunities for the child to point to her eyes. Emphasize that eyes help us see what is around us.

Review

Ask the children to point to their eyes and say their eye color as they leave group time. Be prepared to tell children their eye color if they do not know it.

Review

Ask the children to point to their eyes and say their eye color as they leave group time. Be prepared to tell children their eye color if they do not know it.

Assessment Strategy

Ask each child individually to say what she knows about her eyes.

Emotional Disturbance—Seat the child next to you and affirm her for behaving appropriately.

Other Health Impairment/Attention Deficit Hyperactivity Disorder—Have the child change seating positions or stand if she becomes restless. A good time to do this is when the group examines the glasses and the eye chart.

Orthopedic Impairment—Help the child explore the collection of glasses.

Curriculum Connections

- **Just for Fun**—Bring in enough super-sized sunglasses for the children to wear on the playground. Save them from year to year, so you will always be ready for this lesson.
- **Language and Literacy**—Write *eyes* on several cards and encourage the children to copy or trace the word with their fingers. For young preschoolers, outline each letter in glue and then sprinkle on glitter to make tactile letters to give the experience more meaning.
- **Science**—Suggest that the children use magnifying glasses to look into one another's eyes to see the pupil and pigments.
- **Science/Math**—Working individually or in small groups, suggest that the children graph their eye color. Record the results on a poster board or chart paper that can be shown later as a math activity. Encourage children to graph their family's eye colors at home; make sure that families know about this request first.

CLASS CHART

	HAZEL EYES	BROWN EYES	BLUE EYES	BLACK EYES
Jason				
Micah				
Lucas				
Michelle				
Anna				
Tamika				
Damon				
Marcus				
Shawna				
Oliver				
Rebecca				
Joshua				

Mouth

Time

10–15 minutes

Materials

- Small, unbreakable hand mirrors (one for each child)
- Skull (see the Head lesson plan on page 83) or a picture of a face

Objectives

Children will:

1. Learn where their mouth is on their head or be able to point to it.
2. Demonstrate various ways to use their mouths.

Lesson

- Distribute small, unbreakable hand mirrors to children as they come to Group or Circle Time. Ask them to look at their mouths in the mirror.
- Tell the children that their lips are the fleshy part of their face that covers their teeth. Ask children, "What does the mouth help us do?" Accept all their answers, but lead their conversation to cover the following concepts about the mouth:
  - The mouth helps us talk.
  - The mouth protects our teeth.
  - We can breathe through our mouths.
  - We put food into our mouths.
  - The mouth helps keep food in.
- Show the children where the mouth is on the skull or on the face picture. Remind them that animals have mouths, too.
- Encourage the children to look into the mirrors and use their mouths to form sounds, such as ohs, ahs, oohs, ughs, eees, and so on. Ask them to pretend to be bunny rabbits and fish with their mouths. Ask if anyone can whistle, most children usually develop this skill in the primary grades, but they will enjoy trying. Ask children to blow out air with their mouths or to say "Shhh." Ask, "Did your mouth look different when you made certain sounds?"
- Ask the children to hum a favorite tune. Point out that their mouths are closed while they are doing this.
- Sing this song about the mouth. The tune is "Mary Had a Little Lamb."

My Mouth by Laverne Warner
My mouth can hum and hum and hum, hum and hum, hum and hum;
My mouth can hum and hum and hum, anytime I want.
My mouth can open, open wide, open wide, open wide;
My mouth can open, open wide, anytime I want.

Review

Ask children to name things they can do and say with their mouths.

Assessment Strategy

Show individual children a photograph of a face, asking each to point to the mouth and to show various ways to use their mouths.

My mouth can smile and smile and smile, smile and smile, smile and smile;
My mouth can smile and smile and smile, anytime I want.

Accommodations/Modifications

Autism—Use gestures and demonstration as you talk about what mouths can do. Assist the child in using the hand mirror if needed.

Speech or Language Impairments—When discussing what mouths can do, model the action as you ask what we do with our mouth.

Hearing Impairments—Seat the child across from you so he can see your face and lips as you present the lesson on mouths.

Visual Impairments—Even though the child may not be able to use a mirror functionally, provide one for him. Explain how a mirror is used: we can look at our faces in the mirror and see our eyes, nose, mouth, and hair.

Cognitive and/or Developmental Delays—Provide the child with several opportunities to point to his mouth and say what he does with his mouth, such as talk or eat. Review the concepts throughout the next few weeks.

Emotional Disturbance—Seat the child next to you as you present the lesson on mouths and affirm the child's appropriate behavior.

Orthopedic Impairment—Help the child use the mirror to see his mouth.

Curriculum Connections

- **Art**—Ask a small group of interested children to prepare a mouth mural. They can paste pictures of mouths on a poster board, using cutout pictures from magazines at school or in their homes (with permission). Count the mouths on the poster board for a math activity.

- **Just for Fun**—Ask a family or families to provide enough wax lips for children to have as they leave the classroom at the end of the day.

- **Language and Literacy**—Make a class book about mouths. Give the children magazines and catalogs and invite them to cut out mouths to paste on individual pages.

- **Science**—Have children locate the mouths on their classroom pets.

Teeth and Tongue

Time

15–20 minutes

Materials

- Model of teeth and toothbrush, borrowed from a dentist (optional)
- Commercial poster showing how to clean teeth (optional)
- Book about dental care (see suggestions to the right)

Objectives

Children will:

1. Learn where their tongue and teeth are located.
2. Describe one way they take care of their teeth and tongues.

Preparation

Be sure that children wash their hands prior to the lesson.

Lesson

- If possible, bring a model of teeth and toothbrush to Group or Circle Time and begin by asking children, "What is in your mouth?"
- Show the teeth and engage the children in a discussion about caring for teeth. Demonstrate how to brush teeth with a toothbrush.
- Ask the children to stick out their tongues and point to their teeth. Then ask them to think about what their tongues and teeth help them do. Many children will respond with, "They help us eat" or "They help us talk." Encourage them to talk about how the tongue helps them taste food.
- Find out if there are any children who have lost a baby tooth or who have older brothers or sisters who have. Emphasize the importance of caring for one's teeth throughout life.
- Ask the children to try to "talk" while holding onto their tongues.
- Ask the children to name objects that people lick, such as ice cream cones, lollipops, snow cones, stamps, and frozen desserts. Talk about keeping the inside of their mouths clean so their breath will be fresh.
- Read a book about keeping teeth brushed (see www.americasdentalbookstore.com for titles). Suggested books include *Brush Your Teeth, Please* by Leslie McGuire; *The Berenstain Bears Visit the Dentist* by Stan and Jan Berenstain; *Just Going to the Dentist* by Mercer Mayer; and *Arthur's Loose Tooth* by Lillian Hoban.

Accommodations/Modifications

Autism—Use pictures or clip art as you refer to teeth, tongues, brushing teeth, ice cream cones, lollipops, and so on. When inviting comments from the child, keep the discussion focused on the pictures and on teeth and tongues.

Speech or Language Impairments—When inviting the child's comments, provide assistance if needed by saying part of a sentence and having her complete the sentence. Invite participation as you read the story by asking the child to find various

NUMBER OF TEETH	5	10	15	20	25	30	35	40
Jason								
Lucas								
Michelle								
Anna								
Tamika								
Damon								
Marcus								
Shawna								
Joshua								

Review

Ask children to review why it is important to take care of their teeth.

Assessment Strategy

In small groups, ask each child to say one thing they do to take care of their teeth.

objects represented in the pictures in the books.

Hearing Impairments—Seat the child across from you as you present the lesson on teeth and tongues.

Visual Impairments—Describe your actions as you show how to care for your teeth by brushing them.

Cognitive and/or Developmental Delays—During the discussion, provide several opportunities for the child to show where her teeth and tongue are located. Emphasize that teeth chew food and tongues lick food. Demonstrate the difference between chewing and licking, and ask the child to show you how to chew and how to lick.

Emotional Disturbance—Seat the child next to you as you present the lesson on teeth and tongues.

Other Health Impairment/Attention Deficit Hyperactivity Disorder—At the end of the lesson, have the child get the books from your desk or shelf before you read them.

Orthopedic Impairment—No specific assistance should be needed in this lesson. The child may have difficulty holding her tongue to talk, but do not help her with this for hygiene reasons.

Curriculum Connections

- **Art**—Ask children to use a variety of art media to make teeth models. Styrofoam pieces and playdough might be sufficient, but be open to children's suggestions about what they want to use.
- **Bulletin Board**—Take a photograph of each child's teeth for a class bulletin board.
- **Listening Center**—Make a tape cassette about dental care for children to listen to at their leisure.
- **Math**—Ask children to count their own teeth using small, unbreakable hand mirrors. Record their responses on a classroom chart.

Nose

Time

15–20 minutes

Materials

- Cut-up fruit and vegetables
- Containers that are opaque
- Scissors
- Soft tissues (enough for each child to have one)
- Pictures of various noses (include humans and animals, such as alligator, cow, kitten, dog, zebra, giraffe, and so on)
- *The Holes in Your Nose* by Genichiro Yagyu (optional)

Objective

Children will:

1. Point to their noses on their own bodies.
2. Describe one function of their noses.

Preparation

Prepare Smell Jars by putting fruit and vegetables with distinct odors—such as oranges, bananas, cucumbers, onions, and watermelon—in small covered opaque containers. Punch small holes in the tops of the containers. **Note:** Because the lesson involves several activities, make sure you have all of your materials organized and laid out prior to the lesson. If necessary, move quickly from one activity to the next to maintain the children's attention.

Lesson

- As the children gather for Group or Circle Time, invite them to sniff the Smell Jars and identify the smells.
- With the children, sing the following song to the tune of "Ring Around the Rosie."

    Noses by Laverne Warner
    No—ses, no—ses, no—ses.
    We all smell with noses;
    Sn—iff, sn—iff—
    What do you smell?

- Ask the children how they know what is in each Smell Jar. Open the Smell Jars to discover the contents.
- Show the children pictures of various noses. Ask the children to tell you the differences among the noses, especially animal noses.
- Ask the children to name things they smell in and out of the classroom. If possible, have other objects for children to smell, such as flowers, pickles, paste, glue, markers, or food items.
- Demonstrate how to use a tissue to cover your nose when you sneeze.
- If time is available for a book, read *The Holes in Your Nose* by Genichiro Yagyu or another book about noses.

Review

Ask children to describe the various functions of the nose. Ask them to show how they cover their noses when they sneeze.

Assessment Strategy

Ask each child to name something he can smell.

Accommodations/Modifications

Autism— During the Smell Jar activity, have magazine or clip art pictures of three items in the jars for the child to choose from.

Speech or Language Impairments—During the Smell Jar activity, have magazine or clip art pictures of the items in the jars for the child to choose from.

Hearing Impairments—Seat the child across from you so he can see your lips as you speak. Have pictures to refer to during the Smell Jar activity.

Visual Impairments—When examining noses of various animals, provide toy plastic animals rather than photos for the child to feel. When using the Smell Jars, offer verbal clues about the contents of the jar if needed.

Cognitive and/or Developmental Delays—When presenting the Smell Jars, have objects found in the jars on the table; provide two choices from which the child can select.

Emotional Disturbance—Seat the child near you and affirm him for participating.

Other Health Impairment/Attention Deficit Hyperactivity Disorder—The child may need assistance holding the smell jar to his nose.

Orthopedic Impairment—While reading the story, seat the child next to you and enlist his help in turning pages.

Curriculum Connections

- **Dramatic Play**—Place clown noses and nose masks in the Dramatic Play Center for children's play.
- **Listening Center**—Use a cassette recorder to record the "Nose" song for children to listen to at their leisure. Record some of their answers to the song.
- **Manipulatives**—Enlarge pictures of noses, cut them into pieces and make puzzles for children to put together. Younger children will respond better with a whole nose photograph to use as a guide as they put the puzzle together.
- **Math**—Make a class chart showing everyone's favorite smell. Start out simply with four or five scents children may choose from (such as cinnamon, a rose, soap, orange, and a piece of banana). Expand the choices as necessary. If children have had experiences with forming charts, be more open-ended with children's choices.
- **Science**—Mark the section about noses in a children's encyclopedia. Children can look at the information independently, or you can join them to discuss what is in the book.
- **More Science**—Have more Smell Jars available for children to use to match pairs that smell alike.

MY BODY

Neck

Time

15–20 minutes

Materials

- *I Wonder Who Stretched the Giraffe's Neck* by Mona Gansberg Hodgson (or another book about necks)
- X-ray of a person's neck (optional)
- Turtleneck sweater and scarf

Objectives

Children will:

1. Point to their necks on their own bodies.
2. Describe basic information about the bones and muscles in the neck.

Lesson

- As the children arrive at Group or Circle Time, begin stretching your neck and rolling it from side to side. Ask the children to do the same.
- Engage the children in a discussion about necks by asking them to name all the things their necks can do. Point out that stretching our necks and shoulders helps our bodies feel better.
- Read *I Wonder Who Stretched the Giraffe's Neck* and encourage the children's responses while they listen to the text. Ask children if they know of other animals that have long necks, such as alligators, crocodiles, flamingoes, swans, emus, and horses.
- Tell the children that the neck is the top part of a person's spine; if possible, show them an x-ray of a person's neck. Talk about how the head is joined to the neck.
- Ask the children to feel their necks. Neck bones can be difficult to feel, but they will be able to feel the muscles, which protect the neck.
- Show the children a turtleneck sweater and ask them why it might be called a turtleneck. Show them how a scarf is worn. Remind the children that in winter, a warm scarf keeps the neck and shoulders warm.

Accommodations/Modifications

Autism—Model actions of the neck when asking about things that necks can do.

Speech or Language Impairments—During the discussion of necks, provide clues about things that necks can do. For example, say, "If I want to see what is going on beside me, what do I need to do with my neck? I have to (demonstrate) turn my neck. What do I have to do?"

Hearing Impairments—Seat the child across from you so she can see your lips as you speak. Refer to pictures as you teach.

Visual Impairments—Have the child put her hands on the sides of your neck as you demonstrate what necks can do. Then have the child show you what her neck can do.

Cognitive and/or Developmental Delays—When discussing animal's necks, have the child point to the neck of each animal.

Emotional Disturbance—Seat the child near you during the activity and affirm her for participating.

Review

As the children leave Group or Circle Time, ask them to tell you one thing they know about the neck.

Other Health Impairment/Attention Deficit Hyperactivity Disorder—Have the children stand up while stretching their necks and showing what their necks can do.

Orthopedic Impairment—Help the child move her head to show what necks can do.

Curriculum Connections

- **Art**—Provide playdough for children to mold animals and people with long necks.
- **Dramatic Play**—Add a turtleneck sweater, a woolen scarf, or a muffler to the Dress-Up Center for children's play.
- **Listening Center**—Make a tape cassette of *I Wonder Who Stretched the Giraffe's Neck* for children to listen to at their leisure.
- **Science**—Mark the section on necks in a children's encyclopedia. Children can look at the information independently, or you can join them to discuss what is in the book.
- **More Science**—Have pictures of various animals for children to sort into categories by long-necked animals or short-necked animals.

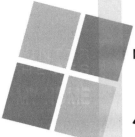

Arms

Time

10–15 minutes

Materials

- Chart paper
- Markers

Objectives

Children will:

1. Describe two jobs they can do with their arms.
2. Demonstrate how they use their arms.

Lesson

- Wear a sleeveless garment when introducing this lesson so children can see your whole arm. Call attention to your arms by flexing them to show children your muscles. The children may imitate you.
- Tell the children that strong arms are helpful in many ways. Ask children to brainstorm ways they use their arms and write their responses on chart paper. Point out the numerous ways children use their arms to help others.
- Talk about the parts of the arm: elbow, forearm, and lower arm. Ask children to feel their arms to see if they can feel their bones.
- Suggest that children move around the room using their arms as airplane wings, birds' wings, or butterfly wings.
- Stand still and ask children to see how tall they are with their arms stretched up high and how wide they are with their arms stretched out.

Accommodations/Modifications

Autism—During the brainstorming on what arms can do, show pictures of activities that cue the child about the actions of arms.

Speech or Language Impairments—During the brainstorming on what arms can do, cue the child by providing hints. For example, say, "I see a heavy box and I want to take it to my mother. What can I do with my arms to get the heavy box? I can lift it."

Hearing Impairments—Seat the child across from you during the discussion so he can see your lips as you speak.

Ask children to name the parts of their arm as you point to them and as they leave for the centers.

Assessment Strategy

Ask each child to describe two jobs he can do with his arms.

Visual Impairments—When talking about the parts of the arm, point out each one to the child. Describe your actions as you write during the brainstorming part of the lesson.

Cognitive and/or Developmental Delays—During the brainstorming on what arms can do, model various actions and have the child tell you what arms can do.

Emotional Disturbance—Seat the child next to you during the discussion and affirm his appropriate behavior.

Other Health Impairment/Attention Deficit Hyperactivity Disorder—During the brainstorming activity, seat the child close to the front so he can watch as you write.

Orthopedic Impairment—Assist the child with arm movements during the part of the lesson when the children pretend to be airplanes, birds, or butterflies.

Curriculum Connections

- **Art**—Ask individual children to fingerpaint with their elbows or their forearms. Make sure you have smocks and clean-up material available.
- **Music**—Encourage the children to make up songs about their arms. Use a cassette recorder to record of their creations.
- **Science**—In a children's encyclopedia, place a bookmark in the section on arms. Children can look at the information independently, or you can join them to discuss what is in the book.

Hands and Fingers

Time

15–20 minutes

Materials

- Gloves of various sizes to fit both adults and children
- *Arms, Elbows, Hands, and Fingers* by Lola M. Schaefer (or another book about hands and fingers)
- X-ray of hands (optional)

Objectives

Children will:

1. Show their hands and fingers when asked.
2. Describe the importance of hands and fingers.

Lesson

- Wear oversized gloves; chant the following rhyme, using appropriate motions to demonstrate:

  Fingers and Thumbs by Laverne Warner
  Fingers and thumbs, fingers and thumbs,
  Show me your fingers; now show me your thumbs.
  They're stuck to my hands, and not in my hair;
  And they aren't much use hanging in the air.

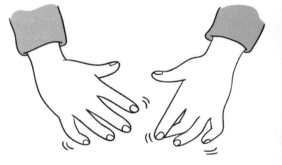

- Ask the children to wiggle their fingers and then their thumbs. Use the word *appendages* to add to the children's vocabulary.
- Demonstrate the pincer grasp and ask children to imitate you. Show children how to make a *fist* and use the term often so they will learn it. Also show children where the knuckles are located. Talk about hands being joined to the arms. If you have an x-ray picture, show children the bones in hands.
- Read *Arms, Elbows, Hands, and Fingers*, giving children an opportunity to respond as the book is read. When you are finished reading the book, ask the children to feel the bones in their hands and fingers.

Accommodations/Modifications

Autism—As you read the story, point to pictures. Review each page before going on to the next.

Speech or Language Impairments—Repeat the vocabulary introduced in the lesson (*thumb, appendage, knuckles, wiggle,* and so on).

Hearing Impairments—Seat the child across from you during the lesson so she can see your lips as you speak.

Review

Repeat the "Fingers and Thumbs" rhyme you used to introduce the lesson.

Assessment Strategy

Ask each child to tell you what she knows about hands and fingers.

Visual Impairments—Point to the parts of the hand on the child so she can follow the lesson. Have the child feel your hand or a friend's fingers as you perform various actions.

Cognitive and/or Developmental Delays—Demonstrate each action of the hands and have the child imitate and name the action. Identify each part of the hand and have the child point to it and name it.

Emotional Disturbance—Seat the child next to you during the activities and affirm her appropriate behavior.

Other Health Impairment/Attention Deficit Hyperactivity Disorder—Seat the child next to you as you read the story and enlist her help in turning the pages.

Orthopedic Impairment—Assist the child in showing, moving, and wiggling her fingers and thumbs.

Curriculum Connections

- **Art**—Show the children how to trace around their hands on paper and cut out their hand shapes. Do a "Hands Around the Room" project or use the cutouts for a bulletin board to spark children's interest in making many sets of hands.
- **Book Center**—Place Bill Martin, Jr.'s *Here Are My Hands* and Lloyd G. Douglas' *My Hands* in the Book Center to enhance children's knowledge of hands.
- **Science**—With small groups of children, compare human hands with dog or cat paws. Talk about the things humans can do with their hands that animals cannot do.

Stomach

Time

15 minutes

Materials

- *What Happens to a Hamburger?* by Paul Showers (or another book about the stomach's function)

Objectives

Children will:

1. Point to their stomach and torso.
2. Describe what stomachs do for their bodies.

Preparation

Send a note home to each child's family asking them to dress their child so they can show their stomachs during Group or Circle Time. Explain the purpose for this activity in your note.

Lesson

- As children arrive at Group or Circle Time, start patting your stomach and say, "Oh, my tummy is growling at me." Ask children what your tummy might be saying when it growls.
- Most children will be happy to pull up their shirts and blouses to show their stomachs. Talk about the belly button and why everyone has one.
- Read a book about the stomach, such as *What Happens to a Hamburger?* by Paul Showers. Ask children what happens when they overeat.

Accommodations/Modifications

Autism—As you read the story, point out pictures on each page and review the content before going to the next page. After finishing the story, ask the child to tell you what the story was about. Tell him that this was a story about how the stomach digests food.

Speech or Language Impairments—Before reading the story, review vocabulary, such as *stomach, digestion,* and *intestines.* Show individual pages in the book to explain vocabulary and then read the story.

Hearing Impairments—Seat the child across from you so he can see your lips as you speak.

Visual Impairments—Describe your actions as you present the lesson. Provide descriptions of the pictures in the book during the story.

Cognitive and/or Developmental Delays—The child should be able to participate and follow the lesson without modifications or accommodations until you read the story. When reading the story, preteach important vocabulary, such as stomach, digestion, and intestines, before reading. As you read, review each page and ask the child to point to items in the pictures.

Review

Ask the children to show their tummies as they go to Center Time.

Assessment Strategy

Ask each child to point to his stomach and torso.

Emotional Disturbance—Seat the child next to you during the lesson and affirm him for participating. Remind the child what everyone must do during Group or Circle Time:

- Keep your hands to yourself.
- Be kind to your friends.
- Take turns.

Affirm the child for appropriate behavior and participation during the lesson.

Other Health Impairment/Attention Deficit Hyperactivity Disorder—Have the child sit next to you as you read the story and enlist his help in turning the pages.

Orthopedic Impairment—Help the child show his stomach.

Curriculum Connections

- **Book Center**—Add *There Was an Old Woman Who Swallowed a Fly* by Hy Murdock to the Book Center. The book shows the woman's stomach as she eats each of several animals and, finally, when it is full.
- **Science**—Talk to small groups of children about the importance of chewing their food thoroughly before swallowing it. Chewing food helps the stomach do its job more easily.
- **More Science**—Make picture cards by cutting out pictures of foods from magazines and catalogs and gluing them onto large index cards. Ask children to sort the pictures into two categories: foods that are good for people and junk food. Ask individual children why junk foods are not good for people to eat.

Lungs

Time

15–20 minutes

Materials

- 2 heavy-duty balloons
- Small paper bags (one for each child)
- *How Do Your Lungs Work?* by Don L. Curry (or another book about lungs)

Objectives

Children will:

1. Describe what their lungs do.
2. Demonstrate how to fill their lungs with air.

Lesson

- Ask the children to breathe deeply and then say, "What are you breathing into your body?" "Where does the air go?" Ask the children to breathe again and to hold their hands on their chests as they breathe.
- Ask the children what is happening to their chests as they breathe in and out.
- Read H*ow Do Your Lungs Work?* or another book that describes the functions of the lungs. Tell the children that everyone needs air to stay alive. Air helps the blood keep the body clean. Remind children that they breathe air in through their noses and mouths.
- Show the children the balloons and demonstrate how they inflate when air is blown into them. Give each child a small paper bag to blow air into to demonstrate how their lungs fill with air when they breathe in air.
- Tell the children they may take their paper bags home at the end of the day to show their families how their lungs work.
- Give the children an opportunity to take the bags to their cubbies in conjunction with the review as they leave Group or Circle Time.

Accommodations/Modifications

Autism—Use pictures and clip art to show the vocabulary used in the lesson: lungs, chest, nose.

Speech or Language Impairments—Review vocabulary before and after the lesson, using pictures or diagrams, such as lungs, chest, nose, breathe.

Hearing Impairments—Seat the child across from you so she can see your lips as you speak. Describe the pictures as you read the story.

Visual Impairments—Let the child feel the balloon as you blow it up. Describe the

Review

As children leave Group or Circle Time, ask them to point to their chests to show where their lungs are.

Assessment Strategy

Ask individual children to describe what their lungs do for them.

pictures as you read the story.

Cognitive and/or Developmental Delays—Give the child pictures of lungs or two unrelated pictures to choose from during the assessment. Ask which one helps us to breathe. Then ask the child what our lungs do. Ask the child to show you how she breathes.

Emotional Disturbance—Seat the child next to you and affirm her for appropriate behavior.

Other Health Impairment/Attention Deficit Hyperactivity Disorder—Seat the child next to you as you read the story and enlist her help in turning the pages.

Orthopedic Impairment—Assist the child in holding the paper bag as she blows air into it.

Curriculum Connections

- **Art**—Give the children straws and tempera paint diluted with water. Suggest that the children fill their lungs with air and blow ink across a piece of paper. The result is a blown paint art product. Dry artwork on a drying rack.

- **Outdoors**—Find dandelions and blow them to watch their spores spread. Encourage children to fill their lungs with air before to blowing the dandelions.

- **Social Studies**—With small groups of children, brainstorm ways that lungs are used for specific purposes: for example, to smell fresh air, after running very fast, before jumping or diving into a pool of water, breathing in before putting your head into water, inflating balloons, blowing dandelions, blowing out birthday candles, and so on. Write the children's responses down to tell the class at a later time.

Legs

Time

15–20 minutes

Materials

- Stuffed toy with prominent legs
- Chart tablet and marker

Objectives

Children will:

1. Point to their legs and know that they each have two legs.
2. Demonstrate one action they can do with their legs.

Lesson

- As children arrive at Group or Circle Time, ask them to sit on the floor with their legs straight out in front of them. Ask them to describe what they notice about their legs and about other children's legs. Ask children if legs are important to the human body. **Note:** If a child in the group has a disability that affects his legs, be sensitive to the comments children make and respond positively when someone notices the child's disability. Provide an opportunity for children with a disability that involves the legs to describe how he copes with the disability, such as using a wheelchair, brace, cane, or other assistive device. Help all of the children observe how the child with special needs copes with his disability.

- Ask the children how they use their legs. Accept all responses, and then ask them to continue to sit and to follow a set of directions: cross your legs, wiggle your legs, hold one leg in the air, hold the other leg in the air, hold both feet in the air, use your legs and arms to make a table, walk a few steps as a crab, do the camel walk, and other motions involving legs. Use a stuffed toy to demonstrate the directions you are giving to the children.

- Ask the children to name animals that have two legs like they have, and record their responses on a piece of chart paper. Ask if they know animals that have more than two legs. Again, record their responses. Keep the chart handy so children can use it at the Art Center for a collaborative project.

- Teach this poem to children:

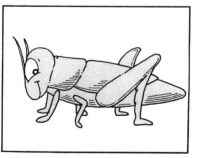

Legs by Laverne Warner
Some legs are short, some legs are long;
I'm glad I have mine to help me along.
When I have to, I can move very fast,
Moving my legs is such a blast!

Review

Ask the children to tell you one thing they do with their legs.

Assessment Strategy

Ask one child to tell you how many legs he has. Then ask the child to tell you two things he can do with his legs.

Accommodations/Modifications

Autism—Provide pictures of animals and insects to help the child to identify animals that have more than two legs.

Speech or Language Impairments—Assist the child in responding to the question about what we do with legs by demonstrating and then naming the action if necessary. Then restate the question.

Hearing Impairments—Seat the child across from you during the discussion so he can see your lips as you speak.

Visual Impairments—When asking what we can do with our legs, let the child feel the stuffed animal as you demonstrate different actions.

Cognitive and/or Developmental Delays—During the assessment activity, provide Picture Communication Symbols or clip art for the child to select from describing what we can do with our legs. When asking how many legs we have, accept two fingers held up as a correct response.

Emotional Disturbance—Seat the child next to you during the lesson and affirm him for participating.

Other Health Impairment/Attention Deficit Hyperactivity Disorder—Have the group stand as they recite the poem together.

Orthopedic Impairment—For children who cannot use their legs easily, the accommodations are described in the lesson. For children who have difficulty with their arms and hands, no accommodations are needed.

Curriculum Connections

- **Art**—Supply the Art Center with magazines so children can cut out pictures of legs to paste onto the chart list they brainstormed during Group or Circle Time. If, for example, they said that a grasshopper had six legs, they could cut out a grasshopper and glue it onto the chart by the word *grasshopper*.

- **More Art**—Provide a pair of worn-out jeans or pajama bottoms for children to stuff with paper or fabric and hang on a clothesline.

- **Dramatic Play**—Place a wheelchair or a pair of crutches in the Dramatic Play Center for children's play.

- **Math**—Count the total number of legs (see the More Art activity) that the class has stuffed and then count the number of pairs of legs.

MY BODY

Thighs

Time
15–20 minutes

Materials
- Toy motorized robot

Objectives

Children will:
1. Identify their thighs as part of their legs.
2. Demonstrate a robot walk.

Lesson

- Begin singing the familiar song, "Heads, Shoulders, Knees, and Toes," as children gather for Group or Circle Time. Point to your thighs and ask children if they know what thighs are.
- Help children understand how thighs help people move their legs, squat, bend, walk, run, and climb stairs. Ask children to walk around the circle without bending their knees, using their thighs for movement. Ask how they felt while they did this.
- Show children how the toy robot walks without bending its knees, using only its thighs. Help the children notice that the stiff-legged walk of the robot slows down its motions, just as it does to humans.
- Teach the children this chant:

  Thighs by Laverne Warner
  Oh, my, I need my thighs.
  My thighs help me rise,
  They are a wonderful prize
  When I want to walk!

  Oh, my, I need my thighs.
  My thighs help me rise,
  They are a wonderful prize
  When I want to run!

  Oh, my, I need my thighs.
  My thighs help me rise,
  They are a wonderful prize
  When I want to dance!

  Oh, my, I need my thighs.
  My thighs help me rise,
  They are a wonderful prize
  When I want to skip!

Review

At the end of the lesson, ask all of the children to touch their thighs.

Assessment Strategy

Ask individual children to show you their thighs.

- Ask children to imitate how a robot walks, runs, dances, and skips as they recite the chant.
- Ask children to suggest other verses; continue the chant as long as children are interested.

Accommodations/Modifications

Autism—When discussing the things thighs help us to do—such as walk, run, climb stairs—demonstrate the actions.

Speech or Language Impairments—When discussing the things thighs help us to do, demonstrate the actions. Then state, "Our thighs help us to _____" and have the child complete the sentence.

Hearing Impairments—Seat the child across from you as you present the lesson.

Visual Impairments—As you sing "Head, Shoulders, Knees, and Toes," touch the child's body parts at the beginning of the song. Let her feel the toy robot as it walks.

Cognitive and/or Developmental Delays—Focus on the critical concept of the lesson and ensure that the child can show you where her thighs are. Once that is accomplished, ask her to show you one thing her thighs help her to do.

Emotional Disturbance—Seat the child next to you and affirm her for appropriate behavior.

Other Health Impairment/Attention Deficit Hyperactivity Disorder—Have the children stand as they recite the chant.

Orthopedic Impairment—During the review and assessment, assist the child in touching her thighs, if needed.

Curriculum Connections

- **Art**—Give children cotton-tipped swabs and other materials to use to make stick people. If it has just rained, go outside and make mud people with mud, twigs, and acorns. Ask individual children to locate the thighs on their stick people.
- **Language and Literacy**—Prepare cards with words that rhyme with thigh. First, conduct this activity orally with small groups of children. Ask children to sort the cards into two piles. One group will have the —igh configuration (high, thigh, and sigh) and the other group will have the —y sound (such as by, try, my, fly, why, dry, and cry). Later, allow children to match the configurations by sight independently. **Note:** This activity is best for five-year-olds. The purpose is to match configurations in words, not to read the words.
- **Science**—Display large pictures of various animals on the Science Table. Ask children to identify the animals' bodies and to identify each animal's thighs.

MY BODY

Feet and Toes

Time

20–25 minutes

Materials

- *Busy Toes* by C. W. Bowie or a similar title, in big book format, if possible
- Various pairs of socks and shoes
- Socks that have toes in them (optional)
- Paper and marker or paint and paper

Objectives

Children will:

1. Learn where their feet and toes are located.
2. Share at least one fact about their feet and toes.

Lesson

- Read *Busy Toes* to the children as they gather for Group or Circle Time.
- After finishing the book, ask the children to take off their shoes and socks so they can see their feet. Ask, "Why do we wear socks? Why do we wear shoes? Why do we need to keep our feet protected?"
- Ask the children to wiggle their toes and feet. Review the well-known nursery rhyme, "This Little Piggy Went to Market." Ask children if they know any other rhymes about their toes or feet. If so, let individuals share what they know with the class.
- Introduce foot-related terminology, such as *heel, sole, toes, footprints,* and *ankle.*
- Show the shoes and socks you have collected. Ask, "Which ones match? How do you know which ones match?"
- If you have a pair of socks with toes in them, show them to the children and have a brief discussion.
- Ask the children to put their shoes and socks back on, providing assistance for children who need help with the task.

Accommodations/Modifications

Autism—"Why" questions are very difficult for many young children with autism, even those who are very verbal. During the lesson, ask where, who, or when questions of the child with autism.

Speech or Language Impairments—When asking what we can do with our feet, demonstrate a few actions, such as pointing, walking, and wiggling. If the child cannot answer, describe your actions and then ask the question again.

Hearing Impairments—Seat the child across from you so he can see your lips as you speak.

Visual Impairments—Describe the pictures in big books as you read them. When discussing the foot-related terms and parts of the foot point to the corresponding parts of the child's foot.

Cognitive and/or Developmental Delays—During the assessment activity, have the child show you what he can do with his feet after putting on shoes.

Emotional Disturbance—Seat the child next to you during the lesson and affirm him for appropriate behavior.

Review

Ask the children to repeat "This Little Piggy Went to Market" at the end of the lesson.

Assessment Strategy

Help the children use paper and a marker to make a footprint of one of their feet for the ongoing portfolio you are developing for each child. Handprints may be included as well, if children want to add theirs to the collection. If possible, have paint available for children to step into and then allow them to step onto a piece of paper. Ask children to identify parts of their feet as the paint is drying. Put the dried product into a portfolio to talk about with families during an upcoming conference.

Other Health Impairment/Attention Deficit Hyperactivity Disorder—Seat the child next to you during the story and have him help you turn the pages.

Orthopedic Impairment—Assist the child in removing his shoes. Help the child make footprints and handprints during the assessment activity.

Curriculum Connections

- **Art**—The portfolio activity described above in the Assessment Strategy section can be classified as an art activity. Provide footprint patterns for children to trace and cut out.

- **More Art**—Print feet and toes on large pieces of poster board. Give children magazines and scissors and ask them to cut out pictures of feet and toes to glue on the poster boards. Display the poster boards on a bulletin board or in the hallway.

- **Social Studies**—Display a collection of different types of footwear—boots, galoshes, tennis shoes, sandals, nurse's shoes, house shoes, wooden shoes, medical boots, and so on—on a Discovery Table for children to explore. Include a shoehorn and a shoetree, as well.

Paint

MY BODY
Skin

Time

20–25 minutes

Materials

- Chart paper and markers (optional)
- Disposable wipes
- Samples of animal fur (optional)

Objectives

Children will:

1. Tell what their skin is.
2. Describe one way to protect their skin.

Lesson

- Engage the children in a discussion about hand washing. Ask, "Why do we wash our hands? Why do we wash our bodies? Is cleaning our body something we need to do regularly?" Ask children to say whether they shower or bathe. (If appropriate for your group, use chart paper and markers to make a graph of their responses.)

CLASS CHART

CHILD'S NAME	SHOWER	BATHE
JEREMY		
TABATHA		
KEITH		
ELIZABETH		
MARCUS		
EDDIE		
DEVON		

- Pass out disposable wipes and let the children pretend to bathe themselves.
- Ask children how dogs behave after they have been bathed. Shake just like dogs do! After settling down again, talk about how the skin covers the entire body. Skin helps us keep our bodies intact. When we scratch our skin or bruise it, then we need to take care of it with lotions, salves, bandages, and other items that help protect the skin.
- Ask children to compare their skin with yours. Tell them that skin changes as people get older. Some children will know their grandparents and will verify that skin begins to show age with lines, wrinkles, and age spots.

Review

At the end of the lesson, ask children to tell you one thing they have learned about their skin.

Assessment Strategy

Ask individual children to describe how their skin is important to their bodies.

- If possible, show the children samples of animal fur and talk about animal skin. Give children an opportunity to talk about why animals have fur and people have skin. (Animals have to stay outdoors most of the time so they must protect their bodies from cold and rain.)

Accommodations/Modifications

Autism—Show the child photographs or clip art pictures to focus on important concepts such as washing, cleaning, bathing, skin, cut, and bandage. Emphasize the fact that skin covers the body. Compare and contrast skin, fur, and scales using concrete items to show the difference.

Speech or Language Impairments—Emphasize and review specific vocabulary used in the lesson: skin, washing, bathing, cut, bandage, and so on.

Hearing Impairments—Have the child sit across from you as you present the lesson so she can see your lips.

Visual Impairments—Describe your actions as you perform them. Let the child feel samples of other body coverings such as fur or scales.

Cognitive and/or Developmental Delays—This child should learn important concepts such as where her skin is and how to care for it. During the assessment activity, have the child show you where her skin is and ask her how to take care of her skin.

Emotional Disturbance—Seat the child next to you during the lesson and affirm her for appropriate behavior.

Other Health Impairment/Attention Deficit Hyperactivity Disorder—Have the group alternate standing and sitting as you present various activities, such as washing or shaking like a dog during the lesson.

Orthopedic Impairment—Help the child perform such actions as washing, shaking like a dog, and so on.

Curriculum Connections

- **Art**—Children have probably done fingerpainting thus far in the school year, but have they tried arm painting? Provide fingerpaint and paper on the school playground for this messy experience. Have smocks available, along with a source of water for cleanup.
- **Dramatic Play**—Place adhesive bandage strips, bandages, and empty lotion bottles in the Dramatic Play Center for children to use to pretend to take care of their skin. Place unbreakable mirrors in the center.
- **Social Studies**—Start a bulletin board with pictures of children of various skin colors. Ask the children to look for pictures in magazines or catalogs that they can cut out and display on the bulletin board. Remind children that skin color makes us look different on the outside, but we are all alike inside.

Hair

Time

15–20 minutes

Materials

- Doll with hair and hairbrush or comb
- *This Is My Hair* by Todd Parr, or another book about hair

Objectives

Children will:

1. Point to their hair.
2. Describe one way to groom their hair.

Lesson

- At Group or Circle Time, ask, "What is on your head that helps keep your head and body warm?" Help them identify their hair, and then continue with the lesson.
- Talk about different hair colors and help the children identify the color of their hair.
- Ask children which other animals have hair. Tell the children that the hair of most animals gets longer during the wintertime, and that many animals shed their hair when the weather starts getting warmer.
- Begin combing or brushing the doll's hair. Tell the children that you are grooming the doll. Ask if they brush and comb their own hair at home. Talk about other ways people groom their hair, such as making braids, using hair mousse, using curling irons and hairdryers, putting ribbons and barrettes in their hair, and so on.
- Read a book about hair to the children, such as *This Is My Hair* by Todd Parr.
- Talk to children about how they keep their hair clean, and then talk about shampoo. Let individual children describe their experiences with hair washing. Use words such as hair follicles and scalp to increase the children's vocabulary.

Accommodations/Modifications

Autism—When talking about animals that have hair, show pictures of animals that have hair and some that do not have hair. Have the child point to the animals that have hair.

Speech or Language Impairments—Before reading the story and starting the discussion, preteach important vocabulary such as hair, shampoo, braids, follicles, and scalp.

Hair

Braid

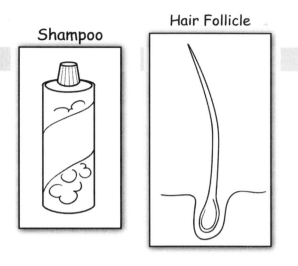

Shampoo

Hair Follicle

Review

Ask children to tell you what they remember about hair grooming.

Assessment Strategy

Ask individual children to name their hair colors.

Show the child pictures and/or objects as you present these concepts.

Hearing Impairments—Seat the child across from you so he can see your lips as you present the lesson.

Visual Impairments—Have the child assist you as you comb the doll's hair. Describe the pictures in the book as you read.

Cognitive and/or Developmental Delays—Use simple, short sentences as you teach. The main concepts you want to stress with this child are "hair" (being able to point to their hair) and grooming (showing how they can brush or comb their hair).

Emotional Disturbance—Seat the child next to you and affirm him for good behavior and for participating.

Other Health Impairment/Attention Deficit Hyperactivity Disorder—When reading the story, have the child sit next to you and let him help turn the pages.

Orthopedic Impairment—Ensure that the child has adapted seating if needed during the circle activity so that he is at the same level as the other children.

Curriculum Connections

- **Dramatic Play**—Place clean, empty unbreakable hair care product bottles and containers in the Dress-Up Center so children can play Beauty Salon or Barber Shop.
- **Language and Literacy**—Work with a small group of children to brainstorm and come up with words that they think rhyme with hair.
- **Math**—Have precut pictures of hair taken from magazines for children to sort by color: blond, brunette, redhead, and so on.

Heart

Time

15–20 minutes

Materials

- Cassette recorder
- *How Does Your Heart Work?* by Don L. Curry

Preparation

Use a cassette tape to record your heart beating.

Review

Ask children to tell you what a heartbeat is. As children leave the circle area, ask them to tell you one thing they learned about their hearts.

Assessment Strategy

Ask individual children to tell you what the heart does.

Objectives

Children will:

1. Tell that the heart pumps blood throughout the body.
2. Tell what a heartbeat is.

Lesson

- As children gather for Group or Circle Time, play the cassette recording of your heart beating. Ask the children to guess what the sound is.
- Tell them that the sound is your heart beating, and that the heart pumps the blood throughout our bodies.
- Read a book about the heart, such as *How Does Your Heart Work?* by Don L. Curry. Let the children respond to the pictures in the book and answer their questions as they arise during the lesson.
- Show children how to feel their hearts beat by placing their fingers over the artery in their neck.

Accommodations/Modifications

Autism—Preteach the vocabulary in the book—heart, arteries, veins, blood, and so on—and refer to the pictures before reading the story.

Speech or Language Impairments—After reading the story, review the vocabulary—heart, arteries, veins, blood, and so on—and talk about what each does.

Hearing Impairments—Seat the child across from you so she can see your lips as you speak.

Visual Impairments—Describe the pictures as you read the story.

Cognitive and/or Developmental Delays—Focus on the function of the heart and direct related questions to the child.

Emotional Disturbance—Seat the child next to you and affirm her for participating.

Other Health Impairment/Attention Deficit Hyperactivity Disorder—Seat the child next to you as you read the story and have her help you turn the pages.

Orthopedic Impairment—Assist the child in feeling her heart beat.

Curriculum Connections

- **Art**—Make heart-shaped patterns out of poster board or cardboard for children to trace and cut out if they wish.
- **Science**—Have a stethoscope available so children can listen to their hearts beat or to other children's hearts beat. They can also listen to the heartbeats of class pets.

INTRODUCTION TO
Families

Time

15–20 minutes

Materials

- Pictures of human families and animal families
- Paper
- Markers

Review

Read the book *Families Are Different* by Nina Pellegrini. Discuss the types of families in the book.

Assessment Strategy

Give the children a sheet of paper and markers and ask each child to draw his family. Ask each child to tell you about his picture. Write their responses at the bottom or on the back of their pictures.

Objectives

Children will:

1. Describe families as groups that take care of one another.
2. Describe who is in their family.

Lesson

- Show the children pictures of human and animal families. Explain that families are groups that take care of one another.
- Talk about who may live in the house together: mother, father, baby, brother, sister, grandmother, grandfather.
- Ask the children who lives in their houses. Sometimes family members live in different houses. Sometimes fathers or mothers live in different houses from their children. Ask the children if they think a baby can live alone without other family members. Explain that babies and children need someone to take care of them. Stress that a family may not always live in the same house, but they still help to take care of each other.

Accommodations/Modifications

Autism—Use Picture Communication Symbols for the family and ask the child to show you who lives in his home.

Speech or Language Impairments—When asking the child who lives in his home, provide suggestions and choices for yes/no responses.

Visual Impairments—Provide family models (people and animals) for the child to touch during the discussion of families.

Hearing Impairments—Point and gesture to pictures when making explanations.

Cognitive and/or Developmental Delays—Speak in short, simple sentences. Allow the child to answer yes/no questions when he is not able to tell you about his family spontaneously or in response to questions.

Emotional Disturbance—Seat the child next to you during the discussion about families.

Other Health Impairment/Attention Deficit Hyperactivity Disorder—Make sure you have the child's attention before you begin the discussion.

Orthopedic Impairments—For the assessment drawing, provide a crayon holder or assist the child in drawing the picture as he tells you what to draw.

Curriculum Connections

- **Blocks/Construction**—Provide families of people to fit into vehicles.
- **Science**—Provide sets of animal and human families for the children to sort.

My Family

Time
15–20 minutes

Materials
- Doll family and dollhouse
- Paper
- Markers

Objectives
Children will:
1. List the members of their family.
2. Draw a picture of their family.

Lesson
- Using a set of family dolls, talk about family members, which could include: mother, father, brother, baby, grandmother, grandfather. Explain that a family is a group of people that care for one another. Each family is different.
- Put the doll family inside a dollhouse. Take out the grandmother and grandfather dolls and explain that some families have grandmothers and grandfathers who live with them and some do not. Take out the baby. Some families have a baby and some do not. Take the mother doll out of the house and explain that some families have mothers who live with them and some do not.
- Line up all the family members and say, "A family is a group of people who help each other and take care of each other."
- Give each child one of the dolls and explain that they are going to help you sing a song about the people in a family. Identify each doll as a specific family member: mother, father, grandmother, grandfather, brother, sister, baby. Sing the following song and cue the children to hold up their dolls as you point to them.

  Where Is the Family? by Sharon Lynch
  (Tune: "Where Is Thumbkin?")
  Where is mother? Where is mother?
  Here she is! Here she is! (hold up doll)
  How are you to-day? Very well, I thank you.
  Run away! Run away! (put doll down)

- Repeat for each family member. End with all in "Where is the family?"

Accommodations/Modifications
Autism—Use Picture Communication Symbols to represent the family members and allow the child to use them to communicate about the family. Ask questions that the child can respond to using the Picture Communication Symbols.

Speech or Language Impairments—If the child is unable to tell you about her family spontaneously or to answer questions about the family, offer verbal choices for the child to select from. Ask the child a question that several other children have responded to so the child can benefit from their language models.

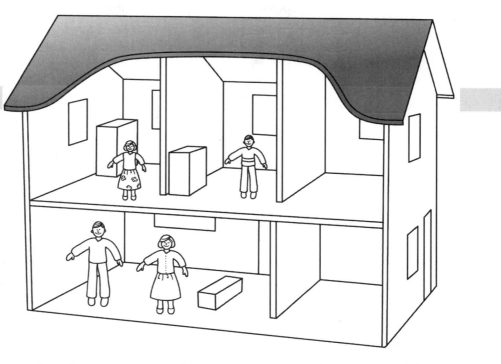

Review

State again that a family is a group of people who care for one another and that all families are different. Ask each child to name the people in her family. Encourage and affirm the children's responses.

Assessment Strategy

Begin making "My Family" books with the children. Each child will make the pages for her own book. Ask each child to name the members of her family. On the first page, each child can paste people cut from die-cuts or a construction paper cutout of a house. Have each child draw her family on the next page. Write down what she says about her family in her book.

Hearing Impairments—Seat the child so she can see your face as you speak. Refer to family members by pointing to the dolls as you speak.

Visual Impairments—Allow the child to hold the dolls as you talk about them.

Cognitive and/or Developmental Delays—Use short, simple sentences as you talk about the family. Allow the child to express herself with words and gestures, and by pointing to the family dolls.

Emotional Disturbance—Seat the child next to you during the discussion of families.

Other Health Impairment/Attention Deficit Hyperactivity Disorder—Use a consistent cue to get the child's attention before beginning the lesson on families and before giving instructions.

Orthopedic Impairment—Provide a glue brush with an adapted holder for the assessment activity.

Curriculum Connections

- **Dramatic Play**—Provide family dolls for use in the Home Living Center.
- **Language and Literacy**—Read and discuss the story *Who's Who in My Family?* by Loreen Leedy.
- **Math**—Have the children count the people in their family.
- **Science**—Provide several sets of animal families in the Science Center. Have the children sort them into family groups
- **Social Studies**—Show pictures of houses and families in other lands. Discuss how they are the same and how they are different. Read *Houses and Homes* by Ann Morris to the children. The book shows houses and homes around the world.

Brothers and Sisters

Time
15–20 minutes

Materials
- Doll family
- *My Brother Never Feeds the Cat* by Reynold Ruffins

Objectives

Children will:
1. Tell whether they have a brother or sister.
2. Tell the names of their brothers and sisters.

Lesson

- Show the children a doll family with a brother and a sister.
- Explain that the topic of the day is brothers and sisters. Some families have more than one child, so they have a brother or sister; other families have one child. Ask the children if they have a brother or sister and what the names of their brothers or sisters are. **Note:** Be sensitive to children who do not have brothers or sisters.
- Read *My Brother Never Feeds the Cat* by Reynold Ruffins. Tell the children that brothers and sisters work together to get things done in a family. Talk about some of the jobs that brothers and sisters take turns doing; for example, feeding the cat, helping mom or dad in the yard, helping mom or dad with the laundry.
- Ask the children if their brothers and sisters have jobs at home. What are the things brothers and sisters do at home together?

Accommodations/Modifications

Autism—Refer to the child's brother or sister by name when discussing siblings. If the child does not have a brother or sister, say so.

Speech or Language Impairments—Call on the child to talk about his brother or sister after others in the class have provided language models.

Hearing Impairments—Seat the child close by and facing you so he can see your face as you speak. Use gestures and make references to pictures and props as you present the lesson.

Visual Impairments—Describe your actions and the pictures in the book during the lesson. Allow the child to hold the brother and sister cutouts and to identify them verbally.

Cognitive and/or Developmental Delays—Use simple language and model pointing to the brother and sister during the assessment activity. During the assessment activity, ask the child if he has a brother or a sister, or if he does not have any brothers or sisters. If the child has a sibling, let him select the cutout representing his brother or sister.

Emotional Disturbance—Seat the child near you as you read the story and present the lesson. Affirm the child for participating with the group.

Review

Ask the children to talk about their brother or sister if they have one. For children who do not have brothers or sisters, encourage them to tell the class about a friend's brother or sister or about another family member.

Assessment Strategy

Using the "My Family" book from the previous activity's Assessment Strategy, ask each child individually if he has a brother or a sister. Select a paper cutout of a boy or girl (or both or several, as the case may be), and have the child paste his brothers and sisters into his "My Family" book. For the child who has no brothers or sisters, encourage him to decorate his "My Family" picture with pets or flowers.

Other Health Impairment/Attention Deficit Hyperactivity Disorder—If the child is becoming restless as you read My Brother Never Feeds the Cat, shorten the text by paraphrasing it. Allow the child to get a drink of water or to put a piece of paper in the trash if he is beginning to get restless.

Orthopedic Impairment—Provide a glue brush, a holder for a glue stick, or hand-over-hand assistance during the assessment activity if the child has difficulty pasting the cutouts on the pages in the book.

Curriculum Connections

■ **Art**—Provide paper plates, yarn, buttons, and markers. Have the children make a mask to look like their brother or sister. Does their brother have brown eyes or green eyes? Is her hair long or short? If the child does not have a brother or sister, he can make a mask that looks like a friend.

■ **Math**—Write each child's name in a line down the left-hand side of a piece of chart paper. Ask each child if they have a brother or a sister and how many. Draw stick figures of brothers and sisters for each child across the page to form a graph. Count the total number of brothers and sisters depicted for the class.

■ **Science**—Show a selection of pictures of animals with their young. Talk about how some animals have many babies at one time. Count the number of brothers and sisters in each picture.

Babies

Time

15–20 minutes

Materials

- Baby doll, basket, blanket
- Baby spoon, bottle, diaper

Objectives

Children will:

1. Describe the characteristics of babies
2. Tell whether or not they have a baby in their family.

Preparation

Place a baby doll in a small basket and cover it with a small blanket. Put it in the Group or Circle Time area.

Lesson

- At Group or Circle Time, ask the children to guess the topic for discussion. Remind them of the other family members that you have discussed. Provide clues until the children guess what you are going to talk about. Then show them the baby doll.
- Ask the children if they remember being a baby. Explain that everyone starts life as a baby. Babies are very small and keep growing until they are grownups.
- Engage the children in a discussion about babies. Ask the following questions:
    - "What do babies eat?" Show them a baby spoon. Ask them to show you how babies eat. Someone has to feed babies but they can eat by themselves as they grow up.
    - "How do babies drink?" Show them a bottle. Invite one of the children to show how to give a baby a bottle.
- Show the children a diaper. Explain that someone has to change a baby's diaper, but that children learn to use the toilet when they get older.
- Show the children baby clothes. Explain that someone has to dress a baby, but older boys and girls can dress themselves.
- Pretend that the baby is crying. Explain that babies cry, but that older boys and girls can use words to tell other people what is happening or how they are feeling.
- Ask, "How do babies move?" Babies have to learn how to hold things, sit up, crawl, and walk. Babies have to learn many things.

Write the
following at the
top of a piece of
chart paper,
"When I was a
baby I used to. . . "
Ask the children to
say what they used
to do when they
were babies.
Follow up by
asking them to
complete the
additional
statement "But
now I…"

Assessment Strategy

Show each child a
baby doll and ask
her to tell you all
about it. Record
what she says. Ask
her if there is a
baby in her family.

Accommodations/Modifications

Autism—Provide clip art or Picture Communication Symbols of things that babies do for the child to refer to. Point to the pictures as you ask the child questions.

Speech or Language Impairments—During the review activity, use gestures to prompt the child if she has difficulty answering questions. During the assessment activity, ask leading questions to scaffold language and cue the child if she does not answer the questions.

Hearing Impairments—Use gestures and make sure the child can see your face as you speak.

Visual Impairments—During the lesson, allow the child to hold objects, such as the doll, the spoon, the bottle, the diaper, and so on.

Cognitive and/or Developmental Delays—During the review activity, provide objects to elicit responses such as the bottle, diaper, spoon, and so on. Provide verbal cues, such as "When I was a baby I used to drink from a _____(hold up bottle)."

Emotional Disturbance—Emphasize that the child is a big girl now and can use words rather than cry to get what she needs. Affirm the child for participation and cooperation.

Other Health Impairment/Attention Deficit Hyperactivity Disorder—Use good eye contact, animated expressions, proximity, and gestures to maintain the child's attention. Call on the child often to maintain engagement.

Orthopedic Impairment—Help the child demonstrate how to feed a baby if she volunteers.

Curriculum Connections

- **Dramatic Play**—Provide a multiethnic collection of baby dolls for the children to play with.
- **Math**—Show pictures of baby animals. Have the children count the number of baby animals in each picture.
- **Social Studies**—Show pictures of babies from other countries and cultures. Talk about how mothers carry their babies. Point out how some things are the same and some are different.

Grandparents

Time

15–20 minutes

Materials

- Family doll set that includes grandparents
- Pictures of grandparents
- Copier

Objectives

Children will:

1. State that grandparents are our parents' parents.
2. Identify a picture of their grandparents by pointing to it.

Preparation

Send a note home asking families to send in photographs or copies of photographs of the children's grandparents. If families send in photographs, make copies of the photographs for the children to handle without damaging the original. If the child's grandparents are not living, the child can still bring pictures of their grandparents. Encourage the child to share his pictures.

Lesson

- Show the children the grandparent dolls in the set of family dolls. Explain that grandparents are special people who care about us. They are our mommy's and our daddy's mother and father. A grandfather is our mother's or our dad's father. A grandmother is our mother's or our dad's mother. Ask the children if they have a grandmother or grandfather. Ask what they call them.
- Show the children the pictures of the grandparents. Ask them to identify whose grandparents they are.
- Invite the children to talk about their grandparents. Where do or did their grandparents live? When do or did they see them? What do they like to do with their grandparents? Emphasize that grandparents are special people. They are our mother's and our father's parents.
- Some children may have grandparents who are in other countries or who live far away, so they may not have pictures. Encourage each child to talk about his grandparents.
- If children do not bring pictures, provide grandfather or grandmother pictures for them to talk about.

Accommodations/Modifications

Autism—Help the child locate the picture of his grandparent by placing a few pictures to select from at a time. Find out some facts about the child's grandparents from his family and provide verbal cues to encourage the child to talk about them.

Review

Mix up the pictures of the grandparents. Select one photo and hold it up for the group to see. Ask the group whose grandfather or grandmother is in the picture.

Assessment Strategy

Have the children paste or draw pictures of their grandparents in their "My Family" books. Ask each child to tell you about his grandparents.

Speech or Language Impairments—Ask the child to tell you about his grandparents after several children have modeled responses in telling about their grandparents.

Hearing Impairments—Make sure the child can see your face as you discuss families.

Visual Impairments—Allow the child to hold the family dolls. Let the child hold the photograph of his own grandparents and encourage the child to show the picture to the class and talk about his grandparents.

Cognitive and/or Developmental Delays—Help the child locate the picture of his grandparents by providing only two pictures to choose from.

Emotional Disturbance—Seat the child near you and encourage him to participate in the discussion of grandparents.

Other Health Impairment/Attention Deficit Hyperactivity Disorder—If the child loses interest, use gestures and call him by name to redirect his attention to the group activity.

Orthopedic Impairment—Help the child draw a picture of his grandparents during the assessment activity.

Curriculum Connections

- **Art**—Have the children make special cards for their grandparents using thumbprint animals. Make the child's thumbprint using an inkpad. With black pen, the children can make their thumbprints into animals such as cats, mice, or monkeys.

- **Language and Literacy**—On chart paper, write a group story about why grandparents are special. Read the story to the children, pointing to each word as you read it. Re-read the story daily, omitting words at the end of the sentence for the children to fill in. Copy the story to send home with the children.

- **Math**—Talk about grandparents being older than our parents. Show a number chart and point out that most grandparents are in their 40s, 50s, or 60s. Show the range of the grandparents' ages and the range of the children's ages on the number chart.

- **Social Studies**—Invite grandparents to the classroom during the week closest to Grandparent's Day, which is the first Sunday after Labor Day. Invite the grandparents to tell the class special stories or to demonstrate their talents.

Family Jobs

Time

15–20 minutes

Materials

- Doll family and dollhouse
- Pictures of people doing jobs at home and jobs outside the home
- *A Clean House for Mole and Mouse* by Harriet Ziefert

Objectives

Children will:

1. Describe the jobs of family members.
2. Tell one job they do around their homes.

Lesson

- Show the children the doll family and the dollhouse. In a family, each person has jobs that they do to help the family. Some people in the family work at home and some work outside the home.
- Take the mother and the father doll out of the dollhouse. Explain that in some families both the mother and father work in factories, offices, or at home.
- Talk about jobs at home: cooking, cleaning, watching children, doing laundry, helping children with homework. Show pictures of people doing those jobs. Engage the children in a discussion about the people who do these things in their homes.
- Show pictures of people working outside the home. Talk about jobs outside the home that the children's family members perform.
- Sing a song about the jobs of family members.

This Is the Way by Sharon Lynch
(Tune: "Here We Go 'Round the Mulberry Bush")
This is way we wash the clothes, wash the clothes, wash the
clothes. (gesture for washing)
This is way we wash the clothes, so early in the morning.

Additional verses include the following. Add appropriate gestures for each verse.
…cook the food…
…wipe the table…
…wash the dishes…
…mop the floor…
…sweep the floor…
…mow the lawn…
…fix the car…

Review

Talk with each child about who in her family does certain jobs at home. Ask the children to describe jobs they can help with at their house.

Assessment Strategy

In each child's "My Family" book, ask her to tell you about the jobs her family members have. Write what the child says on the page in her book.

Accommodations/Modifications

Autism—Show the child pictures or Picture Communication Symbols corresponding to each verse of the song.

Speech or Language Impairments—For the assessment activity, provide picture cues to help the child get started with her descriptions.

Hearing Impairments—During the lesson activity, seat the child across from you where she can see your face.

Visual Impairments—Before singing the song about family jobs, preview the gestures with the children. Provide assistance to help the child perform the actions if she is not familiar with the specific gesture.

Cognitive and/or Developmental Delays—Keep your sentences short as you describe the pictures of various jobs.

Emotional Disturbance—Seat the child near you during the discussion and affirm the child for participating.

Other Health Impairment/Attention Deficit Hyperactivity Disorder—Keep your discussion of jobs brief. Allow the child to get up and put materials on your desk or another task if she needs more activity.

Orthopedic Impairment—For the song about family jobs, help the child to perform the actions.

Curriculum Connections

- **Dramatic Play**—Place props and clothing for various jobs inside and outside of the house in the Home Living Center.
- **Language and Literacy**—Read and discuss *A Clean House for Mole and Mouse* or other books about families and the jobs individual family members do in the home.
- **Listening Center**—Provide tapes with songs about people in the neighborhood and their jobs.
- **Math**—Brainstorm to see how many jobs that the children can think of inside the house and outside the house. Write them on chart paper and count them. Which group has more jobs?

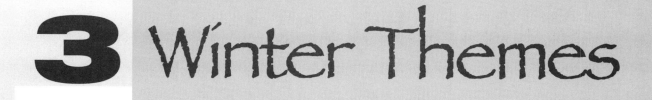

3 Winter Themes

INTRODUCTION TO

My Home

Time

20–30 minutes

Materials

- Pictures different types of homes, such as an apartment, a mobile home, a high rise, a duplex, a single family home, and so on
- Story of "The Three Little Pigs" (many versions are available)
- Straw, sticks, and brick

Objectives

Children will:

1. Know that a home is the place where someone lives.
2. Distinguish between pictures that are homes and pictures that are not homes.

Lesson

- Show the children pictures of several types of homes: a single family home, an apartment, a mobile home, a high rise, a duplex. Explain that homes are where people live. Describe each type of home and where you might find each one.
- Read the story of "The Three Little Pigs." Talk about the types of houses in the story. Ask what type of house was the strongest. Provide straw, sticks, and bricks for the children to feel.

- Discuss why they think the houses of straw and sticks were not as strong as the house of bricks. point out that the homes we live in protect us from things that can hurt us, just like the wolf who could hurt the pigs.

Accommodations/Modifications

Autism—Provide pictures of things that can hurt us and that we are protected from by our homes, such as rain, snow, lightning, wind, bugs, and so on.

Speech or Language Impairments—During the assessment, provide a phrase to help the child get started in telling why she would like a home. For example, "It would be nice to live in a home built of bricks because. . ."

Hearing Impairments—During the lesson and the story of "The Three Little Pigs," seat the child across from you so she can see your face.

Visual Impairments—During the assessment, name each type of home and ask the child what type of home she likes least.

Cognitive and/or Developmental Delays—During the assessment limit the choices to two or three pictures.

Review

Review the sequence of the story with an art project. Provide sticks, straw, and paper "bricks." Let each child select the type of material she refers to use to make a house, and provide tag board and glue for use as the children to build their homes. Use a wolf puppet to come to the home. Ask the children where the wolf will go first.

Assessment Strategy

Show the children pictures of the different types of homes. Ask, "Which home would you like to have when you are grown up? Why?" Then ask the child to tell you about other types of homes.

Emotional Disturbance—Seat the child next to you and affirm the child for sitting, participating, and cooperating during the lesson.

Other Health Impairments/Attention Deficit Hyperactivity Disorder—If the child becomes restless during "The Three Little Pigs," paraphrase the text to shorten the story.

Orthopedic Impairment—Help the child make the house during the review activity.

Curriculum Connections

■ **Language and Literacy**—*Two Homes* by Claire Masurel. Discuss the types of homes in the story.

■ **Science**—In the Building Center, provide many types of materials for building homes: Lincoln Logs, small bricks, wood blocks, and other building materials. Show models of how to use materials to build homes. Encourage children to design and build their own homes.

■ **Social Studies**—Show pictures of homes in other parts of the world. Provide a map so the children can see where these homes are located.

Houses and Homes

Time

20–30 minutes

Objectives

Children will:

1. Describe a home as a place where a family lives.
2. Tell why people live in homes.

Lesson

- Invite the children to tell you all that they know about houses and homes.
- Similar to "Going on a Bear Hunt," recite the following chant about the steps in building a house with the children. You chant the first sentence and the children repeat it the second time. Provide gestures and sound effects for each step.

Let's Go Build a House by Sharon Lynch
Let's go build a house. Let's go build a house.
Okay. Okay.
Let's go. Let's go.
First you dig the ground out. First you dig the ground out.
Then you pour the concrete. Then you pour the concrete.
Then put up the boards. Then put up the boards.
Gotta' lay the floor. Gotta' lay the floor.
We need to build the roof. We need to build the roof.
Gotta' build the walls. Gotta' build the walls.
Now let's lay the bricks. Now let's lay the bricks.
Now we need the windows. Now we need the windows.
Let's put on the doors. Let's put on the doors.
Now let's go inside. Now let's go inside.
Wow! It's a house! Wow! It's a house!

- Engage the children in a discussion about why people live in homes.

Review

Ask the children to show you their "hammers" by holding up their fists. Talk as a group about what is needed to build a house. Go through the motions of building a house. After the house is complete, discuss why people live in houses.

Assessment Strategy

Provide geometric shapes of various colors of paper and ask individual children to use the shapes to build a house. Ask each child to tell you about his home. Ask him to tell why people live in houses or homes.

Modifications/Accommodations

Autism—During the assessment activity, provide yes/no questions if the child does not respond to your request to tell you about his home.

Speech or Language Impairments—Point to various parts of the house during the assessment activity and ask the child to tell you about them. If the child has difficulty with "why" questions, provide an introductory phrase such as, "People live in houses because. . ."

Hearing Impairments—Seat the child across from you so he can see your face during your verbal explanations and during the house-building activity.

Visual Impairments—Assist the child in beginning the movements during the house-building activity.

Cognitive and/or Developmental Delays—Keep your language simple and your sentences short. You may need to help the child build the house during the assessment activity.

Emotional Disturbance—Seat the child near you during the lesson activity and affirm the child by name as he participates in the group activity.

Other Health Impairments/Attention Deficit Hyperactivity Disorder—If the child becomes restless, take a stretch break as a group.

Orthopedic Impairment—During the assessment activity, have the child tell you where to place the geometric shapes as you put them together to build a house.

Curriculum Connections

■ **Language and Literacy**—Read *Our Big Home* by Linda Glaser. Discuss the events in the story and the house as they remember it from the story.

■ **Science**—Provide laminated pictures of animals and their homes. Discuss where the animals live and how their homes protect them.

■ **Social Studies**—Provide models of different types of homes used in the past: caves, sod homes, teepees, log cabins, and igloos, among others. Discuss the places and the people who lived these homes.

My Living Room

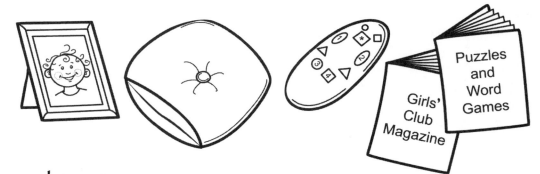

Time

20–30 minutes

Materials

- Large paper grocery or shopping bag
- Objects from a living room; for example, a throw pillow, radio, TV remote control, magazine, book, framed photograph
- Pictures of objects found in a living room; for example, coffee table, sofa, throw pillow, chair, television, DVD player, TV remote control, magazine, tape, CD, CD player, radio, book, framed photograph
- Paper and crayons, markers

Objectives

Children will:

1. Describe the living room as a place where people spend time together.
2. Name the living room as a room in the home.

Preparation

Place commonly found objects from a living room in a large paper grocery or shopping bag (see list in Materials).

Lesson

- One by one, take the living room objects out of the bag. As you remove each object, ask the children to guess what you are going to talk about today. If no one can guess, offer the clue that it is a room in a home. Provide additional clues if needed.
- Show the children pictures of objects found in a living room. Using gestures, demonstrate how each object is used. Next, name the object and say how it is used in a living room.
- Let each child take a turn with a picture of an object found in a living room. First, have the child show how it is used (through gestures), and then have her say how it is used. Affirm the child with a statement that names the object and how it is used in the living room. Emphasize that the living room is a place where people relax and spend time together.

Accommodations/Modifications

Autism—During the lesson, model how an object is used and then state how it is used. Then have the child show you how to use it and tell you how it is used.

Speech or Language Impairments—Provide verbal cues to show what people do in the living room during the assessment activity.

Review

Show the children a dollhouse and pieces of dollhouse furniture, one at a time. Ask the group to tell you if a particular piece belongs in the living room. Then ask them to name the item. Finally, ask them how it is used. If the piece of furniture is used in the living room, place it in the living room of the dollhouse. Talk about the fact that people spend time together in the living room. Ask the children what they like to do in the living room.

Assessment Strategy

Ask the children to draw a living room, then ask each child to tell you about her picture. Probe to find out what the children think people do in a living room.

Hearing Impairments—Seat the child across from you during the lesson activity so she can see your face.

Visual Impairments—Allow the child to feel objects in the bag during the lesson activity. During the review activity, let her hold the doll furniture.

Cognitive and/or Developmental Delays—For the assessment activity, provide verbal choices for what people do in the living room so the child can respond with "yes" or "no." For example, "Do we watch television in the living room? Do we cook in the living room?"

Emotional Disturbance—Seat the child near you during the lesson. Affirm the child for helping and participating.

Other Health Impairments/Attention Deficit Hyperactivity Disorder—Take a stretch break between activities.

Orthopedic Impairment—Assist the child in drawing a living room during the assessment activity, or have her tell you how to decorate the living room.

Curriculum Connections

- **Science**—Prepare a number of "What would happen if…" cards by writing "What would happen if…" on one side of a large index card. On the other side, write, "we did not have…" at the top of the card and glue a magazine picture of an item commonly found in living rooms, such as a couch. Play the "What would happen if…" game, focusing on things found in a living room. Ask one child at a time to draw a card and then invite her to talk about what would happen if we did not have the object pictured on the back of the card, such as a sofa. As a group, talk about what would happen if we did not have the object pictured on the card. Pictures of living room objects include a television, radio, computer, lamp, light bulb, rug, sofa, book, and so on.

- **Social Studies**—Provide pictures of the living area in various types of homes. Be sure to include objects found in the living room: television, computers, telephones, various types of games. Discuss the living room as an area where people like to spend time together. Ask what the children like to do in their living room and discuss differences in the living areas of other types of homes.

The Kitchen

Time

20–30 minutes

Materials

- Large paper grocery or shopping bag
- Items from a kitchen; for example: a can of food, cup, napkin, small pan, large spoon, oven mitt, sponge, fork, and so on
- Pictures of things found in a kitchen and in other rooms in a home

Objectives

Children will:

1. Describe the kitchen as a room where we keep, prepare, and eat food.
2. Name one kitchen fixture.

Preparation

Place items commonly found in a kitchen in a large paper grocery or shopping bag (see the list in Materials).

Lesson

- One at a time, remove items from the bag. As you remove each item, ask the children to guess what you are going to talk about today. If no one guesses "kitchens," provide a clue that you will talk about a room in a home. Provide additional clues if needed.
- Show the group one object and model how it is used with gestures. Then say what the item is and how it is used in a kitchen.
- One at a time, give each child an item that was in the bag. Ask the child to show the group how it is used with gestures only, and then say how it is used. Affirm the child's responses with the phrase, "We use (item the child is holding) with a (another object found in a kitchen). We use the (item the child is holding) in a kitchen," or a similar phrase emphasizing the use of the object in a kitchen.

Accommodations/Modifications

Autism—If the child does not respond to your request to tell you what people do in the kitchen, direct his attention to the pictures one at time.

Speech or Language Impairments—During the assessment activity, use gestures along with the pictures if the child does not respond to your request to tell you what people do in the kitchen.

Hearing Impairments—Seat the child across from you during the lesson and during the review in the Kitchen Center.

Review

Take the children to the Kitchen Center or Home Living Center if you have this center in your classroom. Talk about what you do with equipment or material in the Kitchen Center—and demonstrate how to use each item. Ask the children to tell you what else they have in their kitchens at home.

Assessment Strategy

Collect a set of pictures that show things that are used in a kitchen and things that are used in other rooms of a home. Give a child the pictures and ask him to find the things that go in the kitchen, and to turn over the pictures that do not go in a kitchen. Ask the child to tell you what people do in a kitchen.

Visual Impairments—Allow the child to feel objects in the bag during the lesson activity. During the review activity, let the child hold the objects from the kitchen. Name the items in the pictures during the assessment activity and have the child tell you what people do with each item.

Cognitive and/or Developmental Delays—Limit the number of pictures shown at one time during the assessment activity.

Emotional Disturbance—Seat the child next to you during the lesson. Encourage and affirm his participation.

Other Health Impairments/Attention Deficit Hyperactivity Disorder—Allow the child to stand during the activities if he needs more movement in order to remain focused.

Orthopedic Impairment—Provide hand-over-hand assistance to show how objects are used during the lesson activity.

Curriculum Connections

- **Dramatic Play**—Set up a Kitchen Center in the classroom with table and chairs, stove, sink, dishes, and other kitchen equipment and materials.

- **Language and Literacy**—Read *Two Homes* by Claire Masurel. Discuss the rooms found in each home.

- **Science**—Discuss why it important to keep a kitchen clean. In order to stay healthy, the food we eat must be free of germs. Talk about how germs can get into food if we do not keep the kitchen clean and that we must always wash our hands before handling food. Discuss the fact that some food must be kept cool in the refrigerator or it will spoil. Provide a picture of a pantry, a kitchen cabinet, and a refrigerator, as well as labels and boxes from different types of food. Talk about which can be kept in the pantry and which must be refrigerated.

- **Social Studies**—Discuss the fact that people in other countries also prepare food in kitchens, even if they make different kinds of food. Have a tasting party with foods from other lands. Emphasize the fact that even though we eat different types of food, we all need a place to prepare the food we eat.

My Bedroom

Time

20–30 minutes

Materials

- Large paper grocery or shopping bag
- Objects from a bedroom, such as a pillow, a pillowcase, a sheet, toys, a teddy bear
- Pictures of objects commonly found in a bedroom, such as a bed, a bedspread, a blanket, a pillow, a pillowcase, a teddy bear or stuffed animal, a night light, a nightstand, and so on
- Shoeboxes
- Markers, glue, and other art materials

Objectives

Children will:

1. Describe the bedroom as the place where they sleep.
2. Describe the bedroom as a place where they can play with toys.

Preparation

Place objects commonly found in a bedroom in a large paper grocery or shopping bag (see list to the left).

Lesson

- One at a time, take out the objects. As you remove each object, ask the children to guess what you are going to talk about today. If no one can guess, offer the clue that it is a room in a home. Provide additional clues if needed.
- Show the children pictures of objects found in a bedroom. Using gestures, demonstrate how each is used. Name the object and tell how it is used in the bedroom.
- Let each child take a turn selecting a picture of an object commonly found in a bedroom. First, have the child show with gestures only how the object is used, and then to tell how it is used.
- Affirm the child with a statement that names the object and how it is used in the bedroom. Emphasize that a bedroom is a place to sleep and also to play with toys.

Accommodations/Modifications

Autism—During the assessment activity, provide pictures or objects one at a time to help the child tell what she does in her bedroom.

Speech or Language Impairments—During the assessment activity provide a starter phrase to help the child tell what we do in our bedrooms, if needed. For example, "What do we do in our bedroom? We have a bed to…"

Hearing Impairments—Seat the child across from you during the lesson and review so she can see your face.

Visual Impairments—Allow the child to feel objects in the bag during the lesson activity. During the review activity, let the child hold the pieces of furniture.

Review

Show the children a dollhouse. Then show them pieces of furniture or a dollhouse object one at a time. Ask the group to tell you If the item belongs in the bedroom. Then ask them to name the item. Finally, ask them how it is used. If the item is used in a bedroom, then place it in the bedroom of the dollhouse. Talk about the fact that a bedroom is a place to sleep.

Assessment Strategy

Provide each child with a shoebox to decorate as her bedroom. Provide art materials and other appropriate materials for the child to use to decorate the shoebox. Have the child tell you about her project. Ask the child to tell you some of the things she does in her bedroom.

Cognitive and/or Developmental Delays—During the assessment activity, show the child doll furniture and objects to help her tell you what she does in her bedroom.

Emotional Disturbance—Seat the child near your during the lesson and review, encouraging her to participate and providing attention for appropriate behavior.

Other Health Impairments/Attention Deficit Hyperactivity Disorder—If the child becomes restless, have her collect objects from the lesson and put them in the grocery bag. Then she can put the bag on your desk or in the storage area.

Orthopedic Impairment—Help the child decorate her shoebox during the assessment activity.

Curriculum Connections

- **Dramatic Play**—Provide several beds for the dolls in the Doll Center.
- **Language and Literacy**—Provide story books in the book center that have pictures of beds, such as *Goodnight Moon* by Margaret Wise Brown, "Goldilocks and the Three Bears" (many versions), and "Little Red Riding Hood" (many versions).
- **Science**—Prepare a number of "What would happen if…" cards by writing "What would happen if…" on one side of a large index card. On the other side, write, "we did not have…" at the top of the card and glue a magazine picture of an item commonly found in a bedroom, such as a bed. Play the "What would happen if…" game. Ask one child at a time to draw a card and then invite her to talk about what would happen if we did not have the object pictured on the back of the card, such as a bed. As a group, talk about what would happen if we did not have the object pictured on the card. Pictures of bedroom items include a bed, a blanket, a night light, a nightstand, a lamp, a rug, and so on.
- **Social Studies**—Show pictures of objects used for around the world sleeping. Use a map to designate the country and the object used for sleeping, including a bed, a hammock, a mat, a sleeping bag, a sleeping rug, and so on.

The Bathroom

Time

20 minutes

Materials

- Large paper grocery or shopping bag
- Objects from the bathroom, such as a washcloth, small towel, soap, sponge, toothpaste, toothbrush, hairbrush, comb, adhesive bandage strips
- Box
- Items found in a bathroom and others that are not

Objectives

Children will:

1. Describe the bathroom as a place where they use the toilet, bathe, brush our teeth, and wash our hands.
2. Describe the bathroom as a place where they keep themselves clean.

Preparation

Fill a large paper grocery or shopping bag with commonly found objects from the bathroom (see list to the left).

Lesson

- One at a time, take out each object and ask the children to guess what you are going to talk about today. If no one can to guess, offer the clue that it is a room in a home. Provide additional clues if needed.
- Show the children an object from the bag. Using gestures, demonstrate how it is used. Then name the object and tell how it is used in the bathroom.
- Let each child take a turn with an object found in the bathroom. First, have the child show how it is used with gestures only, and then to tell how it is used. Affirm the child with a statement that names the object and how it is used in the bathroom.

Accommodations/Modifications

Autism—During the assessment activity, hold up the objects one at a time to help the child tell what we do in the bathroom.

Speech or Language Impairments—During the assessment activity provide a starter phrase to help the child tell what we do in the bathroom, if needed. For example, "What do we do in the bathroom? We use soap to …"

Hearing Impairments—Seat the child across from you during the assessment and review so he can see your pace.

Visual Impairments—Allow the child to feel objects in the bag during the lesson activity. During the review activity, let him hold the pieces of furniture.

Cognitive and/or Developmental Delays—Use simple vocabulary words and short sentences as you present the lesson.

Emotional Disturbance—Seat the child next to you during the lesson. Encourage participation and provide plenty of attention for appropriate behavior.

Show the children a dollhouse and pieces of furniture. Ask the group to tell you if each piece of furniture belongs in the bathroom, and then to the name the piece of furniture. Finally, ask them how it is used. Then place the item in the bathroom in the dollhouse.

Assessment Strategy

Provide a box containing some items that go in the bathroom and some that do not. Ask the child to identify the items that go in the bathroom and to tell how each item is used in the bathroom.

Other Health Impairments/Attention Deficit Hyperactivity Disorder—If the child is becoming restless, have him collect the objects that have been used in the lesson and put them back in the paper bag. He can then put the bag in the classroom storage area.

Orthopedic Impairment—Help the child show how the item is used in the bathroom during the lesson activity.

Curriculum Connections

- **Science**—Prepare a number of "What would happen if…" cards by writing "What would happen if…" on one side of a large index card. On the other side, write, "we did not have…" at the top of the card and glue a magazine picture of an item commonly found in a bathroom, such as a sink. Play the "What would happen if…" game. Ask one child at a time to draw a card and then invite him to talk about what would happen if we did not have the object pictured on the back of the card, such as a sink. As a group, talk about what would happen if we did not have the object pictured on the card. Pictures of bathroom items include a bathtub, a shower, a sink, a toilet, a towel, soap, toothbrush, hairbrush, and comb.

- **Social Studies**—Talk about what people did before they had running water and bathrooms. Show pictures of ways that people stayed clean: a pump, or a well for water, a washtub for bathing, bathing in a river, an outhouse for a toilet. Talk about what we would have to do to stay clean if we did not have bathrooms.

My Backyard

Time

20 minutes

Materials

- Picture(s) of a backyard
- Flannel board with a fence
- Flannel board pictures of things that belong in a backyard and others that do not

Objectives

Children will:

1. Describe a backyard.
2. Describe what people can do in the backyard.

Lesson

- Show the children a picture of a backyard. If possible, find a picture of a backyard that is similar to the backyard of one or more of the children. The picture could feature a swing set, a sandbox, a dog, and children playing.
- Talk about the fact that some people have a backyard at their home, and some people do not. People who live in apartments use a playground instead of a backyard.

  Note: Be sure that all of the children in your group feel included in this lesson, whether they have a backyard or not. Depending on where the children in your group live, you may want to shift the focus to playgrounds instead of backyards.

- Talk about the things found in a backyard or on a playground. Ask the children what they like to do outside in a backyard or on a playground. Sing the following with the children.

What Can I Do in My Backyard? by Sharon Lynch
(Tune: "Here We Go 'Round the Mulberry Bush")
What can I do in my backyard, in my backyard, in my backyard?
What can I do in my backyard?
I like to play … (invite the children to say what they like to do in their backyard)

Possible responses include "I like to play on the swings," "I like to dig in the sand," "I like to ride my bike," and "I like to play with my dog." If the children are young or unable to respond, provide picture or object cues.

Review

Show the children a flannel board with a fence representing a backyard. Provide a variety of flannel board pictures and have the children tell you whether a picture belongs in a backyard or if it belongs somewhere else. Examples include a television, a toilet, books, an alarm clock, a computer, canned goods, a package of meat, toothpaste, and so on. Place the items that belong in a backyard on the flannel board. Pictures of back-yard items could include a swing set, a sandbox, a tricycle, toy trucks, children, a dog, and a cat.

Assessment Strategy

Provide pictures of some items which are found in a back-yard and some items which are not. Have the child sort the pictures and tell you what people can do in the backyard.

Accommodations/Modifications

Autism—For the song, provide picture or object cues.

Speech or Language Impairments—Provide a starter phrase during the assessment activity. For example, "In my backyard I like to play with …"

Hearing Impairments—Seat the child across from you so she can see your face during the lesson.

Visual Impairments—As you place items on the flannel board, name and describe them. Name the items in the assessment activity so the child can tell you whether or not they belong in the backyard.

Cognitive and/or Developmental Delays—For the sorting activity during the assessment, show the pictures to the child one at a time.

Emotional Disturbance—Seat the child next to you during the lesson, encouraging participation and affirming her for cooperating and participating.

Other Health Impairments/Attention Deficit Hyperactivity Disorder—Give the child a box to collect the pictures in when you are finished using them. After collecting them, the child can put them on your desk.

Orthopedic Impairment—For the assessment activity, help the child sort the pictures. The child can tell you which are pictures of something one does in a backyard.

Curriculum Connections

- **Math**—Go on a bug hunt over a period of several days (see Science). Count the number of different types of bugs that you find. Graph the different bugs that you find each day using drawings of the bugs and a chart tablet.

- **Science**—Go on a bug hunt and look for bugs that might be found in a backyard. Collect samples of bugs and put them in a plastic display jar. With the children, release the bugs at the end of the day. Explain that the bugs need to hunt for food or they will die. Talk about the things that bugs eat.

- **Social Studies**—Show pictures of different types of homes in different parts of the country. Talk about what a backyard looks like in different places. Show playgrounds and parks that are used by families that live in apartments and high rises.

Fences

Time

20–30 minutes

Materials

- Dollhouse
- Lincoln Logs or other type of blocks
- Small toy plastic dog and small plastic doll
- Paper, glue, and other art materials

Objectives

Children will:

1. Describe why there are fences.
2. Describe three things about fences.

Lesson

- Place a dollhouse on a small table and use Lincoln Logs or other type of blocks to build a fence around the dollhouse.
- Ask the children to guess what you are building. If they do not guess a fence offer clues. Place a toy plastic dog inside the fence and talk about what would happen to the dog without the fence. Place a small plastic doll inside the fence and talk about what would happen to the child without the fence.
- Talk about how fences keep us safe. Fences prevent the dog and the child from going into the street where they could be hurt, and they keep things that can hurt us out of the yard.
- Take a walk outdoors and look for different types of fences.
- Invite the children to talk about all the things they saw on the walk. Point out the fences that you passed and invite the children to tell you about them. Ask what would happen without fences.
- Teach the children the following song:

Now We're Going to Build a Fence by Sharon Lynch
(Tune: "Who's Afraid of the Big, Bad Wolf?")
Now we're going to build a fence, build a fence, build a fence.
Now we're going to build a fence. (pretend to pound with a hammer)
Let's go build it.

Now we're going to dig the holes, dig the holes, dig the holes.
Now we're going to dig the holes. (pretend to dig with a shovel)
Let's go dig them.

Now we're going to set the poles, set the poles, set the poles.
Now we're going to set the poles. (pretend to place the fence poles)
Let's go set them.

Now we're going to nail the boards, nail the boards, nail the boards.
Now we're going to nail the boards. (pretend to nail with a hammer)
Let's go nail them.

Review

Show the children a picture of a wooden fence. Talk about how to build a fence: first you dig the holes, then you set the poles, then you nail the boards.

Assessment Strategy

Provide paper, glue, sticks, pipe cleaners, straws, popsicle sticks, and other fence-making materials. Invite the children to "build" a fence on the paper using their choice of materials. Have the child tell you about the fence he built. Invite him to talk about what would happen without fences. Ask him to tell you three things about fences. Write each on an index card and attach the index card to the child's picture once the glue is set.

Now we've got a big, tall fence, big, tall fence, big, tall fence.
Now we've got a big, tall fence. (put hands in the air)
I can build it! (show muscles)

Accommodations/Modifications

Autism—Provide verbal cues during the assessment activity so the child can tell you three things about a fence.

Speech or Language Impairments—During the assessment activity, provide a starter phrase to assist the child in describing a fence. For example, "We build a fence out of …," "We find a fence …," or "Fences help us to…" If needed, provide the child with verbal rehearsal so he can repeat phrases and then use them spontaneously.

Hearing Impairments—Seat the child across from you during the lesson activity so he can see your face.

Visual Impairments—During the lesson, allow the child to hold objects and explore the layout after you have placed the fence around the house. Verbally describe your actions as you present the lesson.

Cognitive and/or Developmental Delays—Keep your language simple and your sentences short. During the assessment activity, point to items in the child's picture and ask him to tell you about them.

Emotional Disturbance—Seat the child next to you and encourage his participation.

Other Health Impairments/Attention Deficit Hyperactivity Disorder—Have the child collect the materials in a box before beginning the song.

Orthopedic Impairment—Help the child build his fence during the assessment activity.

Curriculum Connections

- **Math**—Make fence sections of craft sticks. Place a different numbers of sticks on each section. Have the children line up the fence sections from largest to smallest and from smallest to largest. Count the number of sticks in each section.
- **Science**—Make corrals on sheets of tag board and laminate them. Provide a number of different types of plastic animals, such as sheep, horses, cows, goats. Have the children sort the animals into separate corrals.
- **Social Studies**—Show pictures of fences from different parts of the country that are made from different materials. Talk about the types of materials used to build fences.

Apartments

Time

20–30 minutes

Materials

- Pictures of various kinds of apartment buildings
- *Harry's Home* by Catherine and Laurence Anholt

Objectives

Children will:

1. Explain that an apartment is a home within a building where many people also have homes.
2. Say whether or not they live in an apartment.

Preparation

Find magazine pictures of different kinds of apartment buildings.

Lesson

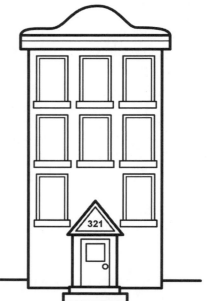

- Show the children several pictures of apartment buildings, including high rise, large complexes, and smaller units.
- Explain that many people live in an apartment building because it has homes for many families. If appropriate, ask the children what it is like to live in an apartment or if they know anyone who lives in an apartment. What do the apartments look like?
- Read the story *Harry's Home* by Catherine and Laurence Anholt or another book about people who live in apartments. Discuss the events of the story and the places in the story where the people live.

Accommodations/Modifications

Autism—During the assessment activity, point to specific items in the picture of the apartment. Ask the child to tell you about each item.

Speech or Language Impairments—During the assessment activity, talk about the specific features of apartments: many people live in them and you find them in the city; of houses: one family usually lives in a house and it has a front yard and a back yard; and of mobile homes: they have wheels and you can take your home with you when you move. Then ask which of these buildings houses the most people. Ask if she lives in an apartment.

Hearing Impairments—Seat the child across from you during the lesson so she can see your face.

Review

Tape bulletin board paper on the wall and draw several apartment buildings on the paper with a black marker to make a mural. Give the children colored markers and tempera paints to decorate the apartments. Talk about the apartments and who might live in each apartment in the buildings.

Assessment Strategy

Show pictures of homes, apartments, and mobile homes. Ask how the pictures are the same and how they are different. Have the child find the pictures of apartments. Ask the child to tell you all about apartments. If the child does not mention it, ask which building houses the most people. Ask the child if she lives in an apartment.

Visual Impairments—Help the child decorate the mural during the review activity, providing hand-over-hand assistance if needed. An alternative to this is to have the child tell you how to decorate the mural. Ask her what to draw in the picture of the apartments.

Cognitive and/or Developmental Delays—During the assessment activity, show the pictures one at a time. Talk about the specific features of apartments: many people live in them and you find them in the city; of houses: one family usually lives in a house and it has a front yard and a back yard; and of mobile homes: they have wheels and you can take your home with you when you move. After this, ask her which building houses the most people. Ask if she lives in an apartment.

Emotional Disturbance—Seat the child next to you. Affirm the child for participating and cooperating.

Other Health Impairments/Attention Deficit Hyperactivity Disorder—If the child becomes restless during the story, paraphrase the text to shorten the story.

Orthopedic Impairment—Help the child decorate the mural during the review activity, providing hand-over-hand assistance if needed.

Curriculum Connections

- **Blocks**—Provide building blocks and a model of an apartment building. See if the children can build an apartment building with the blocks.
- **Math**—On a poster board or a bulletin board, draw several apartment buildings with people's heads in each window. Encourage the children to count the number of apartments in each building and to count the number of people in each building. Which building has the most people? Which building has the most apartments?

Mobile Homes

Time
20–30 minutes

Materials
- Pictures of mobile homes

Objectives

Children will:
1. Describe a mobile home as a home on wheels.
2. Understand that a mobile home can be moved from place to place.

Preparation

Find pictures (from the Internet, magazines, and catalogs) of mobile homes.

Lesson

- Show the children pictures of different types of mobile homes. Explain that a mobile home is a home on wheels that can be moved from one place to another if the owner needs to move.
- Ask the children if anyone has ever moved to a new house. Ask if they had to find a new home or apartment. A mobile home can go with the owner when he or she moves.
- With the children, chant the following like "We're Going on a Bear Hunt." You say the sentence first and then the children repeat it. This chant describes the sequence of constructing and moving a mobile home.

Let's Build a Mobile Home by Sharon Lynch
Let's build a mobile home. Let's build a mobile home.
Okay. Okay. Let's go. Let's go.
Let's go to the factory. Let's go to the factory.
Let's build the floor. Let's build the floor.
Let's build the sides. Let's build the sides.
Let's build the roof. Let's build the roof.
Let's build the walls. Let's build the walls.
Let's put on the wheels. Let's put on the wheels.
Let's put it on the truck. Let's put it on the truck.
Let's go down the road. Let's go down the road.
Let's take it to our yard. Let's take it to our yard.
Now we have our home! Now we have our home!
Let's go inside! Let's go inside!

Review

Provide the children with markers, colored geometric shapes, glue sticks, and the pattern of a rectangular mobile home cut out from tag board. Invite them to decorate their mobile homes. After the child finishes decorating his mobile home, help him use brads to attach tag board wheels to its bottom.

Assessment Strategy

Show pictures of several types of homes, including houses, apartments, and mobile homes. Ask the child to find the mobile home and to tell you about it.

Accommodations/Modifications

Autism—During the assessment, point to specific features of the mobile home and ask the child to tell you about each feature.

Speech or Language Impairments—Provide starter phrases during the assessment activity so the child can tell about the mobile home. For example, "A mobile home can move because it has…" (point to wheels). "You can go inside the mobile home because it has a …" (point to the door).

Hearing Impairments—Make sure the child is seated across from you so he can see your face.

Visual Impairments—Describe the pictures of different types of homes during the assessment activity. Ask the child to identify the type of home you are talking about. After describing the mobile home, ask the child to tell you everything he knows about mobile homes.

Cognitive and/or Developmental Delays—Keep your language simple and your sentences short during the lesson and review. For the assessment activity, limit the choices to two or three pictures.

Emotional Disturbance—Seat the child next to you. Encourage participation and affirm the child for cooperating and participating.

Other Health Impairments/Attention Deficit Hyperactivity Disorder—Have the child hand out and collect materials.

Orthopedic Impairment—Help the child decorate his mobile home during the review activity.

Curriculum Connections

- **Math**—Point out different cities on a map. Select two cities, one where a family once lived in a mobile home and the other where the family subsequently moved their mobile home. Talk about how many miles the home was moved.

- **Science**—Show a picture of a mobile home in a wooded setting. Talk about the desire to live in the woods and the need for protection and shelter. Discuss the things that one might need to be protected from in the woods, such as snakes, animals, bugs, poison ivy, and so on.

- **Social Studies**—Provide pictures of different types of portable homes, including mobile homes, tepees, and tents. Talk about the need for shelter and protection as people travel and move.

INTRODUCTION TO

My Neighborhood

Time

20 minutes

Materials

Photos or pictures of various local neighborhoods showing homes in neighborhoods

Review

Show the children pictures of different neighborhoods. Talk about the fact that a neighborhood is a place where people live, play, shop, and eat. Provide the children with art materials and ask them to make a picture of their neighborhood. After each child has finished, ask her to tell you what she likes to do in her neighborhood. Write what she tells you on the back of her picture.

Objectives

Children will:

1.   Describe their neighborhood as where their home is located in their city or town.
2.   Select pictures that show neighborhoods.

Lesson

■   Show the children a picture of a neighborhood street and its homes and people. Engage the children in a discussion about their neighborhoods, the places in their city or town where they live.

■   Ask the children questions to help them identify their neighborhood:

   ■   Who lives in your neighborhood?
   ■   What do you do in your neighborhood?
   ■   What do you see when you go for a walk in your neighborhood?

■   Sing the following, to the tune of "Who's Afraid of the Big, Bad Wolf?"

Let's Go by Sharon Lynch
Let's go walking down the street, down the street, down the street. (walk in place)
Let's go walking down the street in our neighborhood.
Let's go see who we can meet, we can meet, we can meet. (hand shading eyes, looking)
Let's go see who we can meet in our neighborhood.

■   Ask a child to tell you who she might see on the street in her neighborhood. Continue this song with, "Let's go see what we can see, we can see, we can see. Let's go see what we can see in our neighborhood..." and then ask a child to tell you what she might see in her neighborhood.

■   If appropriate, continue with the following chant, which is similar to "Going on a Bear Hunt." You say the sentence first and have the children echo what you say.

Accommodations/Modifications

Autism—Keep sentences short and use pictures for reference during the discussion. For the assessment activity, model the task of sorting pictures of neighborhoods and pictures that are not of neighborhoods before asking the child to sort the pictures independently.

Speech or Language Impairments—Call on the child during discussions after other children have had an opportunity to model responses.

Hearing Impairments—Seat the child close to you, making sure she can see your face as you speak.

Visual Impairments—For the review activity, assist the child in making her picture. Describe your actions as you do this. For the assessment activity, ask the child to tell you about the neighborhood where she lives.

Cognitive and/or Developmental Delays—Keep sentences short and call on the child after others have modeled appropriate responses. Talk the child through the assessment activity, providing verbal cues.

Emotional Disturbance—Seat the child near the teacher and affirm the child for participating.

Other Health Impairments/Attention Deficit Hyperactivity Disorder—Make sure to keep each activity short and allow a break if the child is beginning to become restless.

Orthopedic Impairment—For the review activity, use hand-over-hand assistance if needed.

Curriculum Connections

- **Language and Literacy**—Read *A Clean House for Mole and Mouse* by Harriet Ziefert. Discuss where Mole and Mouse live and note that they live in different places.

- **Math**—Ask the children to tell you about their pets. Using stickers or drawings and a chart with each child's name, make a graph of the number of pets each child has at home. Compare the number of cats, dogs, and other pets.

- **Science**—Animals live in our neighborhoods, too. Provide miniature toy animals that live in neighborhoods: dogs, cats, fish, turtles, hamsters, birds, and so on. Provide other miniature toy animals that do not live in neighborhoods: dinosaur, lion, elephant, and so on. Have the children sort the animals into two sets: those that live in our neighborhoods and those that do not.

- **Social Studies**—Draw a large map of a neighborhood on butcher paper, or provide a classroom rug with a map of a neighborhood on it. Let the children push cars and trucks down the streets on the neighborhood map.

Neighbors

Time

15–20 minutes

Materials

- Butcher paper
- Markers, crayons

Objectives

Children will:

1. Describe neighbors as people who live or play close to them.
2. Note who are his neighbors are in the classroom.

Preparation

Draw houses on a large strip of butcher paper.

Lesson

- During Group or Circle Time, ask each child to shake hands with his neighbors, the people on either side of him. Explain that neighbors are people who play or live near them.
- Engage the children in a discussion about how one can be a good neighbor. Ask, "What are the things we can do to help our neighbors in our classroom?" Invite suggestions. Possibilities include sharing toys with our neighbors, inviting them to play, telling them when they are doing a good job, and helping them when they are having trouble.
- Talk about neighbors at home. Ask, "Who are your neighbors at home?" They are the people who live next door, across the street, or in your apartment complex.
- Ask, "How can you help your neighbors at home?" Tell the children that they can be friends with their neighbors, bring them food if they are sick, be kind to them, or welcome them when they move into the neighborhood.
- Place the strip of butcher paper with the houses drawn on it on the floor. Suggest that the children draw their neighbors on the butcher paper. Ask them to tell you about their neighbors and write what they tell you on the butcher paper. Invite the children to draw on the butcher paper other things that are in their neighborhood.
- When they are finished, mount the butcher paper on the wall.

Accommodations

Autism—Focus on the fact that the child has neighbors at school. When talking about neighbors at home, refer to the child's neighbors by name (ask the child's family for their names).

Speech or Language Impairments—Provide verbal choices for the child if he is not able to express himself or to answer questions.

Review

When lining up to go outside or to the lunch room, remind the children to be kind to their neighbors. Ask them to name their neighbors after they get in line. Remind them that neighbors are people who play or live near them. When they stand in line, their neighbors are the person in back of them and the person in front of them.

Assessment Strategy

Give the child a piece of paper which has a drawing of the outline of a house. Let him paint the house or decorate it with markers. Ask the child to tell you about his neighbors. Write what the child says on the back of the picture.

Hearing Impairments—Seat the child near you and refer to children or pictures using gestures as you speak.

Visual Impairments—Have the child tell you what to draw on the butcher paper as you assist him using hand-over-hand help.

Cognitive and/or Developmental Delays—Use short simple sentences in your explanations. Focus on the concept of neighbors at school.

Emotional Disturbance—Emphasize the positive as you talk about neighbors: how we can help our neighbors, how we welcome our neighbors. Focus on being a good neighbor at school. Use the term "good neighbor" throughout the day as the children interact with one another.

Other Health Impairments/Attention Deficit Hyperactivity Disorder—Keep discussions short during the lesson. Draw the child back to task if he is distracted during drawing activities. Affirm the child for participating and drawing.

Orthopedic Impairment—Provide a crayon holder for drawing or use hand-over-hand assistance.

Curriculum Connections

- **Language and Literacy**—Place books about neighbors in the Book Center, such as *Miss Penny and Mr. Grubbs* by Lisa Campbell Ernst, *You Can Do It, Sam* by Amy Hest, and *Me and Nana* by Leslie Kimmelman.
- **Math**—Ask the children questions, such as, "How many neighbors do you have? How many people live next door to you?" Count them. "How many people live across the street from you?" Count them.
- **Social Studies**—Show the children a picture of your city or state. Talk about the neighboring cities or states.

Friends

Time

15–20 minutes

Materials

- *My Friends* by Taro Gomi, in big book format, if possible
- Pictures of children playing

Objectives

Children will:

1. Describe a friend as someone that she knows and likes to spend time with.
2. Tell you the name of a friend.

Lesson

- Read *My Friends* by Taro Gomi to the children. Point out that the children in the story are good friends.
- Ask the children how they know that someone is their friend and how they can be a good friend to others.
- Guide the discussion to include the concept that a friend is someone you like to spend time with. Tell the children that everyone in the classroom is a friend to everyone else, playing and spending time together, although we each may have a very good friend or a best friend.
- Explain that it is important to be kind to our friends and that fighting makes friends sad. We are kind to the people in our class because they are our friends. We also have friends in our neighborhood.
- Sing the following song:
- Teach the children the following poem.

  We're Going Out to Play by Sharon Lynch
  We're going out to play.
  We'll take our friends today.
  We're going out to play.
  What will we do today?

- Show the children a group of pictures of children playing. Give each child a turn to tell what they like to do when they play with their friends. "Mason wants to play with the trucks with his friends" or "Shana wants to swing with her friends." Repeat the poem with the action at the end.

  We're going out to play.
  We'll take our friends today.
  We're going out to play.
  What will we do today?

- Go outside with the children. Say, "Let's go outside with our friends."

Review

Sit in a circle and play "Getting to Know You." The first child tells her name (for example, Madison.) The second child says, "Hi, my friend, (Madison). My name is (Caleb)." The third child says, "Hi, my friend (Madison). Hi, my friend (Caleb). My name is (Justin), " and so on around the circle.

Assessment Strategy

Friend or Stranger? Show the child a set of pictures: one set of pictures of their classmates and one set of pictures of children that the child has never met. Ask the child to find the picture of a friend in the class. Then have the child sort the pictures into piles of "friends" and "strangers."

Accommodations/Modifications

Autism—Use pictures from clip art or Picture Communication Symbols when referring to what we like to do with our friends during "We're Going Out to Play."

Speech or Language Impairments—Call on the child after other children have modeled responses during "We're Going Out to Play."

Hearing Impairments—Make sure the child can see the pictures in the book as well as your face as you read *My Friends* by Taro Gomi.

Visual Impairments—When asking the children to sort pictures of classroom friends and strangers during the assessment activity, name the child in a picture and ask the child with visual impairments if this is a friend in your class at school or a stranger.

Cognitive and/or Developmental Delays—Use simple, short sentences when talking about the concept of friends.

Emotional Disturbance—Seat the child near you during the group activities. Affirm the child for participating in activities. If the child has difficulty keeping her hands to herself, provide adequate seating space by placing mats to sit on.

Other Health Impairments/Attention Deficit Hyperactivity Disorder—If it becomes difficult for the child to sit and listen, paraphrase some of the sentences to shorten the story.

Orthopedic Impairment—Help the child sort the pictures of friends and strangers into piles during the assessment activity.

Curriculum Connections

- **Language and Literacy**—In the reading center, provide books about friends such as *Friends Forever: Four Favorite Stories* by Ken Geist (editor), *How to Be a Friend* by Laurie Krasny Brown and Marc Brown, *Do You Want to Be My Friend?* by Eric Carle, or *Little Bear's Friend* by Else Holmelund Minarik.

- **Math**—Using the set of pictures from "Friend or Stranger?" (in the Assessment Strategy at left) count the number of friends and strangers in each pile.

- **Social Studies**—Read books and stories about what friends in other countries and other cultures do together. Talk about the similarities and the differences. Read books such as *Owen & Mzee: The True Story of a Remarkable Friendship* by Deborah Stevenson, *My Friend Isabelle* by Eliza Woloson, *Squanto, Friend of the Pilgrims* by Clyde Robert Bulla, or *Tokyo Friends* by Betty Reynolds.

MY NEIGHBORHOOD

Streets

Time

15–20 minutes

Materials

- Small toy car
- Picture of a car going down a street (optional)
- Different types of small toy vehicles, such as a car, plane, train, boat, bicycle, tricycle, bus, truck, and motorcycle
- Large paper or cloth bag
- Paper
- Markers, crayons

Objectives

Children will:

1. Describe a street.
2. Describe the function of a street.

Preparation

Place the different vehicles inside a bag.

Lesson

- During Group or Circle Time, show the children a small toy car and ask them to guess the topic of the day. Offer clues until someone guesses that you are going to talk about streets.
- Show the children a picture of a car going down the street. Ask them what would happen if we did not have streets. Where would cars go? What other types of transportation do we have? What do boats use instead of streets? What do trains use instead of streets?
- Pull each vehicle out of the bag and ask the children if that vehicle travels on a street. Count the number of vehicles that use streets.

Accommodations/Modifications

Autism—Use short, simple sentences and refer to pictures as you present the lesson.

Speech or Language Impairments—Have the child fill in the answer in response to questions. For example, "Cars go on the _____" or "Boats go in the _____."

Review

Discuss the importance of streets. Ask the children which vehicles use streets. "What would happen if we did not have streets? How would we go from one place to another without streets? What types of things are carried by truck?" Talk about how streets are very important because they make it possible for trucks to bring food and clothes to stores.

Assessment Strategy

Provide paper, markers, and crayons and ask the children to draw a street. Ask them to draw different vehicles that use the street and to tell you about the street they drew.

Hearing Impairments—Make sure the child can see your face and is near you during the discussion parts of the lesson.

Visual Impairments—Help the child draw the street and vehicles during the assessment activity. Ask the child what he wants to draw next. Describe your actions as you are drawing.

Cognitive and/or Developmental Delays—Have the child repeat after you as you discuss the vehicles that use streets and those that do not. For example, "Trains go on tracks," and "Cars go on streets."

Emotional Disturbance—Seat the child near you and encourage the child to respond by directing questions to him when he is likely to be successful.

Other Health Impairments/Attention Deficit Hyperactivity Disorder—Keep the discussions short and animated to hold the child's attention. Allow the child to hold a small object in his lap if it helps him to stay seated.

Orthopedic Impairment—Assist the child in drawing streets and vehicles during the assessment strategy, if needed.

Curriculum Connections

- **Blocks**—Create a Transportation Center with a rug or piece of butcher paper with streets drawn on it. Let the children move toy cars and trucks along the streets.
- **Language and Literacy**—Provide books with stories and pictures of vehicles that use streets, such as cars, trucks, and buses. Possible titles include *Big Joe's Trailer Truck* by Joe Mathieu, *The ABC of Cars, Trucks, and Machines* by Adelaide Holl, *Cars and Trucks and Things That Go* by Richard Scarry, *The Magic School Bus at the Waterworks* and *The Magic School Bus on the Ocean Floor* by Joanna Cole and Bruce Degen, and *I Want to Be a Bus Driver* by Carla Greene.
- **Science**—Talk about how streets are made, usually of cement, tar, and steel rods. What would happen if streets were made of wood? What would happen if streets were made of mud? What would happen if streets were made of grass?
- **Social Studies**—Show the children a road map of your town or city and find the streets where the children live.

Street Signs

Time

20–30 minutes

Materials

- *I Read Signs* by Tana Hoban
- Pictures of street signs, such as Stop signs, Walk/Don't Walk signs, handicapped parking, school crossing, and bike route signs
- Chart paper and marker
- White paper
- Crayons, markers
- Stapler

Objectives

Children will:

1. Identify different street signs.
2. Describe what street signs tell us to do.

Lesson

- Read *I Read Signs* by Tana Hoban.
- Show the children pictures of different street signs and discuss the meaning of each sign.
- Discuss the value of signs—they give us important information to keep us safe on the street.
- Ask the children what street signs they saw on their way to school. Write the street names on a chart tablet and add a small drawing of each.
- Talk about why it is important that we have street signs. Help each child make a street sign book.
- Ask each child to draw a picture or pictures of a street sign and to tell you what each one means. Have them leave a couple of pages blank. Staple the pages together. They can take their books home and add the street signs they see while taking a walk in their neighborhoods.
- Ask them to bring the book back the next day to share with the class. Take a walk around the school to look at signs.

Accommodations/Modifications

Autism—Read each sign aloud and say what it means. For example: "This sign says stop. A car must stop at the stop sign."

Speech or Language Impairments—Have the child finish sentences to describe and name signs. For example: "This sign says _____. The car must stop at the _____."

Hearing Impairments—Seat the child where she can see your face and close enough to hear you as you speak during the discussion activities.

Visual Impairments—For the assessment activity, offer the child clues so she can guess what street sign you are talking about.

Cognitive and/or Developmental Delays—For the assessment activity, tell the child the meaning of the sign and have her select the correct sign from a group of two.

Emotional Disturbance—Seat the child near you during discussions and affirm the child for sitting and participating.

Review

Provide drawings of street signs along with a classroom rug with streets on it in the classroom. Using small cars, show the children how to stop at the stop sign, how to slow down where the sign says *slow,* and to top and look around when the sign says *caution.* Ask a few of the children to show what cars need to do when a sign says, *stop, slow,* or *caution.*

Assessment Strategy

Show the children pictures of street signs. Have them tell you what one of them means.

Other Health Impairments/Attention Deficit Hyperactivity Disorder—During the story, shorten pages by paraphrasing if the story becomes too lengthy for the child.

Orthopedic Impairment—Help the child draw street signs using hand-over-hand assistance.

Curriculum Connections

- **Art**—Cut out different shapes and place them in the Art Center. The children can use crayons, markers or paint to make their own street signs.
- **Language and Literacy**—Write a story about your trip to school, and make sure to include the street signs you saw on the way.
- **Math**—Place construction paper street signs around the room. You can have more than one of each sign; for example: three stop signs, one bike route sign, and five handicapped parking signs. Have the children count the signs and then make a picture graph of the signs in the room.
- **Social Studies**—Create a street map of the school's neighborhood, including the school and the street signs. Encourage the children to make maps of their neighborhoods.

Traffic Signals

Time

20 minutes

Materials

- Green, yellow, and orange circles to represent traffic signals
- Red, green, yellow, black, and orange paper
- Markers
- Crayons
- Scissors
- Glue
- Red, yellow, and green circles

Objectives

Children will:

1. Describe traffic signals look like.
2. Learn the meaning of traffic light colors.

Lesson

- Talk with the children about traffic signals. Do they know what it means when they see a *green* light, a *red* light, or a *yellow* light?
- Play the game of Red Light–Green Light using the colored circles. Show the children how to stop, wait, and go when they see each color. Emphasize that the yellow light means *wait*, and that you will have to stop very soon. The children walk when you show the green circle, wait and prepare to stop when you show the yellow circle, and stop when you show the red circle.
- Recite the following poem and invite the children to say it with you as you repeat it.

  Red, Yellow, Green by Sharon Lynch
  Red, yellow, green,
  Stop, wait, go.
  Red means stop.
  Yellow means wait.
  Green means go.
  Red, yellow, green,
  Stop, wait, go.

- Use small cars to play Red Light–Green Light. Let the children take turns being the leader whose job it is to show the colored circle for *stop, wait,* and *go.*

Accommodations/Modifications

Autism—With the traffic signals, act out the correct action so the child comprehends its meaning.

Speech or Language Impairments—Allow other children to answer questions verbally first, and then call on this child later to review information. Allow the child to show you what the colors mean during the assessment activity.

Hearing Impairments—Seat the child where he can see your face during the lesson activity.

Visual Impairments—Talk about the meaning of the different colors (red, yellow, green) as you present the lesson.

Review

Hold up different colored circles at random times throughout the day to review and practice the meanings of each sign.

Assessment Strategy

Ask the children to tell you the meaning of the different colors of traffic signals.

Cognitive and/or Developmental Delays—Model verbal responses and have the child repeat critical information to you. During the assessment activity, tell the child to show you the color that means stop, wait, or go.

Emotional Disturbance—Emphasize the importance of obeying traffic signs and signals and their purposes, such as, to keep us from being hurt, to keep people safe, and to prevent accidents.

Other Health Impairments/Attention Deficit Hyperactivity Disorder—Seat the child near you during discussions.

Orthopedic Impairment—Help the child construct the traffic signal using hand-over-hand assistance if needed. Provide a crayon holder if the child is able to use one.

Curriculum Connections

- **Art**—Draw and color the signals and tell what each one means. Write down the children's responses.
- **Language and Literacy**—Use chart paper to write a story with the children on different colors of traffic signals. Ask them to tell you about the different signals and what they mean.
- **Math**—In the Math Center, place red, yellow, and green circles. Have the children sort them and count each color or line them up to make a color graph.
- **Social Studies**—Go on a walk around the school community to look at the different signs and signals. Discuss each sign or signal as you walk.

In the Park

Time

20–30 minutes

Materials

- *It's a Go-To-The-Park Day* by Vivian French
- Pictures of different types of parks (optional)
- Pictures of activities and equipment found at each park
- Chart tablet and marker

Objectives

Children will:

1. Describe different activities they can do at the park.
2. Tell you their favorite activity at the park.

Lesson

- Read *It's a Go-To-The-Park Day* by Vivian French to the children and discuss the book with them. Ask them questions about the pictures they saw in the book and what they learned.
- Ask them what they might see at a park or how they might spend the day at a park.
- Show the children pictures of different parks such as local state parks, community parks, and national parks. Explain and show pictures of the different types of equipment that can be found at each of these parks.
- Talk about the different things that people do at a park: play, swing, swim, hike, camp, fish.
- Teach children this song:

   Let's Go to the Park Today by Sharon Lynch
   (Tune: "Who's Afraid of the Big, Bad Wolf?")
   Let's go to the park today, park today, park today.
   Let's go to the park today, park today, park today.
   Let's go have some fun.

   Additional verses:
   Let's go swinging at the park today…
   Let's go swimming at the park today…
   Let's go fishing at the park today…
   Let's go hiking at the park today…

- Make up additional verses with the children.

Accommodations/Modifications

Autism—When discussing the book, keep your language simple. Ask questions the child can answer by pointing to a picture in the book.

Speech or Language Impairments—Call on the child to answer questions about the story after other children have had the opportunity to model responses.

Review

Using a chart tablet, write a group story about visiting a park. Let the children read the story along with you.

Assessment Strategy

Show the pictures of the different parks and have the child tell you about each park. With children who are very young or who have language disabilities, have the child find the picture of a park that you describe. Ask the child what she might like to do at each of the parks.

Hearing Impairments—Make sure the child can see your face and the pictures in the story as you read the book.

Visual Impairments—Describe the pictures as you present each one. Provide artifacts from parks for the child to hold and to feel.

Cognitive and/or Developmental Delays—During the assessment activity, have the child find the picture of the park you are describing.

Emotional Disturbance—Seat the child close to you during the story and discussion.

Other Health Impairments/Attention Deficit Hyperactivity Disorder—If the child becomes restless during the story, paraphrase the text to shorten the story.

Orthopedic Impairment—No accommodations are needed for this lesson.

Curriculum Connections

- **Art**—Encourage the children to use paint or markers to make a picture of a park they would like to visit.
- **Listening Center**—Make a recording of park sounds (for example: birds, children playing and laughing, and so on) and encourage the children to listen to the tape. Provide cards with pictures of each item that makes a sound on the tape and suggest that the children match the sound they hear with the picture of the object that makes that sound.
- **Science**—Take a trip to a park and allow the children to enjoy being outdoors.
- **More Science**—Place objects from a park, such as leaves or pinecones in the Science Center. Provide magnifying glasses so the children can inspect the objects closely.

The Playground

Time

15–20 minutes

Materials

- Pictures of playground items
- Chart tablet and markers
- Butcher paper and markers for mural

Objectives

Children will:

1. Describe a playground.
2. Describe items found on a playground.

Lesson

- Show the children a picture of a swing set and ask them to guess what you are going to talk about today.
- As children guess, introduce additional pictures as clues. Clues might include pictures of a sandbox, a merry-go-round, a seesaw, and a slide. Continue to provide clues until someone guesses that you are going to talk about playgrounds.
- Ask the children to tell you their favorite things to do on a playground.
- Using a chart tablet, write a group story about the playground. Ask each child to tell you one thing to write about the playground.
- Read the story back to the children. With older children, invite them to read it as well.

Accommodations/Modifications

Autism—Use clip art pictures or Picture Communication Symbols for the child to refer to during group discussion.

Speech or Language Impairments—During the discussion of what the children like to do on the playground, provide gesture cues for the child to respond to. Provide verbal choices for the child to select , as well. During the assessment activity, use pictures to help scaffold language.

Hearing Impairments—Seat the child across from you so he can see your face during instruction.

Visual Impairments—Describe the pictures as you present them. For the assessment activity, ask the child to tell you about his favorite things on the playground.

Cognitive and/or Developmental Delays—For the assessment activity, show the child equipment found on the playground. Ask the child to show you which he likes best, and what he likes to do with the equipment.

Emotional Disturbance—Seat the child near you during the discussion activity. Talk about the importance of taking turns, and remind the children about turn-taking before the class goes out on the playground.

Other Health Impairments/Attention Deficit Hyperactivity Disorder—When the child becomes restless during the reading of the group story, let him get a drink of water and then return to the group.

Orthopedic Impairment—When making the group mural, provide a crayon holder or hand-over-hand guidance.

Hold picture cards of the play equipment found on the playground at your school or center. Ask the children to tell you their favorite piece of equipment. Attach the pictures to the wall. Have each child go to his favorite piece of equipment. Count the number of children who choose each piece of playground equipment to determine which is the class favorite. Talk about taking turns and sharing the equipment. End the activity by going out to the playground.

Assessment Strategy

Show the child a picture of the playground and ask him to tell you everything he can about it.

Curriculum Connections

- **Art**—Construct a classroom wall mural of the playground. If necessary, draw the swings, merry-go-round, seesaws, and other pieces of equipment. The children can draw themselves, the grass, flowers, trees, and whatever else they wish. If appropriate, write their descriptions of their artwork on the class mural.
- **Language and Literacy**—Encourage the children to read along with you as you read their group story on subsequent days.
- **Math**—Graph the number of children who choose each piece of equipment on a poster board.
- **Science**—On the seesaw, see what happens when you sit on one side of the seesaw. Talk about the fact that the heaviest person goes down and the lightest person goes up. The heavier person must push up really hard to send the lighter person down.
- **Social Studies**—Make a map of your school with the school playground, classroom, and lunchroom clearly identified.

Where I Live

Time

30–45 minutes

Materials

- *A House Is a House for Me* by Mary Ann Hoberman
- Manila paper
- Crayons

Review

Place copies of the book in the Book Center. Post children's drawings of their home in the classroom.

Assessment Strategy

Discuss the drawings with each child as they are creating them.

Objectives

Children will:

1. Draw a picture of their home.
2. Discuss similarities and differences in their homes

Lesson

- Read *A House Is a House for Me* to the children.
- Have them discuss the different homes where Morty lived.
- Have them describe their own home.
- Ask the children to draw a picture of their home to be displayed on a classroom bulletin board.
- Under each child's home write "This is a house for (child's name)."

Accommodations/Modifications

Autism—Pose forced-choice questions to the child so she can participate in the discussion.

Speech or Language Impairments—Encourage complete sentences in the discussion.

Hearing Impairments—Have the child sit near the story reader.

Visual Impairments—Provide time before you read for the child to see the pictures in the story.

Cognitive and/or Developmental Delays—Pose forced-choice questions to the child so she can participate in the discussion.

Emotional Disturbance—Use eye contact and reinforcement to assist the child in participating in the discussion.

Other Health Impairments/Attention Deficit Hyperactive Disorder—Designate a specific space where the child can sit when listening to the story. Allow the child opportunities to participate in the discussion. Reinforce the child's behavior as she waits for her turn in the discussion.

Orthopedic Impairments—Have the child participate in all activities. Use a Velcro strip or special grips to help the child draw and color.

Curriculum Connections

- **Art**—Provide shoeboxes in the Art Center for children to use to can construct miniature homes.
- **Language and Literacy**—Prepare an album of photos and pictures of various types of homes—such as single-family homes, duplexes, mobile homes, apartment complexes, and so on—and place it in the Book Center for children to "read."
- **Science**—Provide opportunities for children to observe and chart features in their homes.

On a Ride

Time
- 20 minutes (bus ride time)
- 15–20 minutes classroom time

Materials
- Notebook and pen
- Community map (usually available from the local Chamber of Commerce)
- Small sticky labels

Preparation
Prior to this lesson, send permission slips for the field trip to each family. Complete any additional paperwork required by your center.

Review
Place the map in the classroom for individual exploration.

Assessment Strategy
Observe as each child locates places on the community map.

Objectives
Children will:
1. Observe and talk about their community during a bus ride.
2. Find their home on the classroom map.

Lesson
- Gather the children for a bus ride. It can be a regular bus or a bus used for field trips.
- As they board the bus, tell them that during their bus ride they should point out familiar places.
- While you are riding on the bus, ask the children to point out places that are familiar to them. Each time a child mentions a specific place, write down the child's name and the location.
- Upon returning to the classroom, talk with the children about the locations they identified. Ask the children to describe each location.
- Help the class locate the places on a community map. As each child identifies a location, place a small sticky label with that child's initials on that location on the map.

Accommodations/Modifications

Autism—Assign a peer or teaching assistant to point out places on the bus ride to the child.

Speech or Language Impairments—Define new vocabulary while on the bus ride.

Hearing Impairments—Have the child use pictures to represent the places she sees while on the bus ride. During the discussion, let the child sit near the person who is talking.

Visual Impairments—Have the child sit near a window on the bus ride. Describe what you see while on the bus, just as a tour bus driver would do.

Cognitive and/or Developmental Delays— Describe what you see while on the bus, just as a tour bus driver would do. Provide opportunities for the child to see pictures and photographs of the locations along the bus route.

Emotional Disturbance—Assign a peer to discuss the places the children see on the bus ride. Provide opportunities for the child to see photographs of the locations along the route.

Other Health Impairments/Attention Deficit Hyperactive Disorder—Remind the child about safe bus procedures.

Orthopedic Impairments—Seat the child near a window.

Curriculum Connections
- **Language and Literacy**—Provide opportunities for talking about the various locations on the classroom map.
- **Social Studies**—Provide plastic toys of different modes of transportation for children to use to show how people move around a community.

My Address

Time

- 20 minutes for small group time
- 5 minutes for individual practice time, repeated throughout the week

Materials

- Index cards
- Markers
- 5 letter-size envelopes
- Paper or cloth bag
- Sentence strips

Objectives

Children will:

1. Learn what an address is.
2. State their addresses.

Preparation

Draw a house on each of five large index cards. Mark each of the five houses with one numeral from 1–5. Mark each of five letter-size envelopes with one numeral from 1–5. Put the envelopes in a paper or cloth bag. Print each child's name and address on sentence strips.

Mike Smith
123 Elm Street
Anytown, USA 12345

Lesson

- Show the children pictures of five houses numbered 1–5 along with the bag of envelopes.
- Ask the children how to get the letters to the correct house.
- Distribute the envelopes to the children and have them deliver each letter to the correct house.
- Discuss with the children where address numbers displayed on their homes or in their yards.
- Tell the children that the postal worker is able to deliver the mail to the correct house by looking at the address on the envelope and matching it with the address on the house.
- Show the children a piece of mail that you received. Point out your name and address on the envelope. Show the children that the address has both a number and a street name.
- Encourage the children to talk about their addresses.
- Present sentence strips preprinted with each child's address on them.
- Have the child point to their address on their sentence strip and then to say their address.
- If appropriate, help the children write their names on the back of their address strips so they can identify them during independent work time.

Review

Place the address strips in the Literacy Center for children to explore.

Accommodations/Modifications

Autism—Attach picture cues of the child and the child's home to the child's address slip.

Speech or Language Impairments—Encourage the child to speak in complete sentences during the discussions.

Hearing Impairments—Let the child watch the children who are talking. Repeat needed information from the discussions.

Visual Impairments—Write the addresses on sentence strips in large block letters with a dark-colored marker.

Cognitive and/or Developmental Delays—Provide rehearsal time prior to the lesson. Picture clues will assist the child in identifying his address.

Emotional Disturbance—Provide time for the child to share his address. Have the child write his name on the address card.

Other Health Impairments/Attention Deficit Hyperactive Disorder—Designate a carpet square or a specific spot where the child can sit during discussion times. Limit the number of addresses he must sort through to find his own address.

Orthopedic Impairments—Provide materials at the child's level.

Curriculum Connections

- **Art**—Provide opportunities for children to map locations of addresses.
- **Language and Literacy**—Provide opportunities for discussions of addresses.
- **Science**—Provide opportunities for children to observe and chart the addresses of their classmates.
- **Social Studies**—Invite the children to bring photographs of their homes to put on a class bulletin board titled "Our Homes."

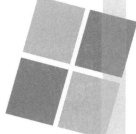

My School Community

Time
30–45 minutes

Materials
- School cutouts
- Tape

Objectives

Children will:
1. Locate specific places in their school.
2. Discuss the roles and responsibilities of people in their school.

Preparation

Before the children arrive, attach school-shaped cutouts to different areas of the building that you will visit with them.

Lesson

- Introduce and recite the rhyme "Going on a School Walk" to the children.

  Going on a School Walk by Sharon Lynch
  We are going on a school walk. (repeat)
  What will we see? (repeat)
  We will find our school helpers. (repeat)
  Let's walk and see. (repeat)

  We will walk to the right.
  We will walk to the left.
  We will walk quietly down the hall
  Looking for school helpers.
  Who will they be?
  Who will they be?
  Let's walk and see.
  Let's walk and see.

- Have the children follow your lead as you recite the rhyme.
- Engage the children in a discussion about the places that they may see on a walk around the school.
- Walk around the school with small groups of children led by you or a parent volunteer. Tell the children to look for school cutouts designating a destination spot (see Preparation).

Review

Talk with the children about the locations in the school that they visited. Have the children select the places they look forward to visiting another time.

Assessment Strategy

Discuss the reasons that each child might visit the various locations.

Suggested locations to visit:

Restroom nearest to classroom	Nurse's office
Attendance office	Cafeteria
Library	Director's (or Principal's) office
Physical Education room	Music room

Accommodations/Modifications

Autism—Talk with the child about the school walk. If possible, walk the route prior to the lesson with the child. Discuss the school helpers you will meet. Use picture cues to assist the child's understanding.

Speech or Language Impairments—Define and name each of the school helpers and what they do to help children, parents, and teachers. Encourage discussion.

Hearing Impairments—Provide picture cues to help the child comprehend the lesson.

Visual Impairments—Pair the child with another child to assist in moving around the school.

Cognitive and/or Developmental Delays—Talk with the child about the school walk. If possible, walk the route prior to the lesson with the child. Discuss the school helpers you will meet. Use picture cues to help her understand the lesson.

Emotional Disturbance—Talk with the child about the school walk. If possible, walk the route prior to the lesson with the child. Discuss the school helpers you will find. Use picture cues to help her understand the lesson.

Other Health Impairments/Attention Deficit Hyperactive Disorder—Discuss the school walk and remind the child about appropriate hallway behavior.

Orthopedic Impairments—Provide a teaching assistant to help the child move around the school as needed.

Curriculum Connections

- **Art**—Provide opportunities for children to draw pictures of one of the locations they visited.
- **Language and Literacy**—Provide opportunities for talking about the locations and the people the children met on their walk.

My Flag—Symbols

Time

30–45 minutes

Materials

- United States flag
- State flag
- Construction paper
- Glue
- Scissors
- Rulers or dowel rods
- Gummed stars or mini pre-cut stars (50 for each child)

Objectives

Children will:

1. Identify symbols of the United States.
2. Create symbols of the United States.

Lesson

- Show the children the flag of the United States and their state flag. Encourage the children to describe the similarities and differences between each flag.
- Ask the children to focus on the United States flag. Discuss the colors, stars, and stripes.
- If appropriate for the children in your class, tell them the order in which their state became part of the United States. Then count with them from left to right and top to bottom to locate their state star on the flag. (See page 337 for a list of the order in which each state entered the United States.)
- Have the children sing "I Love My Flag."

I Love My Flag by Diana Nabors
(Tune: "Three Blind Mice")
I love my flag, my country's flag,
The red, white and blue.
It waves for me and you,
There are 13 stripes of red and white.
It has 50 stars on a field of blue.
The US flag is quite a sight,
It stands for freedom, too.

Accommodations/Modifications

Autism—Encourage the child to participate in the discussion using gestures and close proximity.

Speech or Language Impairments—Encourage the child to participate in the discussion and to use complete sentences. Define any needed vocabulary. Modeling is effective when discussing the stars and the states.

Hearing Impairments—Use gestures when discussing the features of the flag.

Visual Impairments—Give the child ample time to investigate the flag at his eye level.

Engage the
children in a
discussion about
the flag of the
United States, the
flag of their state,
and other symbols,
such as stars,
stripes, and the
eagle, and how
each represents
their state and
their country.

**Assessment
Strategy**

Question each
child about the
flags in the
classroom.

Cognitive and/or Developmental Delays—Encourage the child to use complete
sentences. Define any needed vocabulary. Modeling is effective in discussing the stars
and the states.

Emotional Disturbance—Provide time for the child to observe the classroom flag.
Provide just a few materials at a time so as not to overwhelm the child.

Other Health Impairments/Attention Deficit Hyperactive Disorder—Provide individual
time to handle and observe the flag. Provide a tray for materials to assist in
organizational skills.

Orthopedic Impairments—Provide materials at the child's level.

Curriculum Connections

- **Art**—Provide opportunities for children to create flags.
- **Math**—With individual children, practice counting the stripes and stars of the US
  flag. (How many white stripes? How many red stripes? How many stars?)
- **Social Studies**—Provide other state and country flags and symbols for the children to
  observe and compare.
- **More Social Studies**—With small groups of children, provide opportunities for
  discussing what they like about living in the United States.

Shower Curtain Map

Time
20–30 minutes

Materials
- Large shower curtain liner
- Permanent marker
- Multicolored squares of construction paper
- Double-stick tape
- Wide clear packing tape
- Small toy cars and buses

Review
Provide opportunities for the children to review and use the shower curtain map in the Block Center.

Assessment Strategy
Question each child individually about the locations on the map.

Objectives
Children will:
1. Learn what maps do.
2. Identify various places within their community on a map.

Lesson
- At Group or Circle Time, ask the children questions about their community, such as: "Where do you live?" "Where do you go after school?" "What do you see on your way to school?" and "Where do you and your family shop?"
- As children watch, draw the major streets in the community on the shower liner.
- As the children name different locations in the community, help them place a colored square in the correct location on the shower liner map, using double-stick tape.
- Help the children place their homes on the community map.
- At the end of the lesson, cover all the locations with clear packing tape to fix them securely to the map.
- Place this community map in the Block Center to be used with cars and trucks in the children's imaginative play.

Accommodations/Modifications
Autism—Ask the child to bring in photographs of his home and community.

Speech or Language Impairments—Help the child use correct sentence structure in discussions. Have his draw pictures of places as needed.

Hearing Impairments—Seat the child near the person who is talking.

Visual Impairments—Provide an individual opportunity for the child to be near the map to find specific locations.

Cognitive and/or Developmental Delays—Provide multiple opportunities for the child to observe the map. Have photographs depicting specific locations on the map.

Emotional Disturbance—Provide multiple opportunities for the child to observe the map. Place photographs depicting certain locations on the map.

Other Health Impairments/Attention Deficit Hyperactive Disorder—Provide a time for the child to observe the map and add his home as well as other locations.

Orthopedic Impairments—Provide time for the child to work individually on the map.

Curriculum Connections
- **Art**—Provide opportunities for children to copy or draw their own map using the shower curtain map as a model.
- **Science**—Provide opportunities for children to observe and chart addresses of their classmates on the map.

MY COMMUNITY
Symbols

Materials

- Shower curtain map (see instructions in Shower Curtain Map lesson)
- Construction paper
- Crayons, markers

Review

Discuss the many flags and symbols created by the children and how well each represents the community.

Assessment Strategy

Discuss the reasons why each child created a certain flag or symbol.

Objectives

Children will:

1. Identify community symbols.
2. Create community symbols.

Lesson

- Discuss with the children various locations on their community map, which was made in the previous lesson. Talk about what makes their map unique and different from other maps and communities.
- Invite the children to choose symbols to show everyone that this is their map of their community. Use community flags, school colors and mascots, city or town seals, and street signs to assist in the discussion.
- Brainstorm on ideas for a flag or symbol for your community. If the children need suggestions to get started tell them that an area called Fox Run could have a lag with a fox on it, or a town called Oak Ridge could have a flag with an oak tree or an acorn on it.
- Have each child design a flag or a town symbol. Display them in the classroom.

Accommodations/Modifications

Autism—Provide samples of flags and symbols that may be used.

Speech or Language Impairments—Encourage the child to use correct sentence structure.

Hearing Impairments—Face the child when speaking. Repeat directions as needed.

Visual Impairments—Provide a time for the child to examine the shower curtain map prior to the lesson.

Cognitive and/or Developmental Delays—Provide the child with samples of flags and symbols that may be used. Allow her to work in a small group.

Emotional Disturbance—Provide samples of flags and symbols that may be used. Allow her to work in a small group.

Other Health Impairments/Attention Deficit Hyperactive Disorder—Provide samples of flags and symbols that may be used. Allow her to work in a small group.

Orthopedic Impairment—Provide materials at a level the child can access easily.

Curriculum Connections

- **Art**—Provide opportunities for children to create additional flags and symbols representative of their community.
- **Language and Literacy**—Help the children develop a class chart showing well-known symbols, such as stop signs and other traffic signs, exit signs, sports insignias, commercial logos, and so on.
- **Social Studies**—Provide other community flags and symbols for the children to examine.

INTRODUCTION TO

People at Work

Time

15–20 minutes

Materials

Pictures or
photographs of
various
community
workers, such as
grocer, firefighter,
bus driver, teacher,
nurse, and so on

Review

Ask the children to
name one job their
parent does.

**Assessment
Strategy**

Ask each child to
look at pictures or
photographs of
people in various
careers and to
identify the jobs
they do.

Objectives

Children will:

1. Describe what types of jobs their parents have.
2. Use dramatic play to demonstrate what people do at work.

Lesson

- Ask the children if they know what their parents do when they go to work every day. As they respond, show them a corresponding picture or photograph.
- Tell the children they are going to learn about people at work. Talk with them about the people they see in their communities while they are shopping with their parents or traveling around town.
- Point out the centers, equipment, and toys in the classroom that relate to what people do at work, such as a Grocery Store Center, fire trucks, dress-up clothing for such occupations as nurses or doctors, and so on.
- Discuss with the children the specific workers they will learn about over the next few days, such as a grocer, a bus driver, a firefighter, and others.

Accommodations/Modifications

Autism—Provide assistance and verbal cues as needed.

Speech or Language Impairments—Encourage the child to identify the jobs depicted in available pictures.

Hearing Impairments—Face the child when giving him directions.

Visual Impairments—Provide large pictures and help the child locate the needed pictures when identifying careers.

Cognitive and/or Developmental Delays—Ask the child the name the career he is attempting to identify, then assist in finding the appropriate picture or photograph.

Emotional Disturbance—Support the child while he attends to the task of finding an appropriate picture or photograph during the lesson.

Other Health Impairments/Attention Deficit Hyperactive Disorder—Continually reinforce the child's attention to the task.

Orthopedic Impairments—Provide individual attention to assist the child in describing the career and finding the corresponding picture he needs.

Curriculum Connections

- **Art**—Provide opportunities for children to draw pictures of community helpers that they know.
- **Language and Literacy**—Have the children draw pictures and dictate what they know about their parents and their careers.

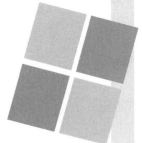

Grocer

Time

20–30 minutes

Materials

- Paper grocery bag
- Non-perishable groceries

Preparation

Fill a paper grocery bag with non-perishable items from a grocery store.

Review

Place the grocery items in centers for individual exploration and dramatic play.

Assessment Strategy

Observe how each child describes the job of a grocer.

Objectives

Children will:

1. Identify things that the grocer does in his or her job.
2. Identify items that are purchased in the grocery store

Lesson

- At Group or Circle Time, show the children a paper grocery bag filled with groceries.
- Take out one item at a time and ask the children to identify each item.
- Discuss the person who helps them and their parents at the grocery store.
- Ask the children to name items they like their parents to purchase at the grocery store.
- Teach children "The Grocer" chant.

The Grocer by Diana Nabors
From him we buy the things that we eat.
Our cereal, bread, vegetables, and meat,
He helps us in any way that he can.
Our grocer is a helpful man.

Accommodations/Modifications

Autism—Provide assistance and verbal cues as needed.

Speech or Language Impairments—Encourage the child to name the items she is placing on the shelf.

Hearing Impairments—Face the child when giving directions.

Visual Impairments—Provide large pictures. Help the child locate the pictures she needs.

Cognitive and/or Developmental Delays—Ask the child what she would like to place on the shelf and assist her in finding the item in the store circular or magazine.

Emotional Disturbance—Provide varied foods and items to stock on the shelves.

Other Health Impairments/Attention Deficit Hyperactive Disorder—Continually reinforce the child's attention to the task.

Orthopedic Impairments—Provide precut items to glue on the store shelf.

Curriculum Connections

- **Art**—Provide cutout pictures of food from grocery store fliers. Suggest that the children create a collage of all the things they like in the grocery store.
- **Language and Literacy**—Display a printed copy of "The Grocer" chant in the classroom. Encourage the children to "read" the chant.

Bus Driver

Time
20–30 minutes

Materials
- *School Bus* by Donald Crews
- Bus driver (invited guest, if possible)
- Manila paper
- Crayons
- List of children's bus numbers

Review
Provide time for each child to discuss their drawing if they wish.

Assessment Strategy
Observe each child participating in the discussion and dramatization of bus safety measures.

Objectives
Children will:
1. Identify things that the school bus driver does in his or her job.
2. Discuss places they see on their bus ride to school.

Lesson
- At Group or Circle Time, read *School Bus* by Donald Crews to the children.
- Engage the children in a discussion about their trips on a school bus and what the bus driver does to keep them safe.
- Ask the bus driver to speak to the children about the rules on the bus and to answer any questions the children have about their bus trip to and from school. If no bus driver is available, you can talk with the children and answer their questions.
- Ask each child to draw a picture of a school bus and to draw himself in one of the bus windows and the driver at the wheel.

Accommodations/Modifications
Autism—Prepare the child for the guest speaker.

Speech or Language Impairments—Encourage the child to ask questions that start with *who, what, when, where,* or *why.*

Hearing Impairments—Have the child sit near the speaker, keeping in mind that the distance from the speaker increases listening difficulty.

Visual Impairments—Have the child sit near the speaker.

Cognitive and/or Developmental Delays—Preteach vocabulary related to driving a bus and riding in a bus.

Emotional Disturbance—Prepare the child for a guest speaker and proper listening behavior.

Other Health Impairments/Attention Deficit Hyperactive Disorder—Prepare the child for the guest speaker and proper listening behavior.

Orthopedic Impairments—Provide a place where the child can be seated with the other children during the guest speaker's presentation.

Curriculum Connections
- **Art**—Provide opportunities for the children to create a school bus using shoeboxes, or work with the children to create a school bus using a large appliance container.
- **Math**—Prepare cards showing different bus styles, such as a school van, a school bus, a city bus, and so on. Suggest that the children arrange the cards in the order of the smallest to the largest vehicle.

PEOPLE AT WORK

Careers A-Z

Materials
- *Community Helpers from A to Z* by Bobbie Kalman
- Chart paper and marker or chalk board and chalk
- Paper
- Crayons, markers, pencils

Review
Provide time for each child to discuss her community helper.

Assessment Strategy
Observe each child as she participates in the discussion.

Objectives
Children will:
1. Identify careers that help the community.
2. Describe the service that each community helper performs.
3. Identify the each community helper uses.

Lesson
- At Group or Circle Time, read *Community Helpers from A to Z* by Bobbie Kalman to the children. Talk about the different community helpers in the book.
- List the community helpers on the chalkboard or on chart paper.
- Ask a small group of three or four children to select one of the listed community helpers and to work together to draw a picture of the helper in their work environment. Or, ask each child to draw her own picture.
- Ask the groups of children or individual children to brainstorm ways that the selected community helper helps in the community.
- Ask each group or an individual child to present their community helper to the rest of the children.

Accommodations/Modifications
Autism—Allow the child to work in a pair rather than a group of four.
Speech or Language Impairments—Encourage the child to verbalize her additions to the drawing.
Hearing Impairments—Provide a space where the child can see the book and the reader.
Visual Impairments—Have the child sit near the book and allow close inspection during drawing time.
Cognitive and/or Developmental Delays—Help the child work with others in the group.
Emotional Disturbance—Select the group that best suits the child.
Other Health Impairments/Attention Deficit Hyperactive Disorder—Provide a carpet square or specified place on the floor where the child can sit during the story reading.
Orthopedic Impairments—Have the child use forms or modified art materials in drawing.

Curriculum Connections
- **Art**—Invite the children to make individual or group poster collages depicting careers they find in magazines. Encourage them to cut out or tear the pictures to glue on the posters.
- **Language and Literacy**—With small groups of children, discuss jobs their families do.
- **Social Studies**—Photograph community figures doing their jobs. Post the photographs on a classroom bulletin board.

Firefighter

Time
20–30 minutes

Materials
- Felt in orange and red
- Scissors
- Pictures of firefighters
- Blanket

Objectives

Children will:
1. Identify things that the firefighter does in his or her job.
2. Identify ways to stay safe from fires.

Preparation

Before the children arrive, cut the orange and red felt into flame shapes.

Lesson

- As children gather together for Group or Circle Time, show them the pictures of firefighters. Ask the children to identify the firefighters in the pictures and to say what the firefighters are doing.
- Allow individual children to discuss fires they may have seen.
- Continue to focus the discussion on who helps people when there is a fire and how they keep others safe. Talk about firefighters in full protective suit, firefighters using air tanks to breathe, and the necessity for everyone to leave a place that is on fire.
- Tell children the basic rules of fire safety:
  - Know two ways out of every room ahead of time.
  - Feel the door. If it is hot, do not open it.
  - Crawl below the smoke.
  - Get out of the building and do not go back in.
  - Call 911 from a neighbor's home.
- Ask the children what they would do if their clothing caught on fire. (The urge for young children is to run away.) Tell them to *stop, cover* their faces, *drop* to the ground, and *roll* back and forth on the ground until the fire is out.
- Have four to six children hold the sides of a blanket at waist level and ripple it to imitate the smoke of a fire. Have the other children practice crawling under this blanket of "smoke."
- Select a child to demonstrate *Stop, Cover, Drop,* and *Roll*. Place felt flames on the child's clothing. As she rolls, the flames will drop to the carpet and the child will have put out the fire on her clothing.

Have the children practice crawling under the smoke blanket and rolling to put out the flames.

Assessment Strategy

Observe each child participating in the discussion and the dramatization of safety measures.

Accommodations/Modifications

Autism—Encourage the child to participate at her comfort level. Provide reinforcement for participation.

Speech or Language Impairments—Encourage the child to verbalize what she is doing as she practices the fire safety activity.

Hearing Impairments—Use gestures and face the child when giving explanations and directions.

Visual Impairments—Provide a peer buddy for the fire safety activity.

Cognitive and/or Developmental Delays—Preteach the activity. Review the information after the activity.

Emotional Disturbance—Allow the child to select a peer buddy for the activity.

Other Health Impairments/Attention Deficit Hyperactive Disorder—Provide a peer buddy for the child.

Orthopedic Impairments—Help the child maneuver through the activity.

Curriculum Connections

- **Art**—Provide opportunities for children to create a fire scene with red, orange, and yellow crayons. Add red cellophane to the Art Center for children to glue to their drawings.
- **Special Art Project**—Bring in a large refrigerator box and encourage children to paint it to look like a fire truck.
- **Social Studies**—Many local fire stations will send a firefighter and a fire truck to your school. Ask if the children can climb on the fire truck and explore its interior and exterior.

PEOPLE AT WORK

Careers

Time

- 5 minutes to distribute materials and give directions for home project
- 30–45 minutes discussion in classroom

Materials

- Home preparation with parent
- Parent letter (see suggested letter on page 183)
- Girl/boy paper doll cutout

Review

Provide time for each child to discuss his career choice.

Assessment Strategy

Observe each child as he participates in the discussion.

Objectives

Children will:

1. Identify careers they would like to have when they grow up.
2. Discuss community helpers, listing their tools, activities, and how the community helper assists the community.

Lesson

- Have the children gather on the rug near the end of the day. Hand each child a paper doll cutout and a parent instruction letter to take home, and ask the children to complete the project at home.
- After the children have returned their completed projects, gather for Group or Circle Time. Ask each child to present his paper doll cutout, describing the community helper represented by the cutout. Read the answer to the questions the family has helped the child to complete (see page 183).
- Discuss each child's answers, but be sensitive to children who may not want to share their information.

Accommodations/Modifications

Autism—Have the child practice his presentation on the community helper he selected.

Speech or Language Impairments—Encourage the child to use complete sentences and correct sentence structure, and provide positive feedback when he does it.

Hearing Impairments—Allow the child to see the paper doll cutouts and pictures as each child discusses his career choice.

Visual Impairments—Rephrase the main points of the child's presentation for the child who may not see the presentation as well as others.

Cognitive and/or Developmental Delays—Ask this child to repeat two main points about the presentation. Assist and clarify as needed.

Emotional Disturbance—Have this child practice his presentation with an adult prior to making it.

Other Health Impairments/Attention Deficit Hyperactive Disorder—Seat the child near an adult during the other children's presentations.

Orthopedic Impairments—Assist as needed with the child's presentation, holding and presenting the paper doll cutout.

Curriculum Connections

- **Art**—Provide opportunities for children to create additional career dolls throughout the week.
- **Math**—Ask individual children to tell what they want to be when they grow up. Record their responses on a class chart.

Parent Letter

Dear Parents,

As part of our unit on People at Work, we are learning how different career opportunities benefit the community. We are also talking about how each of us can grow up to be whatever we want to be. To help reinforce these concepts and ideas, we would like you to help your child dress the attached boy or girl cutout to represent what your child wants to be when he or she grows up, such as an astronaut, a doctor, a nurse, a baseball player, a firefighter, and so on. Please help your child complete the following statements and attach this paper to the boy or girl cutout.

When I grow up I want to be _____.
Because _____.
I can help my community by _____.
I will need to learn _____.

You can use a variety of materials such as pictures, markers, fabric, ribbons, and construction paper to decorate the boy or girl cutout. We encourage you and your child to be creative.

Thank you so much for your help with this activity. Please return the competed project by Monday of next week.

Sincerely,

INTRODUCTION TO

The World Around Us

Time

15–20 minutes

Materials

- A globe
- Map of your state
- Books about the world, such as *The Earth and I* by Frank Asch and Nancy Tafuri's *What the Sun Sees, What the Moon Sees* (in big book format, if available)
- Chart paper and markers or chalk board and chalk

Objectives

Children will:

1. Tell you that they live in the world.
2. Point to the place where they live on the globe.

Lesson

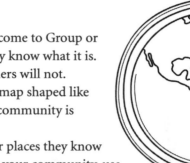

- Have the globe in view as children come to Group or Circle Time. Ask the children if they know what it is. Some children will know, while others will not.
- Tell the children that the globe is a map shaped like the world. Show them where their community is located on the globe.
- Ask the children the names of other places they know about. If they mention a place near your community, use a map of your state to show them where the place is located.
- Read a book about the world around us, such as *The Earth and I,* in big book format if possible.
- Tell the children that over the next few days they will learn about the world. Use the chalkboard or a chart to brainstorm on topics the children think they will be learning about. Write their words on the chart to refer to at a later time. **Note:** NASA has photographs of the world that will complement this lesson; photos are available online at www.nasa.gov/audience/foreducators/k-4.

Accommodations/Modifications

Autism—Assign the child a peer buddy to help him remain on task during Group or Circle Time. Maintain proximity control when handling the globe. If the sound of the chalk on the chalkboard causes sensory overload, consider using a dry-erase board or chart paper during the brainstorming session. Use caution if spinning the globe. A child with autism may use this as an opportunity to engage in self-stimulation behaviors.

Speech or Language Impairments—If the child has a severe speech impairment, allow him to use sign language to tell you about the world. Children can also draw what they know about the world rather than verbalizing the information.

Hearing Impairments—Allow the child to move closer to the globe and to sit in the front during the brainstorming session. Be sure to stay within the child's vision and keep your hands away from your mouth (several children with hearing impairments read lips).

Review

Look at the globe or the map. Ask the children to tell you what they think about the world.

Assessment Strategy

Ask each child to tell you what the map or globe represents.

Visual Impairments—Bring the child closer to the globe so he can see it better. Consider using a globe or a map with a raised surface. Children with more severe visual impairments can relate to the globe tactilely.

Cognitive and/or Developmental Delays—Repeat directions, allowing the child to reword directions (to check for understanding). Utilization of a peer buddy will help the child formulate thoughts into verbal responses.

Emotional Disturbance—Maintain proximity control during the lesson.

Other Health Impairments/Attention Deficit Hyperactive Disorder—A child with ADHD may need to be placed in an area where you can monitor his movement. Using a lap pad will provide the child with a physical cue to remain seated. Allow the child frequent opportunities to move throughout the lesson.

Orthopedic Impairments—A child with an orthopedic impairment may not be able to help put the bulletin board up. However, he can participate by handing pieces over or holding items to be hung up.

Curriculum Connections

- **Art**—Ask the children to work together to build a world. Accomplishing this will require some creative thinking. They might decide to use papier-mâché, salt dough, or a box to create their world. Support their imaginations throughout the process.

- **Bulletin Board**—Ask the children to cut out pictures of the sky, forests, mountains, lakes, and deserts from magazines and attach them to the bulletin board titled "The World Around Us."

- **Science**—Place the map and globe in the Science Center for children to look at during Center Time.

- **Social Studies**—Have a globe available to show children that the earth is made up of water and land. Show how each is represented on the globe. Show children the North and South Poles. Tell them that ice is frozen water.

Dirt and Mud

Time

15–20 minutes

Materials

- Tub of dirt
- Box of wipes or access to a sink
- Classroom plant or two
- Copy of the poem "Mud"

Objectives

Children will:

1. Learn that dirt is the part of the earth that allows plants and animals to live.
2. Name one living thing that grows in the dirt.

Preparation

Bring in a large tub of dirt and place it in the Group or Circle Time area prior to beginning the lesson.

Lesson

- As children gather for Group or Circle Time, allow them to run their fingers through the dirt. Have wipes or a sink nearby for when the children want to clean their hands.
- Talk to children about dirt. Tell them that the outer surface of the earth is where plants grow and animals live.
- Observe classroom plants that are growing in soil. Look outside and see if you can locate grass growing in dirt. Ask children to describe how dirt smells.
- Ask children to tell about times they have played in the dirt. Ask them what happens when water is added to dirt.
- Recite the "Mud" poem (below) to the children, and then ask the children to repeat it with you. Another good poem to use is "Mud" by Polly Chase Boyden.

Mud by Laverne Warner
Mud feels so good.
It's marvelous for play!
Mud makes houses and mud men,
Fences, castles, all kinds of animals, too.
Mud's just great after a rainy day.

Mud feels go good.
It's marvelous for play!
I love to squish it between my fingers,
And most especially between my toes!

Review

Ask the children to tell what kinds of play can happen in dirt and mud.

Assessment Strategy

Ask each child to say something she knows about dirt.

Accommodations/Modifications

Autism—Some children with autism are tactilely defensive. If this is the situation, place the mud into plastic, resealable bags so the child does not have to touch it. Use rubber gloves to provide the same result.

Speech or Language Impairments—Preview the poem with the child prior to saying it aloud with the group. When reciting the poem with the child, you may need to slow down the pace so she can articulate clearly.

Hearing Impairments—Speak clearly when reciting the poem and keep your mouth clear from blockages. Using supportive sign language during the recitation may offer the child an additional means of taking in the verbal language.

Visual Impairments—A child with a severe visual impairment may need increased opportunities to use tactile learning when exploring the plant soil.

Cognitive and/or Developmental Delays—Break tasks down into small components. When seeking direct answers to "What happens when water is added to dirt?" it may be necessary to perform the action to make the abstract idea of mud more concrete.

Emotional Disturbance—Monitor the child's behavior when handling soil.

Other Health Impairments/Attention Deficit Hyperactive Disorder—Allow the child frequent opportunities for movement. Use proximity control and verbal reinforcements to keep her on the actively.

Orthopedic Impairments—If the child is in a wheelchair, be sure to place the dirt in a tub that can be brought to her level.

Curriculum Connections

- **Art/Science**—Place a small tub of mud in the Science Center or Art Center for children to use to make mud creations. Place on wax paper to dry. Better yet, take the artistic endeavors outdoors to dry in the sun. Add twigs and acorns for children to make mud people. Photograph these creations to send home to parents when "The World Around Us" theme is complete.

- **Language and Literacy**—Print the poem "Mud" on a poster and place it near the Art Center for children to "read" as they make their mud creations.

- **Listening Center**—Make a cassette tape of the "Mud" poem for children to listen to at their leisure.

- **Science**—Provide magnifying glasses for children to use to observe dirt more closely. Ask if children have found any small animals living in the dirt.

- **More Science**—Bring in dirt of a different color, texture, or consistency from another area of town. Place these various samples in the Science Center for comparison purposes. Use a children's encyclopedia to determine the names of the soils.

Rocks

Time

10–15 minutes

Materials

- Mystery box
- Variety of rocks in different colors and sizes (at least 40)
- Minerals and rocks chart (available at a teacher supply store)

Objectives

Children will:

1. Identify a rock as different from other objects.
2. Learn one fact about rocks.

Lesson

- Display a mystery box as children come to Group or Circle Time. Show the rocks inside the box, and ask the children where they usually find rocks.
- Divide the group into four smaller groups and give them approximately 10 rocks each. Ask the children to count their rocks and then to arrange them from smallest to largest.
- Ask the children to investigate their rocks and ask them, "Are they all the same? Are some of the rocks darker than others? Do some of the rocks seem harder than others? Why do you think so?"
- Show the minerals and rock chart and tell children that rocks can be classified. Show them rocks that can be classified easily and ask the children to match them with the chart.
- Tell the children that the class is starting a rock collection in the Science Center. Encourage them to bring rocks from home or from outside.

Accommodations/Modifications

Autism—A child with autism may not be able to comprehend concepts such as *different, same, harder, softer,* and so on. Teach concepts using concrete items (for example, a rock is hard, cotton balls are soft). Have cotton balls available. Use five rocks at first and add more rocks as appropriate.

Speech or Language Impairments—Preteach the vocabulary words related to concepts, such as *same/different* and *smallest/largest.*

Hearing Impairments—Keep the child close to the person speaking and giving directions. Check for understanding by having him sign or speak the directions back to you.

Visual Impairments—The child may not benefit from the use of a rock chart unless it is a textured chart with actual rock formations on it. Create a three-dimensional component by using Velcro to add rocks to the chart.

Cognitive and/or Developmental Delays—Use as many concrete items as possible with this lesson, such as adding real rocks to the rock chart. Reduce the number of rocks to four or five at a time.

Emotional Disturbance—Model appropriate behavior when handling rocks. It may be necessary to role play how to handle rocks, how to hand them to friends, and so on.

Other Health Impairments/Attention Deficit Hyperactive Disorder—Use proximity control to monitor impulsive behaviors. For example, while the children are working in groups, periodically walk by offering reinforcement and acting as a physical reminder for the child to remain on task.

Orthopedic Impairments—Be sure the child has materials presented to him at an accessible level. This holds especially true when working in small groups. If a child is in a wheelchair with a tray and the children are using the rocks on the table, he may not be able to reach them. Instead, have the children sort rocks on the child's tray.

Curriculum Connections

- **Art**—Ask children if they can make animals or people from rocks. Provide rocks, glue, markers, and googly eyes to enhance their creativity.
- **Math**—Show children how people counted their flocks of sheep or cattle in ancient times by moving rocks from one side of the gate to another as the animals came into the pen at night. When they had 10 rocks, they exchanged them for one larger rock. This counting system, which we know as the decimal system, allowed people to determine if any of their animals were missing.
- **Science**—Provide magnifying glasses for children to use to observe rocks more closely. Encourage them to find rocks that are alike and place them together on the display. Use a children's encyclopedia to determine the names of rocks.
- **More Science**—Use the minerals and rock chart to classify each of the rocks the groups have used during the lesson. This activity should be completed on the same day as the lesson so children can mak an easier connection to the content of the lesson.

Sky

Time

15 minutes

Materials

- Blanket or sheet for children to sit on outdoors
- Globe used in the introductory lesson
- Photograph of a landscape showing the sky

Objectives

Children will:

1. Point to the sky in a photograph of a landscape.
2. Describe the sky and tell you what is in it.

Lesson

Note: If possible, conduct this lesson outdoors on a sunny day so children can see the sky.

- Gather the children on a large sheet or blanket for Group or Circle Time. Display the globe and tell the children they are going to learn about the sky.
- Show children a photograph of the sky. Ask them if the photograph looks like the sky above them.
- Give them an opportunity to tell what they know about the sky. As they talk, respond to their comments about the sun, moon, stars, clouds, airplanes, birds, and other objects they see in the sky.
- Tell children that the sky is the atmosphere around the planet.
- Ask children to look at the sky and name its color.
- Ask children to rub their hands together in a swishing sound to imitate the sound of rain. While they are doing this, tell them that on rainy days the sky will be cloudy and not blue.
- Read this poem to the children and ask them to make up motions to accompany it.

The Sky by Laverne Warner
I can touch the sky up high.
I can touch the ground below.
The sky is where the clouds appear,
And the ground is where the rain will go.

Accommodations/Modifications

Autism—Break the lesson into smaller tasks for the child. Or create a picture schedule of the steps to provide structure to the lesson. For example, a picture of children walking would represent the first part of the activity and a photo of children engaged in song and hand movements would represent the last part of the activity.

Speech or Language Impairments—Allow the child plenty of time to learn "The Sky" poem. After several recitations, the child will be more likely to join in.

Hearing Impairments—If the child uses sign language, teach her "The Sky" using the proper ASL signs to go with the words. The other children in the classroom will learn the same signs, which will make the child feel more included in the lesson. Be sure to face the child when speaking.

Visual Impairments—Use texture on the photograph of the sky to separate sky, clouds, and land. If you have a child who is blind in your class, it is important to know what represents sky to them. For instance, a specific color, smell, or feeling may be associated with the sky. During the assessment, ask the child, "What things do you hear in the sky?"

Cognitive and/or Developmental Delays—Use concrete examples of things in the sky. For example, if talking about an airplane, have a model airplane available for children to manipulate and identify with. When describing how rain is formed, use sequence cards showing the process from holding water to raining.

Emotional Disturbance—Monitor the child's behavior, frequently offering praise and encouragement. If a child becomes discouraged with incorrect responses, provide choices and more opportunities for success.

Other Health Impairments/Attention Deficit Hyperactive Disorder—If the child exhibits impulsive behaviors while outside, use proximity control when walking. You might assign buddies for the child to hold hands with while walking.

Orthopedic Impairments—If the child is in a wheelchair, she may have a difficult time steering through trees and over rocky or sandy areas. Be considerate of her needs when walking with the children.

Curriculum Connections

- **Art**—Have blue or black construction paper and white paint for children to use to draw clouds.
- **More Art**—Ask a small group of children to make a Sky Mural. Provide a large piece of blue butcher paper for children to draw on or cut out pictures and glue them onto the butcher paper.
- **Language and Literacy**—At story hour, consider reading *It Looked Like Spilt Milk* by Charles G. Shaw.
- **Math**—Cut out pairs of clouds and place them on the Manipulatives Table. Ask children to match the cloud pairs. Start with simple patterns first, increasing the difficulty for children by making the cloud patterns more complex.
- **Outdoors**—When you are on the playground with children, ask them to describe the shapes they see in the clouds.

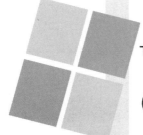

Oceans

Time
20–25 minutes

Materials
- An ocean in a bottle (instructions for making this bottle are found at http://www.gryphonhouse.com/activity/activity.cfm?bookid=18325&page=386)
- Photographs or pictures of oceans and beaches
- *The Rainbow Fish* by Marcus Pfister

Objectives
Children will:
1. Learn that an ocean is a large body of water.
2. Describe ocean water as being salty.

Preparation
Use the instructions for making an ocean in a bottle (see source in the Materials section).

Lesson
- Have photographs of oceans available as children come to Group or Circle Time. Show them the ocean in a bottle.
- Ask children if they have ever been to an ocean. Give them an opportunity to talk about their experiences.
- Hold up the front cover of *The Rainbow Fish* and ask, "What type of animals can you find in the ocean?" After children have named a few, read the book to them, allowing them to make comments as the book is read. Talk about the fish's adventures.
- Ask the children to tell what they liked best about the story or about the fish. Tell the children that they can make an ocean in a bottle in the Science Center after the lesson.

Accommodations/Modifications
Autism—Provide choices when asking what types of animals are found in the ocean. In addition, use concrete objects instead of photographs when describing the ocean.

Speech or Language Impairments—Provide extra time for the child to respond when asking about the types of animals found in the ocean.

Hearing Impairments—Seat the child near the speaker. In addition, when reading the story, add simple American Sign Language signs such as *fish, rainbow, ocean,* and *animals.* Remember to keep hands clear from mouth when reading because the child may have learned to read lips to help him understand the spoken word.

Visual Impairments—Consider using a big book version of *The Rainbow Fish.* If this is not available, allow the child to sit as close as possible to the book. When showing pictures of the ocean to the children, use concrete items to support the photos. Many pet stores sell rocks, seaweed, and other ocean items used in aquariums.

Cognitive and/or Developmental Delays—Offer the child a choice of answers when asking him to identify specific animals that live in the ocean. For example, does a bear or a shark live in the ocean?

Emotional Disturbance—Provide positive feedback to the child when he is sitting appropriately during story time, as well as when he is responding appropriately to questions. For example, by raising his hand.

Child's Name			Date
Story Element	Yes	No	Comments
Knows name of book			
Can identify Rainbow Fish			
Can tell two events that happened in the story			
Can tell why the Rainbow Fish is special			
Can tell why the Rainbow Fish is happy			
Asks to have the book read			
Signature of Evaluator			

Review

Ask children to pretend to swim like fish as they go to centers or to the next activity scheduled for the group.

Assessment Strategy

Ask each child to retell the story of *The Rainbow Fish*. This activity will take a while, so you might want to ask parent volunteers to help out with the assessment. Use the rubric on this page to mark what the child remembers about the story.

Other Health Impairments/Attention Deficit Hyperactive Disorder—The child may have a difficult time sitting still during the reading of the story. Provide carpet squares for him and the other children to sit on to help him identify his place on the floor. In addition, allowing the child to hold an object while the story is being read will keep his hands from touching other children and objects around him.

Orthopedic Impairments—When reading the story to the children, be sure the child can view the book. If the child is in a wheelchair, either move him from the chair so he is level with the book or make sure the book is raised high enough for him to view.
Note: Always check with the child's medical provider or a family member for proper positioning when moving a child out of his wheelchair.

Curriculum Connections

- **Art**—Provide sequins of different colors so children can draw a picture of a fish and attach sequins with glue,
- **Book Center**—Add *The Rainbow Fish* to the Book Center.
- **Math**—Prepare felt fish shapes for children to place onto a flannel board. Challenge children by asking them to count out a certain number of fish. If you use various colors of fish, you can also ask children to match patterns, such as red, blue, gold, red, blue, gold, red, blue, gold, and so on. As children become more proficient with counting and matching patterns, increase the level of difficulty of both activities.
- **Science**—Have materials available so children can make their own ocean in a bottle. This will require adult assistance.

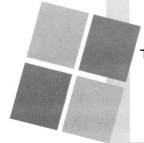

Forests

Time
15–20 minutes

Materials
- *Goldilocks and the Three Bears* by Jan Brett
- Pictures of forests
- Pictures of forest animals or plastic forest animals
- Pictures of a forest, an ocean, a desert, and a field

Objectives

Children will:
1. Describe a forest as a big group of trees that grow together.
2. Learn about the living things they might find in a forest.

Lesson

- As children gather for Group or Circle Time, ask them if they remember the story of "Goldilocks and the Three Bears." Show them a picture from the story and ask if any of the children remember where the three bears lived. Explain that another name for the woods is the *forest*.

- Ask if anyone has ever heard the word *forest*. Explain that forests are places where many, many trees grow together. Places with lots of trees and no homes or buildings are called *forests* or *woods*.

- Show the children pictures of forests (available from USDA Forest Service at http://www.fs.fed.us/). There is a "Just for Kids" section with ideas for children.

- Show pictures of animals found in the forest: squirrels, bears, deer, beavers, moose, foxes, owls, and snakes. Use plastic animals, if they are available. Through gestures, show the movement of each animal and talk about its characteristics. Demonstrate the sound each animal makes.

- Play a game where each person takes a turn pretending to be a forest animal. The children can take one of the pictures and pretend to be the forest animal in the picture.

- Talk about the reasons forests are important: they provide homes for animals, clean air to breathe, and wood for our homes. Teach the poem below if time permits:

Deep, Deep in the Forest by Sharon Lynch
Deep, deep in the forest, (cup hands around the mouth, exaggerating "deep, deep")
What do I see? (place one hand above eyes and move head from side to side)
I see an owl (point forward with index finger)
Saying "hoo-hoo" at me. (point to self when you say "me")

Deep, deep in the forest,
What do I see?
I see a squirrel
Going "click-click" at me.

Deep, deep in the forest,
What do I see?
I see a fox
Smiling slyly at me.

Review

Ask children to name a forest animal as they leave for centers or the next activity.

Assessment Strategy

Show the child pictures of a forest, a desert, an ocean, and a field. Have the child find the picture of a forest and tell you a story about it. With children who are very young or who have language disabilities, have the child find the picture of the forest. If possible, the child can tell you all about the picture or identify items in the picture.

Deep, deep in the forest,
What do I see?
I see a bear
Going "grrr-grrr" at me.

Accommodations/Modifications

Autism—During the game, you may have to let the child know when it is her turn and help her to understand the process of taking turns.

Speech or Language Impairments—The child may benefit from working with a partner when determining animal sounds.

Hearing Impairments—Allow the child to wear an FM system, if available, to enhance the intake of the animal sounds. Allowing the child to make sounds into a PVC phone will enable her to hear her own animal sound more clearly.

Visual Impairments—Provide concrete objects in addition to the pictures presented, such as figures of trees and animals. The child may benefit from enlarged photos.

Cognitive and/or Developmental Delays—Limit the number of steps in each part of the activity.

Emotional Disturbance—Monitor the child's behavior with proximity control; provide positive reinforcement for positive behavior.

Other Health Impairments/Attention Deficit Hyperactive Disorder—The child may become inattentive and impulsive during song movements or when sitting for prolonged periods of time. Consider allowing the child to stand when the story is being read or to wear a weighted vest.

Orthopedic Impairments—Limit the animals the child might select to those that are easier to imitate based on the child's specific orthopedic impairment.

Curriculum Connections

- **Listening Center**—Purchase a cassette or CD of sounds from the forest—bird, bear, owl, snake, frog, rain—and let the children listen to the recording. Provide a card with pictures of the animals or item that makes the sound on the tape. Encourage children to match the animals with their sounds.
- **Math**—Provide pinecones, sweet gum ball, spruce cones, or other types of seed pods from trees in the forest. Working with small groups of children, sort them and count the number of each type.
- **Science**—In the Science Center, provide a stationary magnifying glass and the following materials for the children to inspect: tree bark, pine needles, leaves, and pinecones.

Mountains

Time

20 minutes

Materials

- Clay or playdough
- Pan
- Photographs or pictures of mountains
- Tape
- Globe used in previous lessons

Objectives

Children will:

1. Describe a mountain as a large hill.
2. Point to a mountain in a picture.

Preparation

Use clay or playdough to mold a mountain in a pan. Post pictures of mountains around the room.

Lesson

Note: Using this lesson depends on the geography in your area. If you can look out the window and see mountains, helping children connect with the topic will be easy. Otherwise, have photographs or pictures to assist in their understanding of mountains.

- Start singing "She'll Be Comin' 'Round the Mountain." If you've forgotten the words to this familiar song, many websites and books, including *Wild, Wild West: 25 Songs and Over 300 Activities for Young Children* by Pam Schiller, have the words.
- Show the children the clay mountain in the pan. Tell them that glaciers and volcanic gases helped form mountains many, many years ago. Demonstrate this experience by using a block or a large piece of ice to represent a glacier and plough it into the clay mountain, pushing it upward.
- Point to the globe and remind children that there is lava and hot gases inside the earth. Both change landmass when volcanoes erupt. Be aware of children's responses to this information, making sure that none are fearful as a consequence of the lesson.
- Talk about mountain climbing and snow climbing as sports that some people enjoy. If you live near a mountain or a mountain range, ask the children to name the mountains they know. Spend some time pretending to be a hill, then a mountain. Recite this poem during this movement experience:

Mountains by Laverne Warner
Once I was a small little hill, (curl up in a ball on the floor)
But a glacier came along and pushed me around. (roll over and stand halfway up)
Then lava from inside the earth pushed me up. (stand all the way up)
Now look at me—I'm a great big mountain! (hold up arms above head to show a big mountain)

Review

Ask children to name a nearby mountain or show how they can stand tall like a mountain.

Assessment Strategy

Ask each child to find a picture of a mountain in the room and point to it.

Accommodations/Modifications

Autism—Monitor the child's interaction with the globe as he may spin the globe and use the spinning as a means to self-stem.

Speech or Language Impairments—If the child's impairment is significant, use nonverbal responses and Picture Communication Systems.

Hearing Impairments—Move the child close to where you are demonstrating how glaciers change mountains. Utilize simple sign language activity.

Visual Impairments—Enlarge the photographs to meet the visual needs of the child. The child may also have difficulty understanding his "place in space." He may need help feeling comfortable when engaging in movement tasks.

Cognitive and/or Developmental Delays—Assign a peer buddy to help explain the concepts being taught. It may be helpful to preteach the vocabulary used in the lesson.

Emotional Disturbance—Closely monitor the child when using the block to represent the glacier. This may cause a fearful reaction, depending on the child's life experiences.

Other Health Impairments/Attention Deficit Hyperactive Disorder—Establish physical boundaries for the child when acting out the poem.

Orthopedic Impairments—The child may have difficulty performing the actions to the song. Create motions to the song that he can accomplish successfully.

Curriculum Connections

- **Art**—Have paper cone-shaped cups in the Art Center for children to use to construct mountains. Spark the children's creativity by providing paint and other materials to add trees and snow to the paper cone mountains.

- **Book Center**—Place Viewmasters in the Book Center with slides showing beautiful three-dimensional photographs of mountains or one of the national parks, such as Yellowstone or Glacier National Park.

- **Outdoors**—If there is a hill nearby and weather permits, consider taking the children for a "climb on the mountain."

- **Science**—Have several pans of clay available for children to use to experiment with making their own landforms, including mountains.

Lakes and Ponds

Time

20–25 minutes

Materials

- Photograph of a nearby lake or pond, if possible
- Pictures of lakes and ponds
- *In the Small, Small Pond* by Denise Fleming
- Cutout fish shapes
- Cutout fish sponge shapes

Objectives

Children will:

1. Name two animals that live in a lake or pond.
2. Identify lakes and ponds in pictures.

Preparation

If possible, have a photograph of a lake or pond in the nearby area that children might have visited and would recognize.

Lesson

- Show children a variety of pictures of lakes and ponds.
- Tell children that ponds are smaller than lakes and are often created intentionally and that lakes are formed naturally. Engage the children in a discussion about animals that live in and around lakes and ponds, including turtles, frogs, snakes, fish, and insects.
- Read Denise Fleming's *In the Small, Small Pond* to the children and talk about the plant and animal life around lakes and ponds.
- Teach children the "In the Pond" song about animal life.

In the Pond by Laverne Warner
(Tune: "London Bridge")
In the pond there lives a turtle,
Lives a turtle, lives a turtle.
In the pond there lives a turtle,
See him swimming a–round.

In the pond there lives a frog,
Lives a frog, lives a frog.
In the pond there lives a frog,
Can you hear him croak–ing?

In the pond, I see some fish,
See some fish, see some fish.
In the pond, I see some fish.
Watch their tails go swish, swish.

In the pond live many snakes
Many snakes, many snakes.
In the pond live many snakes,
They enjoy the water.

Minnows swim in the pond,
In the pond, in the pond.
Minnows swim in the pond,
Swimming all a–round.

- Encourage children to add other verses as they learn about animal life in the pond.

Review

Ask children to name all the animals they remember that live in ponds or lakes.

- If children are still interested in the topic, discuss activities people enjoy in lakes and ponds, such as boating, swimming, fishing, water skiing, paddle boating, picnicking, and so on. Ask children to recall what they have done at lakes or ponds. Make sure the children understand that lakes and ponds are dependent upon rainfall to maintain their water level.

Accommodations/Modifications

Assessment Strategy

Ask each child to name two animals that live in ponds or lakes.

Autism—Many children with autism face difficulty in social situations. Modeling of social behaviors, such as singing at an appropriate sound level, might be necessary.

Speech or Language Impairments—Allow the child to use nonverbal responses to questions, such as pointing or using picture symbols. If she has an articulation disorder, let her rehearse the song to practice articulating specific words.

Hearing Impairments—Incorporate simple signs such as those for *lake, pond, frog,* and *fish* into the lesson. Simple sign language coupled with lip reading may enhance the overall transfer of information.

Visual Impairments—Provide concrete examples of lakes and ponds, such as a tub of water and sand to describe a lake or pond. The child may benefit from enlarged photographs with raised surfaces. Move the child close to the materials for better viewing. Provide an opportunity for children to pass pictures around, enabling the child to view the photo at a closer distance.

Cognitive and/or Developmental Delays—Adding movement to the song will help to reinforce the concepts being discussed.

Emotional Disturbance—Reinforce positive behaviors with non-tangible reinforcers such as verbal praise and a thumbs up and/or tangible reinforcers such as stickers.

Other Health Impairments/Attention Deficit Hyperactive Disorder—The child may benefit from moving or taking a break between activity steps. If she exhibits impulsive behaviors when moving from one activity to the next, allow wiggle breaks during the lesson.

Orthopedic Impairments—If hand motions accompany the song, be sure to incorporate motions that the child can perform. For example, if a child is unable to move her arms but can move her legs, add a kicking motion to the song.

Curriculum Connections

- **Art**—Provide sponge pieces in various pond or lake animal shapes. Use them to dip in paint to make a pond collage.
- **Math**—Provide felt pieces cut in the shape of pond animals, such as turtles, frogs, fish, or snakes, for children to count out on a flannel board.
- **Math/Snack**—Provide fish-shaped crackers for snack. Ask children to count ten fish for themselves. If children are already counting to ten, challenge them to move to 15 or 20.

Deserts

Time

15–20 minutes

Materials

- Large plastic tub
- Sand
- Table lamp
- Pictures of the desert
- *Listen to the Desert* by Pat Mora (in a big book format, if possible), time permitting

Objectives

Children will:

1. Name features of a desert.
2. Learn that deserts are hot and dry.
3. Describe the changes in the desert between day and night.

Preparation

Fill a large plastic tub with sand and place a table lamp directly over the sand. Heat the sand approximately 30 minutes prior to the lesson.

Lesson

- Show pictures of the desert to the children as they gather for Group or Circle Time.
- Begin a discussion about what children see in the pictures. Point out the animal and plant life they might observe.
- Explain to the children that in the desert days are very hot and nights are very cold. Have them feel the hot sand at the top of the tub and ask the children when they have felt hot sand before. Perhaps during summers at the beach or even in their backyards.
- Have the children predict what will happen to the temperature when the lamp is turned off. Then turn off the lamp and let the children dig into the sand and feel the change of temperature as they dig further down. Explain to the children that the sun heats the sand in the daylight but that the sand cools quickly in the night as the sun goes down.
- Read *Listen to the Desert,* if time permits.

Accommodations/Modifications

Autism—Check the light before using as any flickering from the lamp may cause the child to fixate or stem off the light. If the child is tactilely defensive, allow him to wear rubber gloves when digging in the sand. He should be able to feel heat and coolness through the gloves.

Review

Remind children of the words *desert, hot,* and *dry* while closing the lesson. Place the tub of sand in the Science Center for children to explore.

Assessment Strategy

Ask each child to describe the temperature of the sand in his own words.

Speech or Language Impairments—Accept the child's nonverbal responses during predictions or possibly allow the child to draw predictions on paper and share the picture with the class.

Hearing Impairments—Move the child closer to the activity and face the child directly when speaking.

Visual Impairments—Enlarge pictures of a desert. The child may benefit more from a physical model of a desert.

Cognitive and/or Developmental Delays—Use caution and monitor the child when he is near the lamp. The child may not understand the concepts of "not safe" or "dangerous." You may need to repeat this lesson over a period of several days for the child to understand the effects of the heat on the sand.

Emotional Disturbance—Provide positive reinforcement, such as offering praise, when the child is following directions and keeping an appropriate distance from the lamp.

Other Health Impairments/Attention Deficit Hyperactive Disorder—Monitor the child around the lamp as he may become impulsive and reach for it. Utilize proximity control and provide positive behavior supports.

Orthopedic Impairments—If the child does not have use of or feelings in his hands, allow him to use his feet to feel the changes in the temperature. He may need assistance in positioning himself to engage in this activity.

Curriculum Connections

- **Art**—Encourage children to use colored sand and glue for sand painting. Provide colored sand and toothpicks for sand art. Place amounts of colored sand in layers in a clear container. Have children use toothpicks to create valleys in the colors.
- **Sand Table**—Provide tubs of sand with small items hidden in the sand for children to locate.
- **Science**—Provide two tubs of sand, one under a lamp and the other covered. Provide large, unbreakable thermometers to record the temperature of surface sand and buried sand. Children will need assistance in understanding how thermometers work. **Note:** Closely monitor the children around the lamp.
- **More Science**—Place a nylon stocking over the top of a large, unbreakable bowl. Place sand in the stocking. Have the children feel the dry sand. Then add a small amount of water to the sand. The children will be able to see the water filtering through the sand quickly, going into the bowl. Discuss the dryness of the desert even with water (rain).

4 Spring Themes

Weather

In the Garden

Manners

Plants

4

INTRODUCTION TO

Weather

Time

20 minutes

Materials

- Box containing a variety of clothing items, such as sweaters, coats, mittens, gloves, snowshoes, scarves, jackets, ponchos, raincoats, rain boots, umbrellas, jeans, socks, boots, sandals, shorts, sleeveless shirts, bathing suits
- Picture cards of common weather conditions, such as a windy day, a rainy day, a snowy day, and so on (use pictures appropriate to your area)

Objectives

Children will:
1. Identify the type of weather in a picture.
2. Select the correct clothing for the weather depicted.

Lesson

- Have the children gather around a large box of clothing items.
- Take one item from the box and ask the children to name the item.
- Give one child a picture card depicting a weather condition.
- Have that child ask a few friends to help her select two items from the box that would be appropriate to wear for the weather in the picture.
- Engage all of the children in a discussion about why certain clothing items are typically worn in the depicted weather scene.
- Repeat this activity for multiple weather scenes.

Accommodations/Modifications

Autism—Allow time before the lesson for the child to examine the clothing items.

Speech or Language Impairments—Encourage complete sentence structure and appropriate word choice during discussion. Define unknown words.

Hearing Impairments—Repeat any instructions, rephrase the discussions, allow the child to sit near the speakers and to maintain close visual contact with you and with the person speaking.

Review

Place the box of clothes and seasonal pictures in centers for the children to continue to explore.

Assessment Strategy

Ask individual children to tell you what they would wear for specific weather conditions.

Visual Impairments—Provide time before the activity for the child to explore and examine the clothing.

Cognitive and/or Developmental Delays—Provide explanation during the discussion as to the reasons for wearing certain clothing. Offer forced-choice options for the child's selection of clothing.

Emotional Disturbance—Provide time for the child to examine the clothing. Encourage her participation in the activity.

Other Health Impairments/Attention Deficit Hyperactive Disorder—Encourage the child to verbalize the items that correspond to the weather condition as she selects the clothing.

Orthopedic Impairments—Provide an opportunity for the child to participate at the same level as other children.

Curriculum Connections

- **Art**—Draw doll figures on paper. Provide collage materials so the children can "dress" the doll figures in appropriate seasonal clothing.
- **Language and Literacy**—Talk with each child individually about the clothes they are wearing that day. Ask them why they made specific choices.
- **Science**—Provide pictures of different seasons and of weather conditions along with pictures of different types of clothing. Ask the children to match the clothing to the appropriate weather or seasonal picture.

Clouds

Time
30–45 minutes

Materials
- Recipe for Whipped Soap Paint
  1 cup Ivory Soap Flakes
  1/3 cup water
- Bowl
- Electric beater
- *It Looked Like Spilt Milk* by Charles G. Shaw
- Blue construction paper
- Marker

Objectives

Children will:

1. Use their imaginations to visualize images in the clouds.
2. Use their fine motor skills to make recognizable shapes in whipped soap paint.

Preparation

In a large bowl, whip the Ivory Soap Flakes and water with an electric beater. Add one drop of blue food coloring or liquid tempera paint for color, if desired.

Lesson

Note: Be sure it is a sunny day with clouds in the sky.

- Tell the children that today they will observe and design clouds.
- Read *It Looked Like Spilt Milk* by Charles G. Shaw to the children.
- After listening to the story, have the children go outside and lie on their backs on the ground to look at the clouds.
- Ask the children to describe what they see in the clouds.
- Give each child an opportunity to share what he sees in a cloud shape.
- Upon returning to the classroom, have the children make cloud pictures with a dab of whipped soap paint on blue construction paper.
- Let each child dictate what they saw in the clouds. Write each child's description on a separate piece of paper.
- When the pages are dry, put them together to make a Class Cloud Book.

Review

Discuss the cloud shapes seen outside. Read the Class Cloud Book. Place the Class Cloud Book in the Book Center.

Assessment Strategies

Note the words that each child uses for his page in the Class Cloud Book.

Accommodations/ Modifications

Autism—Suggest one cloud description at a time. Describe what you see in the cloud.

Speech or Language Impairments—Provide definitions of new vocabulary and encourage the child to use the new vocabulary in the discussion.

Hearing Impairments—Face the child and use gestures to help him understand instructions and concepts.

Visual Impairments—Support the visual activities with sensory or tactile experiences, using tissue, cotton balls, or soft fabric, for example.

Cognitive and/or Developmental Delays—The child may need extended wait time during discussions. Define any new vocabulary.

Emotional Disturbance—Help the child understand what is expected of him.

Other Health Impairments/Attention Deficit Hyperactive Disorder—The child may need assistance to complete the assigned task.

Orthopedic Impairments—The child may need assistance when viewing the cloud formations outside.

Curriculum Connections

- **Art**—Place cotton balls in the Art Center to allow children to design their own cloud pictures using cotton balls, paper, and glue. Place whipped soap in the Art Center to encourage the children to make cloud creations.
- **Listening Center**—Place a taped reading of the book *It Looked Like Spilt Milk* along with copies of the book in the Listening Center for the children to listen and follow.
- **Science**—Place pictures of different types of clouds in the Science Center for children to observe and discuss. Place cloud pictures cards with duplicate shadow outline cards in the Science Center so children can match the clouds with the shapes.

WEATHER

Wind

Time

20–30 minutes

Materials

- Assorted objects, some that are lightweight and some that are heavy—suggestions include block, ruler, pencil, jacket, paper, tissue, flag, ribbon, ball, Frisbee, leaf, scarf, newspaper, backpack
- Tub
- Small jars of soap bubbles and bubble wands, one for each child

Objectives

Children will:

1. Decide which materials in a collection will be moved by the wind.
2. Discuss and define the difference between wind speed and wind gust.

Preparation

Place an assortment of objects in a tub.

Lesson

Note: Conduct this lesson on a windy day.

- Bring the children outdoors for Group or Circle Time and gather them around a tub of materials. See suggestions in Materials.
- Ask the children:
    - What do you feel around you?
    - Can you see it?
    - How do you know it is there?
    - What word is used to describe moving air?
    - Is moving air always the same?
- Ask the children to predict which materials in the tub will be moved by the wind.
- Let the children experiment with each material and sort each object into a "moved" or "not moved" pile.
- Engage the children in a discussion about why some objects were moved by the wind and others not moved.
- Encourage the children to discuss their experiences or knowledge of times when the wind was strong enough to move other items (tornados or windstorms).

Review

Leave selected materials and a paper fan in the Science Center for exploration and experimentation.

- Use bubble soap and a wand to blow bubbles, and ask the children to watch the soap bubbles and describe their movement through the air.
- Give each of the children bubble soap and a wand and let them blow bubbles. Invite them to watch as the wind moves the bubbles through the air.

Accommodations/Modifications

Autism—Provide one item at a time with a description of the item. Verbalize the actions of the wind on each item.

Speech or Language Impairments—Provide definitions of vocabulary and encourage the child to use the new vocabulary in the discussion.

Hearing Impairments—Face the child and use gestures to help her understand the instructions and concepts.

Visual Impairments— Support the visual activities with sensory or tactile experiences. For example, the child may benefit from having water poured on to her hand to help her feel the wind. Or allow her to hold a piece of paper, a tissue, or a scarf between her hands to feel the pressure of the wind.

Cognitive and/or Developmental Delays—The child may need extended wait time during discussions. She may need to see visual representations of events during the discussions (tornadoes and windstorms).

Emotional Disturbance—Provide stabilized boxes for the "moved" or "not moved" items to be placed in.

Other Health Impairments/Attention Deficit Hyperactive Disorder—Provide boxes to separate and organize the items into the "moved" and "not moved" categories.

Orthopedic Impairments—Using a straw or bubble pipe will help the child blow bubbles.

Assessment Strategy

Ask each child to select an item to place either in the "moved" or "not moved" pile. Ask the child his reasons for placing the item in the particular pile.

Curriculum Extensions

- **Art**—Provide paper for children to use to make handheld fans to create wind.
- **Language and Literacy**—Provide picture books of storms and tornados in the Library Center for child to read and discuss.
- **Science**—Have children move water droplets across waxed paper using handheld fans.
- **More Science**—Place objects from the lesson in centers for the children's experimentation and exploration
- **Still More Science**—Place a tub of water and put small boats or rafts in the water for the children to move using handheld fans.

Temperature

Time

20–30 minutes

Materials

- 2 large outdoor thermometers
- Bowl of warm water
- Bowl of ice water
- Calendar chart

Objectives

Children will:

1. Describe what a thermometer does.
2. Practice reading and recording temperatures.

Preparation

Place a large outdoor thermometer in an area outside the classroom that is visible to the children while they are indoors.

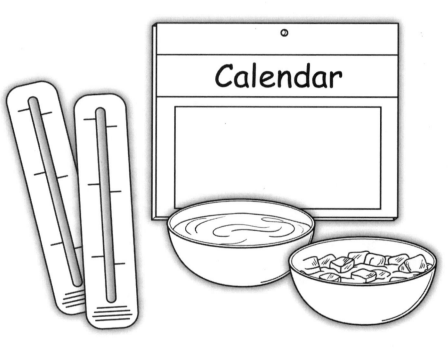

Lesson

- Gather the children on the floor and have them imagine a time when they were very cold, such as a cold, windy, snowy day. Lead the children in pretending to be cold by drawing your arms and legs into your bodies to keep warm.
- Have the children imagine a warm, sunny day. Lead the children in pretending to be warm by relaxing their arms and legs and stretching out.
- Explain to the children that a thermometer reacts in a similar way. When it is cold the red part of a thermometer moves to the bulb at the bottom. The colder the weather, the more the red part shrinks. When it is warm, the red part stretches upward.

Review

Place the two bowls of water and an unbreakable thermometer in the Science Center for the children's individual experimentation.

Assessment Strategy

Question each child individually about how the weather or temperature that day feels to them.

- Show the children a large thermometer.
- Demonstrate how the red shrinks toward the bulb when the thermometer is in the bowl of ice water and how it stretches out when you put it into the bowl of warm water.
- Tell the children where you located the other thermometer outside.
- Over a period of several days and at various times each day, help the children observe the outdoor thermometer and record the temperature on a calendar chart.
- Have the children discuss how the weather feels to them and relate their feelings to the rise and fall of the temperature recorded by the thermometer.

Accommodations/Modifications

Autism—Provide one-on-one time for the child to observe the thermometers and to talk with you about his observations.

Speech or Language Impairments—Define any new words and encourage the child to use the new vocabulary.

Hearing Impairments—Provide visual and gesture cues to help the child understand the relationship of the thermometer reading to the air temperature.

Visual Impairments—When talking, use language as effectively as possible, especially in giving information and directions. Provide verbal orientation if the child appears confused.

Cognitive and/or Developmental Delays—Provide time for the child to repeat the activity. Limit the choices during discussions. Use directional words, such as *right, left, behind, in front of,* and so on, during the lesson.

Emotional Disturbance—Provide time for the child to repeat the activity.

Other Health Impairments/Attention Deficit Hyperactive Disorder—Discuss with the child the need to observe and record temperatures accurately.

Orthopedic Impairments—Provide easy access to the thermometers.

Curriculum Connections

- **Language and Literacy**—Discuss with the children what they like best and least about hot weather and cold weather. Write their responses on a class chart.
- **More Language and Literacy**—Introduce the term *meteorologist* to the children. Discuss the job a meteorologist or weather person does. Write *meteorologist* on your classroom Word Wall.
- **Math**—Compare the temperatures throughout the week, graphing the numbers on a class chart to create a visual representation of temperature changes.

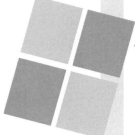

WEATHER

Rain

Time

20–30 minutes on
  day 1
15–20 minutes on
  day 2

Materials

- Small,
  unbreakable
  jars, one for each
  child
- Permanent
  marker
- *Thunder and
  Lightning* by
  Wendy Pfeffer
- Chart and
  markers
- Ruler
- Measuring cup

Objectives

Children will:

1. Observe and record rainfall.
2. Compare rainfall charts.

Note: Plan this lesson when rain has been forecastered.

Preparation

Make each child a rain collection jar by writing one child's name on each jar with permanent marker.

Lesson

- Have the children gather on the floor to listen to *Thunder and Lightning* by Wendy Pfeffer. Encourage them to discuss the amount of rain in the story.
- Give each child the jar with her name on it.
- Talk about the rain that has been forecasted.
- Take the children on a walk around the school. Let each child select a spot to leave her rain collection jar.
- Upon returning to the classroom, ask the children to predict how much rain will be collected in their jar over a 24-hour period.
- Record their predictions on a chart.
  - After the rainfall or the next day, take the children outside again to find their rain collection jars.
  - When children return to the classroom, help them use a ruler to measure the amount of rain in their jars. Talk about the amount of rain that was collected. **Note:** Attach a ruler to the wall above a flat surface (such as a table) at the children's level to help them measure the amount of rain in their jars.
  - Collect ruler measurements and liquid amounts (using a measuring cup) to add details to the discussion about measuring the rain.
  - Compare the actual rainfall collected to the children's predictions and to weather reports on the news or in the newspaper.

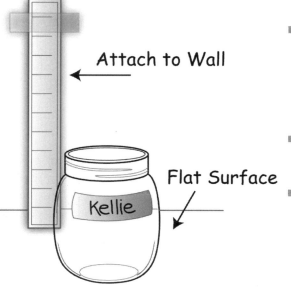

Attach to Wall

Flat Surface

Kellie

Review

Discuss that day's rainfall and any other observations about rain.

Assessment Strategy

Observe each child measuring the rainfall collected in his jar. Assist as needed. Observe the children charting their rainfall predictions and collections.

Accommodations/Modifications

Autism—Guide the child to encourage his participation in the collection of rainfall. Monitor his activity as the children measure and discuss their rain data.

Speech or Language Impairments—Define new vocabulary. Reinforce the child's correct language usage.

Hearing Impairments—Face the child when giving directions. Provide a chart and picture cues to explain the water collection.

Visual Impairments—Allow the child to touch the rain water as she measures her collection.

Cognitive and/or Developmental Delays—Provide a chart and picture cues to explain the water collection.

Emotional Disturbance—Provide a chart and picture cues to explain the water collection.

Other Health Impairments/Attention Deficit Hyperactive Disorder—Provide a chart and picture cues to explain the water collection.

Orthopedic Impairments—Help the child measure the rainfall in her rain collection jar.

Curriculum Connections

- **Art**—Add yellow cellophane to the Art Center so children can make "lightning" in their rain pictures.
- **Language and Literacy**—Individually or in small groups, ask children to tell you what they learned from the book *Thunder and Lightning*.
- **Math**—Compare the rainfall children collected in their jars by posting their chart displays on a classroom bulletin board.

Rain Chant

Time

5 minutes

Materials

Chart paper and marker (optional)

Objectives

Children will:

1. Recite a chant about the rain.
2. Describe their reactions to a sudden rainstorm.

Lesson

Note: This is a good chant or lesson to use if you have been surprised by a sudden rainstorm.

- Gather the children on the floor for Group or Circle Time, for a transition time, or for a scheduled song or fingerplay time.
- Recite the following chant to the children.

Pitter, Patter (author unknown) adapted by Karen Brunson
Pitter, patter, pitter, patter, (hold fingers up and slowly pulsate them like raindrops)
See the raindrops come. (slowly move fingers down)
Pitter, patter, pitter, patter, (hold fingers up and slowly pulsate them like raindrops)
Falling one by one. (slowly move fingers down)

How many raindrops make a storm? (hold arms at sides in questioning motion)
How many raindrops make a storm?
One little raindrop? (hold up one finger)
No, no, no. (shake head)
Two little raindrops? (hold up two fingers)
No, no, no. (shake head)
Millions of raindrops make a storm. (hold all fingers up and pulsate them like
     raindrops)
Billions of raindrops make a storm.

Pitter, patter, pitter, patter, (hold fingers up and slowly pulsate them like raindrops)
(Continue saying "pitter, patter, pitter, patter," quietly fading out.)

- Ask the children to describe how they feel about a sudden rainstorm.
- Teach the "Pitter, Patter" chant to the children. Have them repeat it after you.
- Print the chant on chart paper and recite the chant again, pointing to each word as you say it. Encourage the children to "read" it along with you.

Review

Use the chant during transition times.

Assessment Strategy

Observe each child chanting and making the finger and hand motions to the chant.

Accommodations/Modifications

Autism—Use your fingers to depict raindrops as you introduce the chant. Use picture cues to help the child learn the words.

Speech or Language Impairments—Slowly repeat the chant several times to enable the child to learn it. Review the chant each day until he can say it along with you.

Hearing Impairments—Record the chant on audiotape and have the child practice the chant at Center Time to practice the chant.

Visual Impairments—Give physical prompts and assist physically with movements.
Cognitive and/or Developmental Delays—Use audiotape, wiggling fingers, and picture cues to help the child learn the chant.

Emotional Disturbance—Discuss rainstorms with the child in advance in order to alleviate any fears he may have.

Other Health Impairments/Attention Deficit Hyperactive Disorder—Have the children repeat the chant while sitting, standing, and kneeling to provide opportunities for movement.

Orthopedic Impairments—Assist the child in making motions to go with the chant.

Curriculum Connections

- **Art**—If possible, make spattered chalk artwork by placing children's chalk drawings in the rain for a short period of time. Discuss the results of the rain's impact on the chalk.

- **Language and Literacy**—Ask the children to brainstorm on words that describe how rain sounds. Add these words to the classroom Word Wall.

- **Music**—Invite individual children to use their descriptive words about rain to make up other chants and songs about rain.

Rain Observation

Time

20–30 minutes

Materials

- Digital camera (optional)
- Drawing paper
- Crayons

Review

Later in the day, take another walk to see if there are any trails of water left from the rain.

Assessment Strategy

Discuss and have each child identify what she knows about rain.

Objectives

Children will:

1. Talk about how their environment is affected by rainfall.
2. Record their observations of rain.

Lesson

- Take the children on a walk outside after a rainfall. Have the children look for leaves, grass, buildings, and signs that are still wet with drops of rain.
- Ask the children to explore where the rain goes after it drips from those surfaces.
- Help the children find trails of water in the soil or on sidewalks.
- Have them look for areas where the rain has pooled or puddled.
- Take conventional or digital photographs of rain droplets.
- Return to the classroom for Group or Circle Time and engage the children in a discussion of what they saw. Encourage them to predict what will happen to the rain.
- Ask the children to draw what they saw on their walk outside.

Accommodations/Modifications

Autism—Allow the child to view the digital pictures as you take them.

Speech or Language Impairments—Define new words. Reinforce the child's participation in the discussion.

Hearing Impairments—Keep the child near you during the walk.

Visual Impairments—Have the child view the digital pictures as you take them.

Cognitive and/or Developmental Delays—Cue the child into specific areas to look for rain droplets.

Emotional Disturbance—Invite the child to take pictures to document the walk.

Other Health Impairments/Attention Deficit Hyperactive Disorder—Provide a peer buddy to assist the child during the walk.

Orthopedic Impairments—Provide an easy way for the child to participate in the walk. Provide time for her to go off the path as needed to see the rain "trails."

Curriculum Connections

- **Art**—Have the child draw and paint pictures of rain, using watercolor paint to add raindrops to their art.
- **Listening Center**—Purchase a CD or cassette recording of the sounds of rainfall for children to listen to.
- **Science**—Talk to small groups of children about why the earth needs rain.

Weather Chart

Time

10 minutes a day for a month

Materials

- Calendar chart
- Index cards
- Scissors
- Glue or tape
- Small pictures of rain, clouds, sun, wind, snow, ice

Preparation

Cut index cards to fit into the space for each day on your calendar. Prepare weather cards by gluing or taping a weather picture on to each index card. Prepare enough weather cards for the entire month.

Review

Each day, review the previous day's weather.

Assessment Strategy

Ask each child individually to discuss the current weather and the previous day's weather.

Objectives

Children will:

1. Report the weather they observe each morning.
2. Record the weather on a chart.

Lesson

- Discuss the weather at the beginning of each Group or Circle Time for a period of a month. Each day, select a child to go to a window or door and check the weather.
- Ask this child to select one of the pre-made weather picture cards that matches that day's weather outside. Help the child glue or tape the pictures recording the day's weather on the weather calendar.
- At the end of the month (or at the end of each week), help the children count the number of days in each specific weather category. Engage the children in a discussion of the weather over the past month or week.

Accommodations/Modifications

Autism—Name each of the weather pictures and ask the child to respond to each with a "yes" or "no" as he describes the weather of the day.

Speech or Language Impairments—Encourage the child to use complete sentences when he describes the day's weather.

Hearing Impairments—Use picture cues to help the child discuss the daily weather.

Visual Impairments—Have the child hold and inspect the weather cards as he chooses the day's weather outside.

Cognitive and/or Developmental Delays—Use the picture cards to elicit a "yes" or "no" response to help the child describe the weather.

Emotional Disturbance—Have the child hold the picture cards to assist in selecting the weather for the day.

Other Health Impairments/Attention Deficit Hyperactive Disorder—Have the child count the number of days in each weather category.

Orthopedic Impairments—Use a peer assistant as needed.

Curriculum Connections

- **Math**—Count the number of days with each type of weather. Ask the children to tell you the weather type that occurred most often and the type that occurred least often.
- **Science**—Point out to the children on the weather chart the number of days each type of weather occurred. Ask them to predict the next day's weather.

Trees and Seasonal Changes

Time

20–30 minutes, repeated once a month

Materials

- Tree, located on the playground or near your school
- Small lapboards (or corrugated cardboard)
- Scissors, contact paper (see directions to the right)
- Paper
- Pencils, crayons, markers
- Date stamp (optional)

Objectives

Children will:

1. Observe and document their observations of a specific tree during different seasons of the year.
2. Select their favorite season based on their observations.

Preparation

Make lapboards by cutting corrugated cardboard to a size that fits on a child's lap and covering it with contact paper.

Lesson

- Have the children gather outside around a tree that your class has selected as "their" tree. This ongoing lesson will document one specific tree.
- As the children sit around the class tree, engage them in a discussion about what they see on, in, and around the tree.
- Encourage them to describe the colors, the foliage, the grass, the insects, the surrounding dirt or landscape, and the colors in the sky.
- Ask the children to use the lapboards, paper, crayons, pencils, and markers to draw what they see.
- Help each child write or stamp the date on her picture.
- Repeat this activity each month during the school year.
- Organize the children's pictures into individual "Tree Books" depicting the changes in the tree, the surrounding area, and the weather.

Accommodations/Modifications

Autism—Use picture cues to target the child's observations of multiple aspects of the tree. Develop a dialogue about the tree as the child draws it.

Speech or Language Impairments—Explain any new vocabulary related to the tree.

Hearing Impairments—Use picture cues to target the child's observations of multiple aspects of the tree.

Review

After looking out the window—if you can see the tree—and then looking at their pictures, discuss the changes in the tree with the children.

Assessment Strategy

Ask each child to discuss her tree picture(s).

Visual Impairments—Provide opportunities for the child to touch and smell the tree. Crayon rubbings of the bark will offer an additional dimension to the child's knowledge of the tree.

Cognitive and/or Developmental Delays—Use picture cues to target the child's observation of multiple aspects of the tree. Talk with her about the tree while she is drawing. Allow the child to touch and smell the tree and the surrounding area to add new information to the lesson.

Emotional Disturbance—Engage the child in dialogue as she draws the tree.

Other Health Impairments/Attention Deficit Hyperactive Disorder—Provide picture cues to assist the child in focusing the tree and related details.

Orthopedic Impairments—Provide grips and assists for the crayons. Taping the paper to a lap board may assist the child in drawing.

Curriculum Connections

- **Art**—Provide various art materials so the child can continue creating tree pictures from their observations. During the spring season, remember to add pastel tissue paper to the Art Center so children can add flowers to their trees.

- **Language and Literacy**—Read *The Giving Tree* by Shel Silverstein to the children.

- **Science**—With two or three children, categorize the similarities and differences among their pictures.

Preparing the Garden

Time

30–45 minutes

Materials

- Garden tools, such as shovels, hand shovels, gardening gloves, garden rakes (child-size, if possible)
- Boards, fencing, or any other material to mark the border of the garden
- Compost or soil, enough to fill the garden area
- Sign for garden and permanent marker

Objectives

Children will:

1. Work in the garden.
2. Assist in preparing the soil for a class garden.

Preparation

Using a stick, draw lines in the dirt to mark the edges of the garden area.

Lesson

- Gather the children outside in a specified area that has been designated as the class garden. With the children, note the borders of the garden.
- Working from the center of the garden, demonstrate how to turn the soil to prepare for the class garden.
- As the children help turn the soil using handheld shovels, talk about the soil's color, texture, and moisture content. If the children come across any bugs, insects, or worms, take this opportunity to discuss the habitat of these creatures. Some creatures will be beneficial to your garden and should stay. Others should be removed to other areas where they can continue living without disturbing or being disturbed by the class garden.
- Once the soil is turned, mark the border of the garden with boards, fencing, or other appropriate material. If necessary, fill the garden with compost or soil.
- Prepare a sign for the garden listing the names of children in the class and the date of construction.
- For a week or more, the children can continue turning the soil inside their garden and observing the dirt and life in the garden.

Review

Place soil from the garden in the sand table and allow the children to continue to explore the soil.

Assessment Strategy

Discuss each child's work in the garden. Allow each child to share her experiences working in this garden and in other gardens.

Accommodations/Modifications

Autism—Encourage and help the child participate. Verbalize the process of turning the soil in the garden.

Speech or Language Impairments—Discuss the activity of turning the garden soil and the bugs, insects, or worms that may be found. Encourage the child to use complete sentence structure.

Hearing Impairments—Face the child when talking to him. Model the action of turning the soil.

Visual Impairments—Describe and model the process of turning the soil in the garden.

Cognitive and/or Developmental Delays—Discuss the activity of turning the soil in the garden and the bugs, insects, or worms that may be found.

Emotional Disturbance—Discuss the activity of turning the soil in the garden and the bugs, insects, or worms that may be found.

Orthopedic Impairments—Use Velcro straps to help the child use the hand shovel.

Curriculum Connections

- **Art**—Provide opportunities for the children to draw what they see and what they think the garden will look like when it is in bloom.
- **Language and Literacy**—Provide opportunities for the children to make a book charting the timeline of the plant growth or garden changes.
- **Science**—Plant and tend to seeds in the classroom. Match the new growth to pictures of plant life.

IN THE GARDEN
Planting Seeds

Time

20–30 minutes

Materials

- Selected packets of seeds for planting
- Small handheld shovels
- Watering cans, purchased or made (see directions for making watering cans in Preparation)

Objectives

Children will:

1. Plant seeds in the prepared garden.
2. Observe and discuss the growth of seeds.

Preparation

Make watering cans from old plastic quart- or gallon-size water jugs, removing the cap. Before the children arrive, use a nail to pierce small holes in the upper three inches on the side opposite the handle.

Lesson

- At Group or Circle Time, gather with the children near the prepared garden and check to see if the soil is soft enough to plant seeds.
- In groups of four to six, have the children take turns planting seeds in areas of the garden. This should be a group project (rather than designating a single area for each child) in order to alleviate individual disappointment if some plants do not grow as expected. With group areas, there is a greater likelihood that the seeds planted in each area will sprout and grow. The group effort will foster a sense of community among the children.
- Once the garden is planted, continue to have the children observe, water, and tend the garden on a daily or weekly basis.

Accommodations/Modifications

Autism—Select a participation group so the child participates in the planting of and tending to the garden and in discussing garden activities.

Speech or Language Impairments—Encourage and reinforce the child's efforts to use correct sentence structure. Define unfamiliar words.

Hearing Impairments—Face the child when talking. Select a participation group so the child participates in the planting of and tending to the garden and in discussing garden activities.

Visual Impairments—Define unfamiliar vocabulary. Select a participation group so that the child participates in the planting of and tending to the garden, and in discussing garden activities.

Review

Each day, discuss the planting of the seeds and observe any growth. Weed the garden of unwanted growth.

Assessment Strategy

Observe each child planting her seeds.

Cognitive and/or Developmental Delays—Have the child participate with a small group of friends. Repeat directions as needed.

Emotional Disturbance—Have the child decide if she would like to work with other children, with you, or plant the seed by herself.

Other Health Impairments/Attention Deficit Hyperactive Disorder—Monitor the child's engagement. Help the child focus by verbally repeating the directions for planting.

Orthopedic Impairments—Help the child get to the appropriate level of the garden for planting.

Curriculum Connections

- **Art**—Provide opportunities for children to draw pictures of themselves and others planting seeds.
- **Language and Literacy**—Offer opportunities for children to discuss the feel of the soil. Provide descriptive words for them to use in conversations about the garden. Have the children prepare an audio tape to sequence what they did to plant the garden. Adding photographs will enhance the activity.
- **Science**—Plant and tend to seeds in the classroom. Use actual photographs of the children and the garden to enhance their concept knowledge of plant growth. Match the new growth to pictures of plant life.

Caterpillars

Time

20–30 minutes

Materials

- Poster board
- Scissors
- Template of butterfly (see illustration)
- *The Very Hungry Caterpillar* by Eric Carle
- Tissue paper pieces
- Glue
- Water
- Paintbrushes

Objectives

Children will:

1. Describe the metamorphosis of a caterpillar to a butterfly.
2. Imitate the dance of metamorphosis.

Preparation

Use the butterfly in the illustration as a guide to make a butterfly pattern. Cut one poster board butterfly shape for each child in your class. Thin the glue with water.

Lesson

- Read the book, *The Very Hungry Caterpillar* by Eric Carle.
- Recite the following and demonstrate the actions of this metamorphosis dance for the children.

Metamorphosis Dance, with motions added by Diana Nabors

A little egg lay on the leaf. (curl up in a ball as an egg)

Then one day out popped a tiny caterpillar. (pop up and stand straight and tall, keeping hands and arms close to the body wiggle from side to side)

*The caterpillar began to eat and eat and eat. (*use hands to gather and eat food, then begin to widen foot stance, bend backwards and use hands to show a "full belly")

Then the caterpillar spins a chrysalis and goes to sleep. (lie on the floor with hands at sides and roll back and forth until becoming still)

The caterpillar sleeps for about two weeks, (close eyes and remain still)

Then begins to waken. (slowly open eyes and stretch)

Out comes a beautiful butterfly. (place hands on hips to form wings and walk around room "showing off" the beautiful colors)

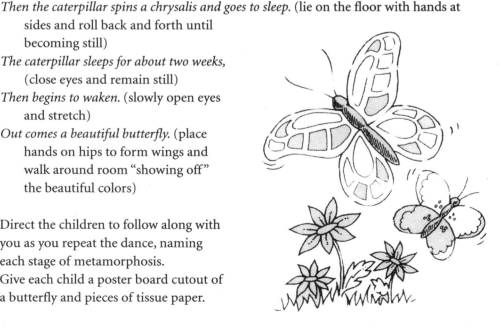

- Direct the children to follow along with you as you repeat the dance, naming each stage of metamorphosis.
- Give each child a poster board cutout of a butterfly and pieces of tissue paper.

Review

While the children are creating their butterflies, talk with them about the stages of metamorphosis and the metamorphosis dance.

Assessment Strategy

Observe each child creating his butterfly and participating in the metamorphosis dance.

■ Help the children use the thinned glue to attach pieces of tissue paper to their butterfly cutouts, creating their own beautiful butterflies.

Accommodations/Modifications

Autism—Provide opportunities for the child to interact using short phrases enhanced by you.

Speech or Language Impairments—Define new vocabulary. Encourage the child to use complete sentences in the discussion.

Hearing Impairments—Let the child sit near you when you read the story.

Visual Impairments—Provide seating near you when you read the story. Have art materials accessible to the child.

Cognitive and/or Developmental Delays—Encourage the child's participation through verbal praise.

Emotional Disturbance—Encourage the child's participation through verbal praise and gestures.

Other Health Impairments/Attention Deficit Hyperactive Disorder—Stand near the child to help him with body awareness, or use a carpet square or towel to designate his area.

Orthopedic Impairments—Place thinned glue in a low lip bowl or flat tray. Use Velcro straps to help the child manipulate the paintbrush.

Curriculum Extensions

■ **Language and Literacy**—Discuss how caterpillars become butterflies. Suggest that the children draw pictures to go with the book.

■ **Math**—Point out the symmetry of a butterfly's coloration.

■ **Science**—Discuss the meaning of the word *metamorphosis*.

Ant Watch

Time

20 minutes outside followed with observation checks at 30-minute intervals

Materials

- Cardboard
- Scissors
- Chart paper and marker
- Typical picnic foods that ants might like, such as peanut butter, jelly, tuna fish, orange slices, and crackers
- Picnic basket (use a box or a bag if you do not have a picnic basket)
- Plastic spoons

Objectives

Children will:

1. Observe ants in their habitat.
2. Predict which food will attract the most ants.

Preparation

Cut cardboard into 3" squares. Place the food items in a picnic basket (or in a box or a bag).

Lesson

- Gather the children outdoors near an anthill to predict what the ants will choose to eat. Make sure the children are standing near, not in, the area of ant traffic.
- With the children, brainstorm food items the ants would be attracted to and predict which will be most popular. Record their ideas on chart paper.
- Return to a non-ant area and show the children various foods one might find in a picnic basket.
- Divide the children into groups of two or four children.
- Help each group select one of the foods so each group has a different food. Have them place a tablespoon-size portion of each food on a cardboard square.
- Have them leave the food near where the ants have been noticed. (Place each cardboard square of food around the anthill (or several anthills if you find more than one anthill.)
- At five intervals of 30 minutes each, have the children check their food squares and count the number of ants on each one.
- After each observation time, help the children graph the number of ants on their cardboard square.
- Engage the children in a discussion about the ant activity. Check their original predictions.
- Talk about any food that has been moved and any that has not been moved by the ants during the two-hour activity.

Review

With the children, discuss their findings and chart the differences among them.

Assessment Strategy

Talk with each child about her findings and check her predictions of the ants' favorite food.

Accommodations/Modifications

Autism—Use verbal cues to help the child attend to the ants and their trails.

Speech or Language Impairments—Encourage the child to use complete sentences in the discussion about ants and their environment.

Hearing Impairments—Use visual gestures to help the child attend to the task of observing ants.

Visual Impairments—Dialogue with the class as you help the child prepare the food squares for observation purposes.

Cognitive and/or Developmental Delays— Dialogue with the class as you help the children prepare the food squares for observation purposes.

Emotional Disturbance—Help the child predict what the ants will do when the food squares are placed near the anthill.

Other Health Impairments/Attention Deficit Hyperactive Disorder—Through dialogue and verbal cues, help the child observe and discuss how the ants respond to the food.

Orthopedic Impairments—Assist the child in moving around the anthill without disrupting the other children as they observe the ants.

Curriculum Connections

- **Art**—Provide several sizes of Styrofoam balls and chenille sticks (also known as pipe cleaners) for children to use to create ant creatures.
- **Dramatic Play**—Add a picnic basket, napkins, and eating utensils to the Home Living Center so children can pretend to go on a picnic in their dramatic play.
- **Math**—Count the number of ants on the playground, graph the ant count, and share the results of the graphs with another class or with families.
- **Science**—Observe the ants and the feeding process of ants. Develop a science log booklet that includes children's drawings of the Ant Watch.

Birds

Time

- 15 minutes during the first lesson
- 5 minutes over the next few days

Materials

- Sack of birdseed
- Small paper cups
- Feather duster
- Scissors
- Paint
- Paper

Objectives

Children will:

1. Observe and discuss information about birds in their habitats.
2. Imitate bird behaviors.

Preparation

For a few days prior to the lesson, ask the children to observe the birds outside. On the day of the lesson, pour a small amount of birdseed into a small paper cup, filling one for each child. Cut individual feathers from a feather duster.

Lesson

- After the children have had a few days to observe the birds outside, talk with them at a Group or Circle Time to predict what the birds will eat.
- Give each child a small amount of birdseed to spread on the playground.
- Over the next few days, have the children watch the birds feeding on the playground.
- Encourage the children to note which times of the day they see more birds feeding and which times they see fewer birds feeding.
- Suggest that the children use feathers as paintbrushes in the Art Center.
- Encourage the children to paint pictures of the birds they see with the feather brushes.
- During transition times throughout the day, encourage the children to move like the birds they have observed.

Accommodations/Modifications

Autism—Use verbal cues to help the child observe birds and spread birdseed.

Speech or Language Impairments—Encourage the child to use complete sentences in the discussion of the birds and their behaviors.

Hearing Impairments—Use visual gestures to help the child attend to the task of observing birds.

Visual Impairments—Talk with the child as you call attention to the birds and their behaviors.

Review

Discuss with the children their observations of the behavior of birds.

Cognitive and/or Developmental Delays—Talk with the child as you provide seeds for children to use to feed the birds.

Emotional Disturbance—Help the child predict what the birds will do when birdseed is spread on the playground.

Other Health Impairments/Attention Deficit Hyperactive Disorder—Through dialogue and verbal cues, assist the child in observing and discussing the bird feeding activity.

Orthopedic Impairments—Assist the child if he needs help distributing the birdseed.

Assessment Strategy

Ask each child to tell you what birds eat.

Curriculum Extensions

- **Art**—Point out all of the various colors of birds to encourage the children to use many colors in their pictures of birds.

- **Math**—Count the number of birds seen at any one time and chart the results.

- **Science**—Take photographs of the birds and the feeding times of the birds to display in the Science Center or on a classroom bulletin board.

- **More Science**—When some of the seeds cast for the birds begin to sprout, call the children's attention to these new plants.

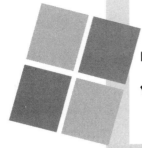

Worms

Time

- 20 minutes
- 5-minute observations during the next two weeks

Materials

- Clear, unbreakable, gallon-size jar
- Moist potting soil
- 3-5 earthworms
- Food for the worms (unsweetened cornflakes and lettuce)
- Large strip or sheet of black paper that fits around the jar
- Tape
- Gravel

Objectives

Children will:

1. Identify an earthworm.
2. Note the characteristics of earthworms.

Preparation

Fill the jar with 1" of gravel, 3"–5" of potting soil, and a few earthworms. Add food for the worms, such as unsweetened cornflakes and lettuce. Cover the jar with a large sheet or strip of black paper. Secure with tape.

Lesson

- At Group or Circle Time, show the children the jar you prepared. Ask them if they think anything is living inside the jar, and then remove the black paper from the jar.
- Have the children observe the jar of soil. Carefully remove an earthworm from the jar. Hold the worm in your hand. Allow the children to look at the worm, and then place the worm back in the jar.
- Allow the children to continue to observe the earthworms as they tunnel through the soil in the jar.
- Place the black paper around the jar when the children are not observing the earthworms. Doing this will encourage the worms to leave the dark middle of the jar, and their tunnels will be more evident when you remove the black paper.
- Tell the class that the tunnels the earthworms make keep soil fertile and aerated.

Review

Continue the discussion and observation of the worms over a period of two or three weeks.

Assessment Strategy

Talk to each child about her observations of the worms to assess what she has learned from the demonstration.

Accommodations/Modifications

Autism—Prior to the lesson, provide a time for the child to watch the worm's movements.

Speech or Language Impairments—Verbalize what the children are seeing in the worm's movements. Define any new vocabulary.

Hearing Impairments—Provide a separate time for the child to watch the worm's movements.

Visual Impairments— Provide a separate time for the child to watch the worm's movements. Allow the child to touch the worm, if desired.

Cognitive and/or Developmental Delays— Provide a separate time for the child to watch the worm's movements. Supervise the child in touching the worm, if desired.

Emotional Disturbance— Provide a separate time for the child to watch the worm's movements. Supervise the child in touching the worm, if desired.

Other Health Impairments/Attention Deficit Hyperactive Disorder—Provide guidance and reinforcement during the lesson.

Orthopedic Impairments—Provide an opportunity for the child to manipulate the jar to observe the worms.

Curriculum Connections

- **Language and Literacy**—Find children's encyclopedias that show earthworms in their natural environments. Place these in the Book Center for children to enjoy.
- **Science**—Take a Nature Walk during the week to find earthworms in their natural environments.
- **More Science**—Place a cookie sheet with soil on it in the Science Center so children can make their own earthworm tunnels with their fingers.

Worm Art

Time

15–20 minutes

Materials

- String
- Scissors
- Washable paint
- Trays
- Two earthworms on a moistened, smooth tray
- Art paper

Preparation

Cut string into 10" lengths. Pour paint into trays.

Review

Keep pieces of string and paint in trays in the Art Center for a week so all of the children have multiple opportunities to create "worm art."

Assessment Strategy

Observe the child as he is creating his artwork using a variety of materials.

Objectives

Children will:

1. Talk about creatures that live in the garden.
2. Recreate the movement of worms through art.

Lesson

- Show the children two earthworms on a moistened tray. Discuss the movement of the earthworms along the tray. Return the worms to the jar from the previous lesson or put them back into the soil outside.
- Have the children visit the Art Center in small groups to create their own worm art.
- Have the children dip a piece of string in a tray of washable paint, and then slowly drag it across paper to create their own art design. Remind them to keep the string close to the surface of the paper, just like worms move along the ground. **Note:** Reminding children to keep the string on the paper (like worms on the ground) and to move the string slowly across the page avoids messy painting experiences.

Accommodations/Modifications

Autism—Prior to the lesson, provide a time for the child to watch the worm's movements.

Speech or Language Impairments—Verbalize what the child is seeing in the worm's movements. Define any new vocabulary.

Hearing Impairments— Provide a separate time for the child to watch the worm's movements.

Visual Impairments— Allow the child to touch the worm, if desired.

Cognitive and/or Developmental Delays— Provide a separate time for the child to watch the worm's movements. Supervise the child in touching the worm, if desired.

Emotional Disturbance— Provide a separate time for the child to watch the worm's movements. Supervise the child in touching the worm, if desired.

Other Health Impairments/Attention Deficit Hyperactive Disorder—Provide verbal guidance and reinforcement during the lesson.

Orthopedic Impairments—Provide longer string for the child to pull across the paper.

Curriculum Connections

- **Language and Literacy**—Develop small-group discussions of the worms as children observe them in the Science Center. Invite children to think of words that describe their movements, such as *wiggly, jiggly, squirmy*, and so on.
- **Outdoors**—Encourage children to move around the playground like earthworms.

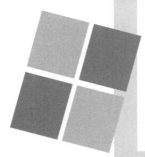

Plant, Bark, and Leaf Rubbings

Time

20–30 minutes

Materials

- Large sack for collecting items
- Magnifying glass(es)
- Paper
- Crayons
- Class book pages

Review

Place the class book and rubbings in a special interest center for children to look at and discuss.

Assessment Strategy

Observe individual children while they collect their debris and make their rubbings.

Objectives

Children will:

1. Collect different plants and parts of plants (plant debris) as they clean the garden.
2. Use the debris to create art with plant, bark, and leaf rubbings.

Lesson

- After a windy day, have the children gather around the garden to clean up the school grounds or garden. **Note:** For the safety of the children, clear away any trash from the school grounds or garden before they arrive.
- Collect items that have fallen into the class garden or playground with the children.
- Have them place any item from nature—such as leaves, pieces of bark, and pine needles—into the collection bag.
- When you return indoors, engage the children in a discussion about how the items ended up in the garden or on the playground. Place some of the items on a classroom table and let the children use a magnifying glass to inspect them.
- Show the children how to use soft crayons and paper to make rubbings of these items from nature. Help the children label their found items from the garden and create a class book titled "Items Found in the Garden."

Accommodations/Modifications

Autism—Encourage the child to participate in the discussion of the items picked up from the garden.

Speech or Language Impairments—Encourage and reinforce the child's use of correct and complete sentence structure.

Hearing Impairments—Face the child when speaking to her.

Visual Impairments—Help the child find and talk about the items from the garden.

Cognitive and/or Developmental Delays— Help the child find items from the garden.

Emotional Disturbance— Help the child find and talk about the items from the garden.

Other Health Impairments/Attention Deficit Hyperactive Disorder—Help the child maintain her focus by asking her questions about the items she has selected.

Curriculum Connections

- **Art**—Children might want to make collages with the items they collected from the garden.
- **Language and Literacy**—After the children have completed their artwork, discuss the variations among the rubbings.

INTRODUCTION TO

Manners

Time

15–20 minutes

Materials

- Puppet theatre or large box with hole for puppet stage
- 2 puppets

Objectives

Children will:

1. Know that manners consist of being polite so that they can live and play with other people.
2. Differentiate between polite and rude behavior.

Preparation

Set up a puppet theater, or make a large box into a puppet stage.

Lesson

Note: Do this lesson during Group or Circle Time, or later on in the day, preferably before centers, lunch, or free play.

- Introduce one puppet as Miss Manners. Tell the children that Miss Manners likes to be nice to other people and that she has good manners.
- Then introduce the other puppet as Miss Rude. Tell the children that Miss Rude is selfish and does not care how others feel. **Note:** Alternately, the puppets can be "Mr. Manners" and "Mr. Rude," "Manners the Mouse" and "Rude the Rabbit." Use your imagination.
- Compare and contrast how Miss Manners and Miss Rude act in certain scenarios, such as chewing their food, using tissues when they cough or sneeze, sharing toys, and using napkins.
- Set up a puppet theater (a large box or a table turned on its side).
- Give each child a chance to be Miss Manners and to be Miss Rude. Talk about how it makes them feel when someone uses good manners and when someone is rude to them.

Accommodations/Modifications

Autism—Use pictures or clip art to depict for example, pictures that show chewing, sneezing, playing with toys, and chewing with one's mouth closed.

Review

On a poster board, draw a line down the center, and write *DO* on one side of the page and *DON'T* on the other side. Have the children tell you what they do to show good manners and what they should not do. Write down their suggestions. If possible, draw diagrams based on what the children say.

Assessment Strategy

Observe individual children as they go through their day to see which manners they need to work on and which they have mastered.

Speech or Language Impairments—Use specific gestures or sign language to show good manners and bad manners to a child who is a reluctant speaker and who has language delays. If a child has expressive language problems, allow him to point to pictures that show both good and bad manners rather than responding verbally. Let a child who is unable to speak participate by using Picture Communication Symbols clip art depicting good and bad manners.

Hearing Impairments—Seat the child near the front of the group. Use gestures, pictures, and objects during the activity.

Visual Impairments—Let the child touch props that accompany the instructions, such as a tissue, small toys, and a napkin.

Cognitive and/or Developmental Delays—As you conduct the activity, rephrase your instructions and your comments using simplified language. If needed, use prompts when the child takes a turn with Miss Manners and Miss Rude.

Emotional Disturbance—Seat the child with behavior problems near you when you introduce the puppets.

Other Health Impairments/Attention Deficit Hyperactive Disorder—Be sure you have the child's attention before you introduce the lesson. Use a predictable strategy to get the child's attention, such as holding up one finger before introducing the puppets. Seat the child near you.

Orthopedic Impairments—For the child with severe fine motor problems, provide an adapted holder for the puppets.

Curriculum Connections

- **Book Center**—Place books about manners in the Book Center. Suggestions include *The Berenstain Bears Forget Their Manners* by Stan and Jan Berenstain, *Manners* by Aliki, and *Soup Should Be Seen, Not Heard* by Beth Brainard and Sheila Behr. This book is written for older children, but the pictures in the book will be useful when the lesson is introduced.
- **Dramatic Play**—Place the DOs and DON'Ts list above the Kitchen Center. Remind the children to use their good manners when they are playing in the kitchen.
- **Math**—Count the number of DOs and DON'Ts on your manners poster.
- **Social Studies**—Talk about manners in other cultures and in our culture. For example, in some cultures it is considered good manners to burp or belch out loud after a meal! Discuss other differences in manners in other lands.

Sharing

Time

15–20 minutes

Materials

- Stuffed animals, one for each child
- Bag
- Pudding cups and spoons, one for each child

Preparation

Put a number of stuffed animals in a bag. Make sure there are enough for each child.

Objectives

Children will:

1. Describe why it is important to share with their friends.
2. Describe how they feel someone shares or refuses to share

Lesson

- Gather a small group of children. Give one child a stuffed animal to hold and say, "Here. You can play with this *(name of the stuffed animal)*. Let's share the animal." Ask, "How do our friends feel when we share with them?" Then grab the toy and say, "I want *(name of the stuffed animal)*. It's mine." Ask, "Is this sharing? How do people feel when someone grabs their toy?" **Note:** Giving children examples of negative behavior can be helpful when teaching a concept to children with cognitive difficulties.

- Now talk with the children about what happened. Encourage them to say why they think it is important to take turns and to share. Talk about how it makes them feel when someone shares toys with them and then takes the toy away.

- Distribute one stuffed animal to each child. Ask the children how they feel when other people share with them.

- Take an armful of stuffed animals out of a bag and say, "You can't have these. They are all mine." Ask the children how they feel when someone hogs all of the toys.

- Introduce the song "The More We Share Together."

The More We Share Together adapted by Sharon Lynch
(Tune: "The More We Get Together")
The more we share together, together, together,
The more we share together, together, together,
The happier we'll be.
With your toys and my toys,
With my toys and your toys,
The more we share together, the happier we'll be.

The more we share together, together, together,
The happier we'll be.
With your blocks and my blocks,
With my blocks and your blocks,
The more we share together, the happier we'll be.

- At Snack Time, divide the class in half. Give each child in one half of the class two pudding cups; give each child in the other half two spoons. Explain that they have a wonderful snack of chocolate pudding. But who can eat it? In order to eat it, each child must find a friend to share with him.

Review

Using a picture schedule of the day, talk with the children about all of the things they can do throughout the day to share with their friends.

Assessment Strategy

Observe the children during free play, Center Time, and on the playground to notice who is successful in sharing and who needs to learn more about sharing.

■ At the end of Snack Time, review the experience of sharing. Sing "The More We Share Together" again to close the activity.

Accommodations/Modifications

Autism—Use clip art or pictures to show the following: animals, happy, sad, angry, pudding, spoon, sharing. As you talk about sharing, pair a picture with the action you are describing.

Speech or Language Impairments—Use gestures or sign language to promote the participation of a child who is a reluctant speaker or who has language delays. For a child with expressive language problems, allow her to point to pictures rather than responding verbally. Let a child who is unable to speak participate by using Picture Communication Symbols or clip art.

Hearing Impairments—Seat the child near you during the lesson. Pair gestures and objects with verbal explanations throughout the lesson.

Visual Impairments—Provide opportunities for the child to touch the stuffed animals, pudding containers, and spoons as you explain the lesson.

Cognitive and/or Developmental Delays—As you explain the lesson, rephrase your explanations with short, simple speech accompanied by gestures referring to the stuffed animals, pudding, and spoons.

Emotional Disturbance—Seat children with behavior problems near you as you take stuffed animals out of the bag and share the snack.

Other Health Impairments/Attention Deficit Hyperactive Disorder—Seat the child near you. Before taking each stuffed animal out of the bag, make sure you have her attention.

Orthopedic Impairments—Place the stuffed animal in the child's hand if she has difficulty holding objects.

Curriculum Connections

- **Block Center**—Provide room for several children to play together and share the cars and trucks.
- **Book Center**—Place two comfy chairs where children can share books together.
- **Math**—At Snack Time, slice a pizza for the children to share. Count the number of children and slice the pizza into the correct number of pieces, counting aloud as you cut. Ask the children if there is enough for everyone to share.
- **Science**—Explain that most animals and people do not live alone, that they live in groups and must get along in groups. Provide sets of animals in a box. Have the children sort the animals by species.
- **Social Studies**—Provide pictures of people in other countries and cultures who live in groups and must share their food, their work, and their homes.

MANNERS

Saying "Please" and "Thank You"

Time

15–25 minutes

Materials

- Toys
- Crackers

Objectives

Children will:

1. Say "please" and "thank you" as they share with their classmates.
2. State why it is important to say "please" and "thank you."

Lesson

- Introduce the concept of using good manners by stating why it is important to say "please" and "thank you" to others.
- Give a child a toy and explain that you are going to use good manners to ask him to hold the toy. Say, "May I hold the *(name of the toy)*, please?"
- Then give another child a toy and say, "Give me that *(name of the toy)*."
- Ask the children which approach uses good manners. Which makes them want to share with others? Explain that you will be talking about saying "please" and "thank you," which are often called "magic words." Using "please" is a polite way of asking someone to do something; saying "thank you" shows that we are grateful when someone gives us something or does something nice for us.
- Talk about different experiences the children might have had with other children using "please" and "thank you" when they were sharing. Discuss why it is so important to say "please" and "thank you."
- Pass out crackers. Remind each child to use the magic words of "please" and "thank you" if they want a cracker.

Accommodations/Modifications

Autism—Emphasize that the child needs to look at the person he is speaking to when he says "please" and "thank you."

Speech or Language Impairments—Use sign language and verbal models to prompt the child to use the words "please" and "thank you."

Hearing Impairments—Seat the child near you. Use signs for "please" and "thank you" as you teach the lesson.

Visual Impairments—As you give the child the toy or the cracker, explain what you are doing verbally.

Cognitive and/or Developmental Delays—Use signs to prompt the child to say "please" and "thank you."

Review

Role play the use of "please" and "thank you" prior to Center Time. Remind children as they go into centers that they need to use the magic words of "please" and "thank you" when they play with their friends. Ask the families to remind their children to use "please" and "thank you" at home.

Assessment Strategy

Observe the children as they interact with their peers during Center Time and on the playground. Notice which children use "please" and "thank you" regularly and which children need reminders.

Emotional Disturbance—Seat the child next to you while you are presenting the lesson. Have several other children model the use of "please" and "thank you" before you ask this child to use the magic words.

Other Health Impairments/Attention Deficit Hyperactive Disorder—Emphasize the fact that the child will need to pay attention and to wait his turn. Use a gesture such as holding up one finger to gain the child's attention before giving instructions. Use a sign for "wait" to remind the child to wait his turn.

Orthopedic Impairments—Encourage the child to use both hands to hold the toy at midline. This is helpful when children have difficulty with grasp and release. Hand-over-hand or other forms of assistance are often useful when the child eats the cracker.

Curriculum Connections

- **Language and Literacy**—Write a story on chart paper about using good manners such as saying "please" and "thank you." Ask each child to contribute to the story.
- **Math**—Make a bar graph showing how many times "please" and "thank you" are used during Circle Time, Center Time, or during an entire day.
- **Social Studies**—Talk about the way other countries say "please" and "thank you." For example, in Spanish the word for "thank you" is "gracias."

MANNERS

Conversations

Time

20–30 minutes

Materials

■ Nerf ball
■ Several puppets

Objectives

Children will:

1. Participate in a conversation.
2. Use the following conversational skills: waiting for their turn to talk, looking at the person who is talking, using their inside voice, and ending a conversation.

Lesson

■ Begin the lesson by explaining to children that a *conversation* is when we talk to each other.

■ Say, "It's like a ball game." Throw the ball to one of the children. "I take my turn to talk, then you take your turn to talk." Ask the child to throw you the ball.

■ Throw the ball to another child. Say, "I take my turn, then you take your turn." Ask the child to throw the ball to you.

■ Throw the ball to several children, emphasizing taking turns.

■ Ask the child to throw the ball to a friend. Say, "John takes his turn, then Judy takes her turn."

■ Explain that when we have a conversation, we take turns talking.

■ Use puppets to demonstrate appropriate and inappropriate ways to carry on conversations. **Note:** Providing positive and negative examples can be helpful when teaching children with special needs.

■ When you are working with the puppets, ask the children to tell you which scenario presents the following: waiting one's turn to talk, looking at the person who is speaking; using inside voices; or ending a conversation appropriately. Have the child use one of the puppets and you use the other.

■ Examples of positive and negative scenarios include the following: having the puppet wait rather than interrupt; looking at the conversational partner rather than looking in the opposite direction; using an inside voice rather than yelling; and saying, "I have to go now. See you later" rather than walking away in the middle of a conversation.

Accommodations/Modifications

Autism—Preteach the following concepts: inside voice versus yelling; interrupting versus waiting your turn; looking at the speaker versus looking away. Work with the families and the child's speech-language pathologist whenever possible. Make cue cards using drawings and words to remind the child to use an inside voice, to wait her turn, and to look at the speaker.

Review

Write the words "How to Have a Conversation" at the top of the poster board. Ask the children to tell you things they need to remember about carrying on a conversation. Use markers to write what they say on the poster board.

Assessment Strategy

Using a doll family, ask each child to help you with a family conversation. Have the child tell you what the dolls need to do when they have a conversation (wait to take a turn, look at the person talking, and politely end the conversation). If necessary, provide prompts to help the child remember.

Speech or Language Impairments—Rehearse verbal responses and provide cue cards with drawings before eliciting the child's response for inside voice versus yelling, interrupting versus waiting your turn, and looking at the speaker versus looking away.

Hearing Impairments—Seat the child near the speaker. Rehearse verbal responses.

Visual Impairments—Gain the child's attention before throwing the ball. Instruct the child to turn toward the child she is talking to.

Cognitive and/or Developmental Delays—Use verbal prompts and cue cards when asking the child to wait for her turn. Model the responses with several children before asking the child to take her turn.

Emotional Disturbance—Have the child sit or stand near you. Model the responses with several children before asking the child to take her turn.

Other Health Impairments/Attention Deficit Hyperactive Disorder—Have the child stand or sit near you. Gain her attention with a consistent cue such as holding up one finger before giving instructions.

Orthopedic Impairments—Help the child catch the ball and place the puppets on her hands.

Curriculum Connections

- **Book Center**—Place two cozy chairs side-by-side to encourage the children to have conversations while reading together.
- **Dramatic Play**—Provide costumes, props, and two toy microphones to encourage social conversation during dramatic play. These props work especially well in the Home Living Center and the Kitchen Center.
- **Science**—Provide science books with pictures of the mouth, eyes, and ears so children can see the parts of the body engaged in carrying on conversations.

Table Manners

Time

30–35 minutes

Materials

- *The Berenstain Bears Forget Their Manners* by Stan and Jan Berenstain
- Paper plates, cups, utensils, napkins
- Puppet
- Cookies or crackers

Objectives

Children will:

1. Give at least one example of table manners.
2. Distinguish between good manners and bad manners.

Lesson

- At Group or Circle Time, read *The Berenstain Bears Forget Their Manners.*
- Ask the children what they know about manners at the dinner table. If the children do not know, review the table manners they should use: chew with your mouth closed, use your spoon and fork, keep your elbows off the table, use your napkin to wipe your mouth, and ask politely for things that you need.
- With a puppet, paper plates, utensils, cookies or crackers, cup, and napkin, model examples of good and bad manners.
- Ask the children to tell you whether (the name of the puppet) is using good manners or bad manners. Remind children to use their good manners during Snack Time.

Accommodations/Modifications

Autism—Use Picture Communication Symbols or clip art to provide pictorial cues for the child during the group discussion.

Speech or Language Impairments—Provide a lead-in sentence as you encourage the child to express his opinion during the group discussion. For example: "What do we need to remember about our mouths when we chew. We chew with our mouth _____ (closed)."

Hearing Impairments—Seat the child near the front of the group. Use concrete objects and pictures during the group discussion.

Visual Impairments—Provide verbal explanations of good manners. It may be necessary to use physical cues to assist the child on occasion.

Cognitive and/or Developmental Delays—Use short, simple sentences in your explanations. Use pictures and objects for the child to see. You may need to provide physical cues on occasion.

Emotional Disturbance—Seat the child near you. Provide positive attention for the child's appropriate behavior throughout the lesson.

Other Health Impairments/Attention Deficit Hyperactive Disorder—If the child becomes restless, have him get the objects you need for the lessons. This gives him an opportunity to move about.

Orthopedic Impairments—Be aware that a child with orthopedic problems may have difficulty chewing with his mouth closed, as well as with eating neatly.

Review

On a chart tablet or poster board, draw a line down the middle. Label one side "Good Manners" with a smiling face and the other side "Bad Manners" with a sad face. Ask individual children to tell you things to write on the Good Manners side and on the Bad Manners side.

Assessment Strategy

Before Snack Time each day, ask one child to tell the class what they need to remember about good table manners. Make a list of what each child says. After each child has had a turn talking about good manners, post their lists near the snack tables.

Curriculum Connections

- **Art**—Have the children make their own placemat out of construction paper so they can set up their place setting for Snack Time.
- **Book Center**—Provide books on manners in the book center. Suggestions include *Manners* by Aliki and *Soup Should Be Seen, Not Heard* by Beth Brainard and Sheila Behr.
- **Language and Literacy**—Ask the children to work with each other to decide on class rules for manners. Write what they say on a poster board and post it in the classroom. Put small drawings or clip art beside each rule to help them remember.
- **Math**—Have the children estimate how many paper plates, napkins, cups, and utensils it will take so everyone in the class has one. Give them a chart of children's names and have the children mark down the number down of each item on hand.
- **Science**—Stress the importance of manners for good health, cleanliness, and limiting the spread of germs. Manners that keep us in good health include taking small bites, chewing with our mouths closed, using our napkins, and washing our hands.
- **More Science**—Show a picture of the stomach and explain that a burp comes from swallowing air. When we eat too fast, we swallow a lot of air that can give us a stomachache if we do not burp or belch.
- **Social Studies**—Talk about manners and customs in different countries and cultures.

MANNERS

Sneezes and Runny Noses

Time
30 minutes

Materials
- Animal puppet
- Dolls
- Tissues

Objectives
Children will:
1. Describe what to do when they sneeze.
2. Describe what to do when they have a runny nose.

Lesson
- Engage the children in a discussion about runny noses and sneezes.
- Introduce an animal puppet to the class and explain that Mr. Dog has a cold so he is sneezing and has a runny nose.
- Have the puppet sneeze, and then politely ask the puppet, "Please do not sneeze on me." Tell the puppet that you can get germs that make you sick from his sneeze and that he must cover his mouth and nose when he sneezes.
- Cover Mr. Dog's mouth and nose with a tissue as he sneezes.
- Explain that Mr. Dog also gets runny noses. Tell the children why it is important to wipe your nose with a tissue when they sneeze (it stops the spread of germs). Using Mr. Dog, demonstrate how to wipe your nose with a tissue when you sneeze. Thank Mr. Dog for wiping his nose with a tissue.
- Engage the children in a discussion about why it is important to cover your mouth and nose when you sneeze, to blow your nose into a tissue, and to put used tissue in the trash.
- Show the children a large doll. Tell the children that the doll has a cold. Ask what happens when someone has a cold.
- Demonstrate how to use a tissue on the doll when she sneezes or has a runny nose. Show another type of doll and explain that he, too, has a cold.
- Ask a few children to demonstrate what to do when the doll sneezes or has a runny nose.
- Give each child a tissue and ask them to role play how to use the tissue for a sneeze or a runny nose.
- Have the children put their tissues in their pockets in case they have to sneeze or wipe their noses.

Show pictures of people who have colds. Ask the children what they do when they have a cold. Ask what would happen if we did not have tissues.

Assessment Strategy

Observe the children throughout the day, noticing whether they use their tissues to cover their noses. Have each child demonstrate how to use the tissue and ask her when she needs to use a tissue.

Accommodations/Modifications

Autism—Have other children model responses before asking the child with autism to respond.

Speech or Language Impairments—Ask the child *who, what, when,* and *where* questions during the lesson to promote language development. If the child has difficulty, provide a sentence for the child to complete. For example: "Where do we put our tissue when we finish with it? We put the tissue in the _____."

Hearing Impairments—Use concrete objects in the lesson and model appropriate responses for the child.

Visual Impairments—Describe what you are doing, and let the child hold concrete objects as you provide verbal explanations.

Cognitive and/or Developmental Delays—Keep your sentences short and let other children model responses before you call on the child.

Emotional Disturbance—Seat the child near you and positively involve the child in the activity.

Other Health Impairments/Attention Deficit Hyperactive Disorder—Provide stretch breaks between activities for the entire class.

Orthopedic Impairments—Hand-over-hand assistance is often helpful for the child who has difficulty with reach and grasp.

Curriculum Connections

- **Language and Literacy**—Write a group story on chart paper about what to do in case of a sneeze or runny nose. Ask each child to contribute part of the story. Write down each child's contribution.
- **Science**—Discuss germs, and how they spread. Draw pictures or provide pictures of germs or of items or situations that could cause germs from magazines. Describe germs as "small dots in the air that fly when you sneeze or cough."
- **Social Studies**—Discuss what people did before we had tissues. Show the children a handkerchief and explain that they may have family members who use handkerchiefs. Would you rather use a tissue or a handkerchief?

Thinking of Others

Time
20–30 minutes

Materials
- Magazines
- Scissors
- Index cards
- Glue or tape
- *Alexander and the Terrible, Horrible, No Good, Very Bad Day* by Judith Viorst
- Photographs or pictures of faces expressing the following feelings: happy, sad, scared, excited, angry, silly, lonely, and so on

Preparation
Prior to the lesson, select magazine pictures that show children and adults expressing various feelings. Cut out the pictures and glue them on index cards.

Objectives
Children will:
1. Describe feelings with specific situations.
2. Describe feelings associated with pictures of faces.

Lesson
- Tell the children that everyone in the class has different feelings and that each day brings different moods.
- Explain to the children that they will not always feel the same as their friends and that is fine. Also explain that expressing their feelings is a good thing.
- Help the children understand the importance of showing consideration for other people's feelings. It is important to help our friends when they are having a hard time.
- Read and discuss *Alexander and the Terrible, Horrible, No Good, Very Bad Day* by Judith Viorst. Talk with the children about how Alexander felt when negative events occurred. Talk about Alexander's feelings throughout the day. Discuss the importance of talking about how you feel.
- Show the children the index cards with pictures of faces that depict various feelings. Ask the children to describe how the person in the picture feels. Ask them what they think happened to make the person _____ (happy, sad, and so on).
- Have one child draw an index card. Look at the picture and then say, "I feel _____ (the feeling on the face of the person pictured) when…" and ask the child to say when he feels happy, sad, angry, and so on. Continue with additional children.
- Sing the following song with the children.

If You're Happy and You Know It
If you're happy and you know it, clap your hands,
If you're happy and you know it, clap your hands,
If you're happy and you know it, then your face will surely show it.
If you're happy and you know it, clap your hands.

If you're angry and you know it, stomp your feet,
If you're angry and you know it, stomp your feet.
If you're angry and you know it, then your face will surely show it.
If you're angry and you know it, stomp your feet.

If you're sad and you know it, wear a frown,
If you're sad and you know it, wear a frown,
If you're sad and you know it, then your face will surely show it,
If you're sad and you know it, wear a frown.

Review

Play a game, "How would my friend feel if…" On one side of small construction paper cards or index card write "How would my friend feel if…." On the other side, describe different situations, such as "she won a race," "someone took her toy away," "he cut his finger," "no one would play with her," and so on. Read each card to the children. Scaffold their responses as needed to promote consideration of others.

Assessment Strategy

Show each child the index cards with faces depicting feelings (happy, sad, mad, surprised, afraid, and so on). Ask him to tell you the feeling shown on the face and ask him to tell when he feels that way.

If you're happy and you know it, clap your hands,
If you're happy and you know it, clap your hands,
If you're happy and you know it, then your face will surely show it.
If you're happy and you know it, clap your hands.

Accommodations/Modifications

Autism—During the review, use familiar scenarios that depict concrete examples of feelings. Accentuate the feelings on your own face. Describe feelings exhibited during the day.

Speech or Language Impairments—Ask the child to select the feeling (from pictures on cards) rather than tell the feeling at first. Then ask him about the feeling in the picture. If needed, name the feeling and have the child repeat after you.

Hearing Impairments—Seat the child near you. Emphasize the feelings associated with the pictures. Allow the child to use the feelings cards to show how she feels.

Visual Impairments—Describe feelings verbally. Make sure the tone of your voice corresponds to the expression on your face.

Cognitive and/or Developmental Delays—Let the child choose the feeling card to describe the feeling in the situation. Use your voice to emphasize the feeling. Begin with a few feelings that you have emphasized with this child (happy, sad, angry).

Emotional Disturbance—Encourage the child to verbalize and describe him feelings throughout the day as you observe them. Refer to actual situations where you observed the child's feelings when explaining the lesson. For example, talk about how the child felt last week when someone else took the truck he was playing with.

Other Health Impairments/Attention Deficit Hyperactive Disorder—Have the child get materials to be used in the later steps of the lesson. This enables him to move about more frequently.

Orthopedic Impairments—Assist the child in drawing cards if he has difficulty using his hands.

Curriculum Connections

- **Art**—Have children make puppets to express their feelings.
- **Listening Center**—Provide a tape or CD that has "If You're Happy and You Know It" on it for children to listen to.
- **More Listening Center**—Record the story of *Today I Feel Silly and Other Moods That Make My Day* by Jamie Lee Curtis for the children to listen to.
- **Writing Center**—Write a group story on chart paper about what makes each person happy.

How to Listen

Time

20–30 minutes

Materials

- Picture of a person with the following parts visible: eyes, ears, mouth, hands, feet, head
- Doll or puppet
- Small chair or mat

Objectives

Children will:

1. Name several appropriate behaviors to use when listening.
2. Describe what one does with at least three body parts when listening.

Lesson

- During Group or Circle Time, show the children a picture of a person.
- Ask the children to tell you what part of the body they use when they listen. Affirm the children when they tell you they listen with their ears.
- Explain that ears are for hearing and listening, but when they listen, they also use other body parts. Ask the following questions:
  - What do you do with your eyes when you listen? (you watch the person talking)
  - What do you do with your mouth when you listen? (you close it)
  - What do you do with your feet when you listen? (you keep them on the floor)
  - What do you do with your hands when you listen? (you keep them in your lap)
  - What do you do with your seat when you listen? (you sit in your chair or on your mat)
  - What do you do with your brain with you listen? (you think about what is being said)
- Ask the children to tell you the things they do when they are listening.
- Demonstrate how to listen with a puppet or doll. Put the doll or puppet in a small chair or on a mat to show how to listen.
- Remind the children how to listen with all of their body parts. Demonstrate correct and incorrect ways to listen. Ask them to say whether you were a good listener or not. Ask them what you need to do when you listen.
- Have the children show you how to listen with all of their body parts, reminding them what they need to do with their ears, eyes, mouth, hands, feet, seat, and brain.

Accommodations/Modifications

Autism—Use line drawings or clip art to show the specific parts of the body that are used to listen. Model what to do to listen with each part of the body.

Speech or Language Impairments—Provide verbal models of responses. When it is the child's turn to respond, supply the first part of the sentence and let the child complete it. You can use picture cues for the child.

Review

Give the children markers and paper. Ask them to draw pictures of people who are good listeners. Ask the children to tell you about good listening. Write what each child says on the back of her pictures.

Assessment Strategy

Observe the child to see if she is using good listening behaviors. If a child is not listening, ask her to tell you what she needs to do to be a good listener. If necessary, cue her about parts of her body that she can use for good listening.

Hearing Impairments—Seat the child near you and make sure that the child can see clearly as you use the puppet or doll. Provide picture cues and references to concrete objects as you present the lesson.

Visual Impairments—Describe what you are doing as you demonstrate actions with the puppet or doll. Then ask the child to tell you if the puppet is a good listener.

Cognitive and/or Developmental Delays—Use short, simple sentences, rephrasing after you provide explanations. Point to specific parts of your body as you make explanations. Use gestures and modeling as you present the lesson.

Emotional Disturbance—Have the child sit near you during the lesson.

Other Health Impairments/Attention Deficit Hyperactive Disorder—Make sure you have the child's attention before demonstrating with the puppet and before providing explanations.

Orthopedic Impairments—Provide an adaptive holder for the child's marker so she can draw a picture during the Assessment Activity.

Curriculum Connections

- **Art**—Let the children listen to classical music or other instrumental music as they draw pictures.
- **Language and Literacy**—On poster board, write suggestions on "How to Be a Good Listener." Draw diagrams or use clip art and post the suggestions near the circle area.
- **Listening Center**—Record interesting sounds and challenge the children to identify the sounds, testing their listening skills.

INTRODUCTION TO

Plants

Time

20 minutes

Materials

A variety of plants (flowers, vegetables, potted plant, cactus, and so on)

Review

Provide time for the children to observe various plants: flowers, ivy, grasses, and ferns. Provide time for the children to draw different pictures of plants.

Assessment Strategy

Discuss the observations of plants with each child.

Objectives

Children will:

1. Identify what a plant is.
2. Name at least one plant.

Lesson

- Show children various plants. Include flowering plants, ivy, grasses, and ferns. Talk to them about what plants are. Tell them that there are two types of living things: plants and animals.
- Talk with the children about the characteristics of plants. Pass plants around and let the children look at them and handle them gently.
- Show the children the roots of the potted plant. Make sure the plant is replanted, stressing to the children that potted plants need our help to survive.
- Tell children that we also eat plants. Point out that vegetables are plants.
- As they leave for centers or the next activity of the day), ask them to name at least one plant.

Accommodations/Modifications

Autism—Position the child so he will have easy access to the plants during the lesson.

Speech or Language Impairments—Use forced-choice questions to elicit responses from the child.

Hearing Impairments—Use cueing and gestures to help the child understand the directions.

Visual Impairments—Provide verbal directions and dialogue to help the child understand the content of the lesson.

Cognitive and/or Developmental Delays—Use picture cards in conjunction with showing the plants to help the child understand the lesson.

Emotional Disturbance—Provide positive feedback to the child as you share the content of the lesson.

Other Health Impairments/Attention Deficit Hyperactive Disorder—Provide assistance with turn-taking. Having a specific place for seating will help the child know his body space area.

Orthopedic Impairments—Help the child as he observes and touches the various plants shown in the lesson.

Curriculum Connections

- **Language and Literacy**—Read Shel Silverstein's *The Giving Tree* to children.
- **Math**—Prepare plant and animal cards and place them on the Manipulatives Table for children to sort.

Celery

Time
- 20 minutes
- 10–20 minutes, four hours later

Materials
- Bunch of celery
- Knife (teacher only)
- 2 large jars of water
- Food coloring

Preparation
The day before the lesson, place a bunch of celery out at room temperature. (The celery needs to be at room temperature for about 8 to 10 hours before the lesson.)

Review
Keep the two jars of celery out for the children to observe over a period of a few days.

Assessment Strategy
Ask each child to talk about the changes she noticed in the celery stalks.

Objectives
Children will:
1. Identify celery in a group of vegetables.
2. Observe and describe the movement of water through a stalk of celery.

Lesson
- Gather the children after they have played outside. Talk about how they are thirsty and want a drink, and talk about other things that drink water.
- Lead the discussion to include the concept that plants need water.
- Show the children the limp bunch of celery that has been left at room temperature overnight. Explain that plants drink water, too.
- Cut the celery at the base of the stalk. In one jar of water, place four stalks of celery. In the other jar, add eight drops of red food coloring to the water and then place four stalks of celery in that jar.
- Later that day (about two hours later), gather the children together and look at the celery stalks in the two jars. Help them notice that the celery is no longer limp and is refreshed, just as they get refreshed when they drink water.
- Then look at the celery stalks in the colored water and examine the straw-like lines in the celery that show how the colored water traveled up the celery stalks.

Accommodations/Modifications
Autism—Emphasize the concept of drinking water is something that both people and celery stalks need to revive and to grow.

Speech or Language Impairments—Define unknown words.

Hearing Impairments—Face the child when talking.

Visual Impairments—Provide time for up-close inspection of the celery stalks.

Cognitive and/or Developmental Delays—Provide adequate discussion time.

Emotional Disturbance—Provide adequate discussion time. Pose questions to be sure the child understands. Allow reiteration of the concept of drinking water.

Other Health Impairments/Attention Deficit Hyperactive Disorder—Provide directions to maintain focus on the concepts.

Orthopedic Impairments—Provide time for the child to inspect the celery stalks.

Curriculum Connections
- **Science**—Observe what happens to celery and to a white carnation placed in a glass of colored water. Explain to children why these plants change colors.
- **More Science**—Provide sequence cards for children to show the transference of colored water through a plant.

Apple Tree

Time

25 minutes

Materials

- Basket of apples, one for each child
- String
- Scissors

Objectives

Children will:

1. Identify an apple when they see one.
2. Participate in the "Apple Tree" song.

Lesson

- Gather the children on the rug at Group or Circle Time. Place a basket containing different varieties of apples on the rug.
- Talk with the children about the different colors of apples.
- Give each child an apple to observe closely.
- Help each child cut a piece of string the length of the circumference of the apple, and then put the strings in order from longest to shortest.
- Cut slices of the various apples so the children can taste the different apples.
- Talk with the children about their taste preference in apples.
- Sing the following "Apple Tree" song with the children.

Apple Tree Song by Diana Nabors
(Tune: "Three Blind Mice")
My apple tree,
My apple tree,
Gives apples to me,
Gives apples to me.
My apple is big as you can see.
My apple is as round as it can be.
I'll eat my apple 1, 2, 3,
Yum, yum, yummy.

Review

Provide time for the children to observe the various apples.

Accommodations/Modifications

Autism—Help the child place her string in the correct place lengthwise among the other strings. Provide guidance so she participates in observing and ordering the string lengths.

Speech or Language Impairments—Provide definitions for unknown words. Reinforce the child for participating in the group.

Hearing Impairments—Use gestures and modeling to emphasize directions and activities.

Visual Impairments—Remember that the child's knowledge will be enhanced as she touches and manipulates apples.

Cognitive and/or Developmental Delays— Allow the child to hold and explore the apples. Provide guidance so the child participates fully.

Emotional Disturbance—Provide guidance to the child so that she can participate fully.

Other Health Impairments/Attention Deficit Hyperactive Disorder—Provide guidance to allow the child to focus and participate fully in the ordering activity.

Orthopedic Impairments—Provide individual time for the child to manipulate the apples with adult assistance.

Curriculum Connections

- **Snack**—With the children, cut, core, and place apples in a crock pot with 1 cup of water for each five apples. Cook the apples for two hours on high heat. Once cooled, the children can taste the cooked apple and sing the "Apple Tree" song.
- **Science**—With the children, cut open an apple and examine its insides. Observe and smell apples of different colors and types. Enjoy a taste experience.
- **Language and Literacy**—Provide opportunities for children to dictate stories about apples. Ask parent volunteers to write the stories for the children.

PLANTS

Bulbs

Time

20–30 minutes

Materials

- Basket of various bulbs
- Pictures of flowers that grow from each bulb, if possible
- Small scale

Objectives

Children will:

1. Measure the weight of various bulbs.
2. Participate in a poem about flowers.
3. Plant bulbs and watch for growth.

Lesson

- At Group or Circle Time, show the children the basket of bulbs. Give each child a bulb to hold and examine.
- Engage the children in a discussion about bulbs. Ask them questions about the bulbs they are holding. Suggestions include:
    - Will the plant that grows from your bulb be a big plant or a small plant?
    - What color flower will grow from your bulb?
- If possible, show the children pictures of the plants that will grow from each bulb.
- Teach the children "Flowers" and encourage them to follow you as you perform the actions.

> **Flowers** by Diana Nabors
> *I'm a little flower*
> *Sleeping just below the ground.* (curl up)
> *I'll raise my head up. See me grow.* (raise head and begin to grow)
> *And I'll stretch my leaves side to side.* (sway side to side)
> *My roots will grow way, way down.* (stomp feet)
> *I'll lift my head, so that I can say,* (nod head)
> *"I'm glad to see this bright new day."*

- Help the children weigh the different bulbs and order them from lightest to heaviest.
- Plant the bulbs in the classroom garden and observe them until blooms appear.

Accommodations/Modifications

Autism—Use picture cues for *light* and *heavy* for weighing the bulbs. Reinforce the child's participation in the group discussion. Assist the child with motor sequences for the poem.

Speech or Language Impairments—Use forced-choice questions to elicit responses from the child. Repeat the poem throughout the unit.

Review

Provide time for the children to reweigh the bulbs in centers prior to planting them.

Assessment Strategy

Ask each child to predict the plant that will grow from the bulb.

Hearing Impairments—Use cueing and gestures to help the child understand the directions. Use pictures as an aid for the poem.

Visual Impairments—Provide verbal directions and dialogue to assist with the poem and directions. Allow the child to touch and hold the various bulbs as he participates in the sequencing activity.

Cognitive and/or Developmental Delays— Use space holders for the bulbs to assist in sequencing. Using picture cards will help with direction and activity comprehension.

Emotional Disturbance—Provide positive feedback in the poem and sequencing activity. Preteach the strategy of trial-and-error to assist in modification of a sequence as new items are added.

Other Health Impairments/Attention Deficit Hyperactive Disorder—Provide assistance with turn-taking. This can be done verbally or through gestures. Having a specific place for seating will assist the child in knowing his body space area.

Orthopedic Impairments—Provide opportunities at the child's level. Assist the child in manipulating the bulbs and moving during the poem. Describe the actions associated with the poem verbally to assist the child.

Curriculum Connections

- **Dramatic Play**—Place gardening tools in the Home Living Center so children can pretend to develop a garden for their home.
- **Movement**—Provide opportunities for children to demonstrate with their bodies how bulbs grow.
- **Science**—Place bulbs in the Science Center so children can do independent weighing and measuring.

Carrot Top

Time

5–10 minutes a day over a series of 5 days to 2 weeks

Materials

- Large (3-pound) bag of carrots (do not use "ready to eat" baby carrots or carrot sticks)
- Cutting board
- Knife (teacher only)
- Bowl
- Toothpicks
- Small unbreakable jars
- Water

Objectives

Children will:

1. Identify a carrot in a group of vegetables.
2. Observe and discuss changes in a carrot top.

Preparation

Before the children come to Snack Time, place a bag of carrots on the table. Using a cutting board and knife, cut off the top of each carrot and place the tops in a bowl. Wash and cut the remaining carrots into carrot sticks for snack.

Lesson

- When the children come to the snack table, show them the bowl of carrot tops and ask them what they think should be done with the tops. Ask them, "Can these carrot tops grow?'
- Engage the children in a discussion about the possibility of the carrot tops growing.
- Pierce three to four toothpicks into the sides of each carrot top. Place each one over a jar of water. (The carrot is held in place by the toothpicks resting on the sides of the jar.)
- Fill each jar with enough water so the bottom part of the carrot top is covered with water but not fully submerged.
- Over a period of time, look at the carrot tops to observe its growth. Some carrot tops will flower if cared for over a long period of time.

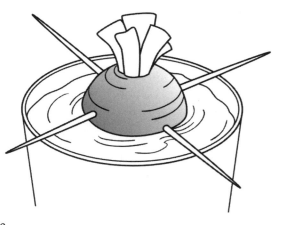

Accommodations/Modifications

Autism—Provide individual time to discuss and observe the carrot tops.

Speech or Language Impairments—Encourage the child to use complete sentence structure during discussion.

Review

Place the carrot tops in the Science Center for individual observation.

Assessment Strategy

Discuss and question each child about the growth of the carrot top. Help the child learn that the small part of the carrot provides the food that helps the carrot top grow.

Hearing Impairments—Rephrase the children's statements using visual cues and gestures.

Visual Impairments—Provide time for the child to inspect and manipulate the carrot tops with supervision.

Cognitive and/or Developmental Delays— Provide time for the child to inspect and manipulate the carrot tops with supervision. Define new vocabulary words, such as *root, root hairs, top, bud,* and *water* as the child inspects the carrot.

Other Health Impairments/Attention Deficit Hyperactive Disorder—Prior to the activity, discuss with the child what will happen during the lesson. Explain that it will take days for the growth to appear on the carrot tops.

Orthopedic Impairments—Provide time and assistance for the child to hold and inspect the carrot top.

Curriculum Connections

- **Art**—Provide opportunities for children to draw or paint the growth of plants.
- **Language and Literacy**—Provide sequence cards for children to order the sequence of plant growth. These cards may need to be teacher-made.
- **Science**—Take photographs of the carrot tops growing over the course of time so children can observe the differences for themselves.

Potato

Time
- 20 minutes initially
- 5–10 minutes daily for 3–4 weeks

Materials
- 2 potatoes
- Large unbreakable jar of water
- Small shoebox with a lid
- Tape
- Toothpicks
- Water

Review
Provide time for the children to observe the potato over a period of a few days.

Assessment Strategy
Individually, provide time for each child to observe the potato over a period of a few weeks.

Objectives

Children will:
1. Observe and name the parts of a plant.
2. Observe and discuss plant growth.

Lesson
- Show the children two potatoes, a jar of water, and a small shoebox. Ask the children if they think the potatoes can grow, and what the potatoes need to grow. After the initial discussion, place one potato inside the shoebox and tape the lid shut.
- Add water to the jar. Place toothpicks in the other potato so it can rest on the rim of the jar, with half of the potato above the rim and the other half in the water.
- Ask the children to predict how each potato will grow.
- Over the next two weeks, observe the growth of the potato in the jar of water. (Add water as needed to keep the bottom of the potato submerged in water.) Do not look at the potato in the shoebox. After two weeks, look at both potatoes. Notice any root growth or stem growth. If desired, cut out potato eyes, with about a 1" cube of potato around each potato eye, and transplant the potato into a garden or in a pot.

Accommodation/Modifications
Autism—Dialogue with the child about the possible growth of the potato.

Speech or Language Impairments—Use forced-choice questions to help the child discuss and predict the potato's growth.

Hearing Impairments—Have the child tell you her predictions of the potato's growth to make sure she understands.

Visual Impairments—Place the potato in water in a location that makes it easier for the child to view it. This may include touching with assistance.

Cognitive and/or Developmental Delays—Ask the child to verbalize and gesture to predict the potato's growth.

Emotional Disturbance—Dialogue with the child about the possible growth of the potato and other items in the classroom. Reinforce positively, when she participates in the discussion.

Other Health Impairments/Attention Deficit Hyperactive Disorder—Encourage the child's prediction abilities.

Orthopedic Impairments—Place the potato in water in a location that is easily accessible for close inspection.

Curriculum Connections
- **Science**—Observe the potato in the water. Help children notice when the eyes begin to sprout. Be sure to have a before photograph available, so children will be able to describe the changes when the potato plant is fully grown.

Leaf Collage

Time
20–30 minutes

Materials
- Small bags (one for each child)
- Wire screen
- Scissors
- Duct tape
- Glue and paper
- Box with sides, large enough to fit a sheet of paper (copy boxes work well)
- Toothbrushes
- Paint

Preparation
Give each child a small bag to collect a few leaves and nature items. Away from the children, cut a piece of wire screen slightly larger than the box. Cover all the edges with duct tape.

Review
Provide time for the children to observe the splatter-painting process.

Assessment Strategy
Discuss with each child the nature items he collected.

Objectives

Children will:
1. Discuss differences in leaves on the tree and those who have fallen from the tree.
2. Use items from nature to develop a leaf collage.

Lesson

- At Group or Circle Time, engage the children in a discussion about the different leaves they saw and collected outside during the nature walk.
- Ask each child to look in her bag and select a few leaves and nature items to glue onto his collage. Provide paper and glue for each child to create a college.
- Work with one child at a time to help the children spatter-paint their collages. Have each child places his collage inside the box then place the screen over the top of the box.
- Help the child dip a toothbrush in a little bit of paint and then brush it across the screen, creating a splatter of paint on the leaves and other nature items inside the box.

Accommodations/Modifications

Autism—Provide assistance with the paint splattering process. The child may choose to use a small sponge across the screen to make the splatters.

Speech or Language Impairments—Encourage the child to use complete sentences when discussing the leaves.

Hearing Impairments—Have the child repeat directions to be sure he understands. Use gestures and face the child when talking and giving directions.

Visual Impairments—Use bright paint colors. Understand that the child may want to splatter a lot of paint.

Cognitive and/or Developmental Delays—Have the child repeat the directions to check for understanding. Be present during splatter-painting.

Emotional Disturbance—Have the child repeat the directions to be sure he understands. Be present during splatter-painting if this is a new painting technique.

Other Health Impairments/Attention Deficit Hyperactive Disorder—Have the child repeat the directions to be sure he understands.

Orthopedic Impairments—Provide a large grip on the toothbrush to assist in palm grasp as he paints.

Curriculum Connections

- **Language and Literacy**—Post the collages on a bulletin board and provide opportunities for children to discuss their creations with others.
- **Science**—Talk with each child individually about the leaves and nature items they have collected. Help them learn the appropriate names for each item.

Grass "Heads"

Time

30–45 minutes

Materials

- Individual-size milk cartons or plastic cups in size similar to the milk carton (one for each child)
- Sharp scissors or ice pick (teacher only)
- Construction paper
- Crayons, markers
- Glue
- Small pebbles
- Potting soil
- Rye grass seeds
- Tray
- Small watering can

Objectives

Children will:

1. Plant and observe the growth of grass.
2. Name their grass "head" plants.

Preparation

Away from the children, use a sharp pair of scissors or an ice pick to pierce a few small drainage holes in the bottom of each milk carton or plastic cup. Put the scissors or ice pick out of the reach of the children when you are finished. Cut construction paper into strips that fit around the milk carton or plastic cup.

Lesson

- Tell the children that they will be making grass "heads." Allow each child to select one of the clean milk cartons or plastic cups.

Potting Soil

1" Gravel

- Help each child wrap her carton with a construction paper strip, making creases around each corner. Unwrap the paper and let the children decorate their construction paper strips with a face or other design. When they are finished, help the children rewrap the milk carton or paper cup and attach the paper to the carton or cup.
- The next step is to add 1" of small pebbles to the bottom of each milk carton or cup, and then fill the carton or cup with potting soil.
- Help the children sprinkle a teaspoon of rye grass seeds on top of the potting soil. Place their grass "heads" on a tray.
- Place the tray of the children's grass "heads" near a window.
- The children can take turns watering the tray of plants daily.
- As the rye grass sprouts, the grass "heads" will appear to grow "hair."

Review

Each day, encourage the children to observe the changes in their grass "heads."

Assessment Strategy

Ask each child about the changes in the plants. If appropriate, ask each child to make drawings of the changes in their grass "heads."

Accommodations/Modifications

Autism—Verbalize the instructions for the child during the lesson.

Speech or Language Impairments—Reinforce the child when she uses complete sentence structure.

Hearing Impairments—Face the child when speaking.

Visual Impairments—Verbalize instructions for the child during the lesson.

Cognitive and/or Developmental Delays—Verbalize instructions for the child during the lesson. Assist as needed.

Emotional Disturbance—Verbalize instructions and provide guidance for the child during the lesson.

Other Health Impairments/Attention Deficit Hyperactive Disorder—Verbalize instructions and provide guidance for the child during the lesson.

Orthopedic Impairments—Provide materials at the child's level.

Curriculum Connections

- **Just for Fun**—Ask children to name their "grass heads." Help them make cards to place beside their "grass head."
- **Language and Literacy**—Provide opportunities and assistance for children to make a timeline book of the plant growth or garden changes.
- **Science**—Plant and tend to seeds in the classroom. Match the new growth to pictures of plant life. Have samples of various types of grasses for children to compare.

Flowers

Time

20–30 minutes

Materials

- Construction paper
- Scissors
- *The Tiny Seed* by Eric Carle
- 12" garden box
- Marigold seeds
- Potting soil
- Watering can

Objectives

Children will:

1. Name the parts of a flower.
2. Discuss plant and flower growth.

Preparation

Cut out construction paper petals, flower centers, stems, and leaves.

Lesson

- At Group or Circle Time, read *The Tiny Seed* by Eric Carle aloud. Ask the children what a seed needs to grow. Discuss problems that a seed might have as it develops into the large sunflower.
- With the children, plant marigold seeds in a small garden box in the classroom.
- Allow the children to water the seeds. Place the garden box by a window in the classroom.
- Allow the children to care for the seeds as they sprout and bloom.
- Encourage the children to use construction paper petals, flower centers, stems, and leaves to make flowers for display in the classroom.

Review

Provide time for the children to re-read the book The Tiny Seed in the Book Center.

Assessment Strategy

Provide time for each child to observe the flowers over a period of a few weeks.

Accommodation/Modifications

Autism—In a one-on-one situation, dialogue with the child about the growth of the flower and of other plants growing in the classroom. Use forced-choice questioning to continue the discussion.

Speech or Language Impairments—Use forced-choice questions to continue the discussion and prediction of the flower growth. Reinforce the child's use of correct sentence structure and word choice.

Hearing Impairments—Have the child verbalize his predictions of seed growth to assess her comprehension.

Visual Impairments—Provide seedlings in a location easily accessible for close inspection. This may include touching with assistance.

Cognitive and/or Developmental Delays—Have the child verbalize and use gestures for his predictions of the flower growth to enable you to assess his comprehension.

Emotional Disturbance—Dialogue with the child about the possible growth of the seeds and other items growing in the classroom. Reinforce discussion participation

Other Health Impairments/Attention Deficit Hyperactive Disorder—Encourage the child's prediction abilities. Help him keep a daily log of growth. Relate growth with the child's predictions.

Orthopedic Impairments—Provide planted seeds in a location easily accessible to the child.

Curriculum Connections

- **Art**—Ask a local florist to donate wilted flowers to your classroom. The children can rub the flower petals on paper to make a delicate art product.
- **Language and Literacy**—Ask children to name their favorite flowers. Add the names of the flowers to the classroom Word Wall.
- **Science**—Have flower seed packets available for children to sort and match.

5 Summer Themes

Just for Fun

Games and Sports

Let's Pretend

Vacations

INTRODUCTION TO

Just for Fun

Time

20 minutes

Materials

- *Clap Your Hands* by Lorinda Bryan Cauley, in big book format if possible
- Pictures of children having fun (optional)

Review

Ask children to describe what "just for fun" means.

Assessment Strategy

Survey children individually to find out if they know what the phrase "just for fun" means.

Objectives

Children will:

1. Name one activity they do or their family does for fun.
2. Describe their favorite fun activity.

Lesson

- As children arrive for the lesson, begin to giggle or laugh.
- Tell the children that over the next few days they will talk about things that are just for fun.
- Read *Clap Your Hands* by Lorinda Bryan Cauley or another suitable book. Talk with the children about how people clap their hands when they are having fun.
- Ask the children to think about ways they and their families have fun. Ask them to talk with their families that night about fun things they do together.

Accommodations/Modifications

Autism—Use pictorial cues of feelings such as, *happy, sad, afraid, excited,* and *lonely.*

Speech or Language Impairments—Provide a lead-in sentence as you encourage the child to express his opinion during the group discussion.

Hearing Impairments—Rehearse verbal responses before eliciting the child's response for fun things that families do together.

Visual Impairments—If possible, read a big book version of *Clap Your Hands.* If props are available to support the book, allow the child to hold and manipulate the props.

Cognitive and/or Developmental Delays—Have several pictures available of families having fun, and ask the child to select a picture that shows how his family has fun.

Emotional Disturbance—Model the responses with several children before asking the child to respond to the various questions asked in the lesson.

Other Health Impairments/Attention Deficit Hyperactive Disorder—Secure the child's attention before transitioning from one part of the lesson to another.

Orthopedic Impairments—If the child is not able to clap his hands, provide another way for him to show delight, such as tapping a drum.

Curriculum Connections

- **Discovery Center**—Set up a Just for Fun Center, with items such as Mr. Potato Head, magic slates, Silly Putty, finger and glove puppets, and books about having fun.
- **Language and Literacy**—Read nonsense poems, such as "Eletelephony" by Laura E. Richards or "Grizzly Bear" by Denise Austin to a small group of children. Talk with the children about the poems.

JUST FOR FUN

Kites

Time

20 minutes

Materials

- Kite
- *Kites* by Demi
- Paper and art materials for drawing kites

Review

Ask the children to tell you what they learned in the lesson.

Assessment Strategy

Observe the children drawing kites. Note which children choose to draw kites and which do not.

Objectives

Children will:

1. Describe a kite.
2. Attempt to fly a kite.

Lesson

- Have a kite available as children arrive at Group or Circle Time for the lesson. Talk about why a kite might be considered a "just for fun" item.
- Tell the children that the topic of the day is kites. Ask the children if they have ever flown a kite. Read a book about kites. Demi's *Kites* is a good choice.
- Let children discuss what they see around them as you read the story. Tell them that kite flying will be an outdoor event later in the day.
- Tell the children there are materials in the Art Center that they can use to draw pictures of kites or to build a kite.

Accommodations/Modifications

Autism—Have other children model responses before asking the child with autism to discuss what she sees around her during the story.

Speech or Language Impairments—Ask the child *who, what, when,* and *where* questions during the activity to promote language development. If the child has difficulty, provide a sentence for her to complete.

Hearing Impairments—Seat the child near the front of the group. Use concrete objects and pictures during the group discussion.

Visual Impairments—Use as many concrete items as possible to support the book about kites. This will increase the child's participation in the discussion of the story.

Cognitive and/or Developmental Delays—Rephrase explanations you give children by using short, simple sentences.

Emotional Disturbance—Seat the child near you and involve the child in the lesson. Praise the child for her participation.

Other Health Impairments/Attention Deficit Hyperactive Disorder—Ask the child to get materials to be used later in the lesson; for example, to get the kite book from a table or shelf, enabling the child to move about.

Orthopedic Impairments—If necessary, assist the child by providing hand-over-hand support during the lesson.

Curriculum Connections

- **Book Center**—Place books about kites in the Book Center for children to "read" at their leisure.
- **Outdoors**—Fly kites assisted by family volunteers.

Umbrellas

Time

25–30 minutes

Materials

- Several children's umbrellas
- Book about umbrellas, such as *Yellow Umbrella* by Jae-Soo Liu
- Variety of fabrics (one or two should be waterproof)
- Bowl
- Pitcher of water
- Poem about umbrellas, such as "U Is for Umbrellas" by Phyllis McGinley

Objectives

Children will:

1. Describe how umbrellas are used.
2. Demonstrate how to use an umbrella.

Lesson

- Have two or three children's umbrellas available when starting the lesson. Ask the children if they can guess that day's topic of discussion.
- When they respond with the word *umbrellas*, ask how many of them have their own umbrellas. Ask, "When do people need umbrellas? Are umbrellas always helpful? What happens to an umbrella when the wind blows too hard?"
- Read a book about umbrellas, giving children opportunities to share with the class their experiences with umbrellas.
- Ask these questions:
  - What are umbrellas made of?
  - Is the fabric they are made of important?
- Demonstrate what happens to fabric when it gets wet. Ask children why they think nylon and plastic fabrics do not let water through.
- Use the words *handle, shaft, button, slide,* and *spokes* as you look at and describe the umbrella. Ask children what people can use in place of umbrellas. A good poem to read with this lesson is "U Is for Umbrellas" by Phyllis McGinley.

Accommodations/Modifications

Autism—This lesson has several steps. Break it down into specific tasks that are each represented by picture icons. For example, one picture would be of an umbrella, the next a pitcher of water, and then a picture of children listening to a book. Use a visual cue to indicate an upcoming transition, such as a wave of your hand.

Speech or Language Impairments—When asking children about their experiences with umbrellas, use a lead-in sentence such as, "I used an umbrella once when . . ." Provide choices to children when asking them what can be substituted for an umbrella.

Review

Point to parts of the umbrella and ask children to name each part while they are still in the group.

Assessment Strategy

Ask each child to demonstrate how to use an umbrella.

Hearing Impairments—Place the child close to you during the discussion time and the story time. Integrate simple sign language for key words such as *umbrella, button, slide,* and any other lesson-related words.

Visual Impairments—Allow children to hold the umbrellas and to feel the umbrella as you get the fabric wet.

Cognitive and/or Developmental Delays—Provide opportunities for the children to make choices. For example, instead of asking when people need umbrellas, ask, "Do you need an umbrella when it is raining or when it is sunny?"

Emotional Disturbance—Discuss safety and how to handle and open umbrellas properly before letting the child hold the umbrellas. Ask the child to rephrase the safety rules to be sure he understands the rules. If you are concerned about him using inappropriate behaviors, stand near him.

Other Health Impairments/Attention Deficit Hyperactive Disorder—Allow the child to participate in the fabric and water activity. Sitting for too long may be difficult; this will give him an opportunity to move about.

Orthopedic Impairments—Make sure the materials you are examining and the demonstration are accessible to the child. Demonstrate the fabric and water activity at the child's level.

Curriculum Connections

- **Dramatic Play**—Include umbrellas in the Dramatic Play Center. Demonstrate to children how dancers use umbrellas in their routines, or invite in a family volunteer with talent in this area to visit the classroom.
- **Outdoors**—Take umbrellas to the playground on hot days. Remind children that umbrellas can protect people from the sun as well as the rain.
- **Snack**—Add party umbrellas to beverages served at Snack Time.

JUST FOR FUN

Spinners

Time

25–30 minutes

Materials

- Pinwheels (one for each child)
- *Charlie Needs a Cloak* by Tomie dePaola, or another book about clothes being made by spinners
- Spinning wheel or a picture of one
- Classroom fan
- Pictures of a windmill and other things that spin
- Whirligig (optional)

Objectives

Children will:

1. Demonstrate how to spin.
2. Name an object that spins.

Lesson

- Bring a pinwheel to Group or Circle Time and blow on it to show children how it works. Pass out a pinwheel (spinners) to each child as they arrive for the lesson. Show children how to blow, swing, or flick the pinwheel to make it move. Allow them to play with them for a few minutes.
- Tell children that some people call them *pinwheels* and others call them *spinners*. Ask if anyone knows something else that is called a spinner. Someone might mention that tops are called spinners.
- Collect the pinwheels and tell children you are going to talk about another type of spinner today.
- Read *Charlie Needs a Cloak* (or another book about spinning wheels). Display a real spinning wheel or a picture of one. Tell children that spinners were used to make clothes a long time ago.
- Show the children other things that spin, such as classroom fans, or pictures of things that spin, such as windmills. Tell the children that wind provides breezes to cool us down. Point to the classroom fan as an example of a spinner.
- At the end of the lesson, tell children that people can spin around, too. Ask a few children at a time to demonstrate how to spin. Ask them to describe what happens when people spin too quickly or for too long. Caution children to stop spinning after a few spins.

Accommodations/Modifications

Autism—Some children with autism will use the spinner as a self-stimulation device. Monitor the child when she is spinning the pinwheel. If a child becomes self absorbed in the spinning, she may not take in additional information being presented.

Speech or Language Impairments—Use gestures or sign language to help a child who has language delays or who is a reluctant speaker.

Hearing Impairments—Use simple sign language as you introduce new vocabulary, such as *windmill* and *spinning wheel*.

Review

Ask children to tell you what they learned about spinners during the lesson.

Assessment Strategy

Ask each child to spin around a specific number of times. Ask each child if she can name something that spins.

Visual Impairments—Providing items or props to support the photos will give the child a better understanding of the items being discussed. This is especially important if the child has never been exposed to these items. Use caution when asking a child with a visual impairment to spin. Some children with visual impairments may experience severe dizziness after only a few spins.

Cognitive and/or Developmental Delays—As you conduct the activity, rephrase your instruction and comments using simplified language. If needed, use prompts when reading *Charlie Needs a Cloak*. Explain vocabulary introduced in the book that may be unfamiliar to the child.

Emotional Disturbance—Stand near a child who may exhibit behavior concerns.

Other Health Impairments/Attention Deficit Hyperactive Disorder—Ensure that you have the child's attention before introducing the activity. Use a predictable strategy to get the child's attention, such as holding up one finger before children are to start spinning. Provide both verbal and non-verbal cues when children are to stop spinning.

Orthopedic Impairments—The child may not be able to spin around for the assessment portion of this activity. Replace this assessment with another activity that meets the lesson objective.

Curriculum Connections

- **Art**—Help the children make their own pinwheels. Instructions can be found at . Supervise the children closely during this activity.
- **Connecting with Home**—Find a volunteer to demonstrate spinning wheel techniques for the children.
- **Manipulatives**—Place a few toys that spin, such as tops and spinner, in the Manipulatives Center for children to play with. For more curious children, Anatex produces a Paddle Wheel Wall Panel allows children to explore how a spinning mechanism works.
- **Outdoors**—Invite children to spin around outdoors. Caution them to spin for a short while to avoid getting dizzy.

Merry-Go-Rounds

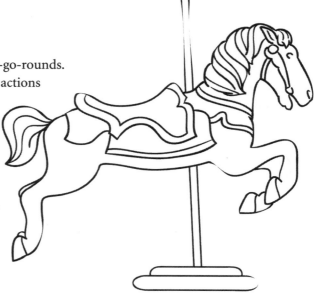

Time

25–30 minutes

Materials

- Pictures of merry-go-rounds
- *The Memory Horse* by Troon Harrison, or another book about merry-go-rounds
- Stick horses (optional)
- Carousel music (optional)

Objectives

Children will:

1. Describe one fact about merry-go-rounds.
2. Demonstrate merry-go-round actions (through the "Merry-Go-Round" poem).

Lesson

- Find pictures of merry-go-rounds to show the children as they arrive for the lesson.
- Ask the children if they know what a *merry-go-round* is. Tell them that sometimes merry-go-rounds are called *carousels*.
- Engage the children in a discussion about merry-go-rounds. Ask the children if they have ever ridden on a merry-go-round. Read a book about merry-go-rounds or show pictures of them. A good book to share is *The Memory Horse* by Troon Harrison.
- Ask children what they think it is like to ride on a merry-go-round. Introduce the poem below and ask children to add appropriate motions. If stick horses are available, children can ride them as they chant the poem.

Merry-Go-Round Poem by Laverne Warner
Merry-go-rounds go up and down, up and down, up and down.
When I'm up, my partner is down.

The horses are pretty and brown, pretty and brown, pretty and brown;
The horses ride all over town.

Come go with me up and down, up and down, up and down.
I love to ride all around!

- If carousel music is available, play it as the children chant the rhyme and pretend to ride around the circle.

Review

Ask the children to say the poem with you or to complete the end of a line as a review.

Assessment Strategy

Show a picture of a merry-go-round to each child one by one. Ask him to tell you what it is.

Accommodations/Modifications

Autism—Have picture icons available that show the sequence of movements that the child will be doing as he chants of the poem. For example, use icons representing hands up, hands down, around, and riding. Use a visual cue to let the child know that one part of the lesson has ended and you will be transitioning into the next part.

Speech or Language Impairments—If the child has articulation disorders, he may have a difficult time with the pace of the chanting. Practice the chant slowly and repeatedly before chanting it to music.

Hearing Impairments—If playing carousel music, allow the child to stand closer to the player and to feel the vibrations of the music.

Visual Impairments—Provide props to support the discussion and the book reading. When discussing merry-go-rounds, share with the child a sample of music that is associated with a carousel.

Cognitive and/or Developmental Delays—Preteach the hand motions that will be used to accompany the poem.

Emotional Disturbance—Provide positive reinforcement for participating appropriately in the discussion as well as during the chanting of the poem.

Other Health Impairments/Attention Deficit Hyperactive Disorder—Stand near the child if you anticipate impulsive behavior.

Orthopedic Impairments—When the children are learning hand motions to accompany the poem, be sure to select movements that a child with a specific orthopedic impairment can manage.

Curriculum Connections

- **Art**—Children can fashion horses from playdough or salt dough. Provide a circular base where they can place their creations. This will enhance the horse's appeal as a merry-go-round figure.

- **More Art**—Have materials available so children can make stick horses, including broomstick handles, socks or small pillows to stuff horse's heads, yarn for manes, ribbon or rope. Most preschoolers will need adult assistance to build a stick horse. Have family volunteers available to help them.

- **Outdoors**—Use the stick horses to ride on the playground or to simulate a merry-go-round.

- **Special Field Trip**—If a carnival is in town, take children on a trip to ride the merry-go-round. This experience could open up an avenue for discussions about Ferris wheels, car rides, special events, food, or art contests.

JUST FOR FUN

Magic

Time
15–20 minutes

Materials
- An magician (optional)
- Magician's wand (purchased or teacher-made)

Review
Ask the children to tell you which magic trick they liked best.

Assessment Strategy
This lesson is just for fun, so no assessment is needed. You may ask individual children who are willing to demonstrate a trick they have learned.

Objectives
Children will:
1. Name one magic trick.
2. Describe a magic trick they enjoy.

Lesson
- If possible, invite an area magician or an older child who can do magic tricks to visit your class as a performer. If you want to do your own magic tricks, *Mark Wilson's Complete Course in Magic* by Mark Wilson is a good resource for learning how to do magic tricks.
- Ask the children if they have ever seen a magic act or a magician. Introduce your guest performer and tell the children that the person will perform magic tricks. Talk with the children about where they might see a magician.

Accommodations/Modifications
Autism—Magic is an abstract concept. Be sure the magician is an adult and is aware of the child's disability, and knows that children with autism often take words literally.

Speech or Language Impairments—Use a lead-in sentence when asking the child how a magician performs her tricks. During review, provide choices as to which trick the child liked best rather than offering an open-ended question.

Hearing Impairments—Allow the child to move closer to the show. If the magician is soft-spoken, provide a small microphone for her use.

Visual Impairments—Allow a child with a visual impairment to hold and manipulate some of the items used in the magic trick.

Cognitive and/or Developmental Delays—When teaching a magic trick, use simple language and model each step of the trick for the child.

Emotional Disturbance—Encourage and praise the child's participation in the activity.

Other Health Impairments/Attention Deficit Hyperactive Disorder—Use proximity control to prevent impulsive behavior.

Orthopedic Impairments—Make sure the child can see and participate in the magic show.

Curriculum Connections
- **Book Center**—Place *Mark Wilson's Complete Course in Magic* in the Book Center. Although this book is written for children ages 9-12, some children will enjoy looking at the pages to find out how tricks are achieved.
- **Dramatic Play**—Add a magician's cape, wand, and top hat to the Dramatic Play Center to encourage the children's play.

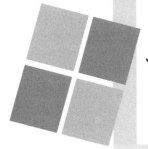

Bubbles

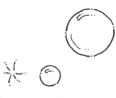

Time

10 minutes

Materials

- Tubs
- Bubble soap
- Utensils to make bubbles, such as whisks, wire spatulas, slotted spoons

Preparation

Place a small tub of bubble soap in the Group or Circle Time area and a few tools to make bubbles. Place an additional tub of bubble soap in the Water Table.

Review

Ask the children to blow a bubble as they leave the Group or Circle Time area.

Assessment Strategy

As children participate in Bubble Day, ask each child to tell you what is needed to make bubbles.

Objectives

Children will:

1. Blow bubbles with a variety of tools.
2. Describe bubbles in their own words. **Note:** Declare a specific day as Bubble Day. Ask family volunteers to help children enjoy making, blowing, and chasing bubbles.

Lesson

- Dip one of the tools into the bubble soap and wave the utensil to make bubbles.
- Ask the children what the bubbles are and if they have ever made bubbles at home. Tell them you have placed a tub of bubble soap in the Water Table or in the Water Play area for them to experiment with later.
- Tell the children they need bubble soap and a bubble tool to make bubbles.

Accommodations/Modifications

Autism—Create a picture chart of how to make and use bubbles. Model how to use the various tools children will use to create bubbles.

Speech or Language Impairments—During the assessment, let the child choose and point to picture icons representing bubble soap and bubble-blowing utensils.

Hearing Impairments—Place the child closer to you when you are discussing bubbles. Use simple signs to support spoken words such as *bubble*, *water*, *soap*, and *play*.

Visual Impairments—Allowing the child to feel bubbles as they are blown and to place his hands into bubble soap will help him understand how bubbles are formed.

Cognitive and/or Developmental Delays—Model how to blow bubbles. Have the child focus on forming his mouth and blowing out air.

Emotional Disturbance—Clearly explain how to handle the bubble utensils and model their use. Provide praise when the child uses the utensils correctly.

Other Health Impairments/Attention Deficit Hyperactive Disorder—The child may become impulsive when allowed to use the utensils. Monitor his behavior.

Orthopedic Impairments—The child may have a difficult time blowing a bubble. Show the child how to wave the bubble wand.

Curriculum Connections

- **Art**—Provide bubble soap and paper for the children. Ask children to blow bubbles so they hit the paper and make a wet imprint. When the children are satisfied that the paper is wet enough, let the bubbles dry to create an art design.
- **Connecting with Home**—Ask children's families to help child find bubbles at home (in the bathtub, in the washing machine, in the kitchen sink, and other places in the home).

Glitter

Time

15–20 minutes

Materials

- Index cards and marker or chalkboard and chalk
- Glitter in several different colors
- Paper and glue (put newspaper under the paper to protect the floor)

Objectives

Children will:

1. Use glitter to prepare an artistic product.
2. Describe the characteristics of glitter.

Preparation

Write *glitter* on a chalkboard or on a large index card. On additional index cards, write words that rhyme with *glitter*, such as *litter, hitter, knitter, sitter, bitter, fitter, jitter, pitter, quitter, titter, twitter,* and *flitter*.

Lesson

- Have several bottles of glitter in front of you as children gather for the lesson. Ask them if they know what is in the bottles.
- Ask children to tell you what they know about glitter.
- Show children the word *glitter* on the index card or on the chalkboard. Ask if they recognize the words written on the index cards. (See suggestions in the Preparation section).

  Note: Some of the children who are more experienced with phonemic awareness activities will do well with this aspect of the lesson.
- Demonstrate how to draw a picture with glue, and then shake glitter on top of the glue. Tell children they will make a picture with glitter later in the day, if they choose.

Accommodations/Modifications

Autism—Assist the child as she prepares her glitter pictures by using family volunteers or classroom peers to guide her through the process.

Speech or Language Impairments—The child may have difficulty with the phonemic awareness activity. Add a clapping motion to syllables and stress the ending "–itter" sound of each word. This should help her understand the pattern in the words.

Review

Ask children to say one word that rhymes with glitter as they leave Group or Circle Time.

Assessment Strategy

At the end of the day, ask each child to show you the artwork she made with glitter. Use this opportunity to determine how well children are progressing toward representation in their artwork.

Hearing Impairments—The child may have a difficult time with rhyming words. Specific impairments may cause a reduced ability to hear specific tones in certain sounds of letters. If possible, finger spell the initial sounds of each word. Real words, such as *litter, sitter, knitter,* and *flitter,* can be signed for the child.

Visual Impairments—Allow the child to feel the texture of the glitter. You may need to place her hand on the glitter if this is the first time she has been exposed to glitter. Have available a picture created with glue and glitter. Allow the child to run her hands over the dried picture after you demonstrate the process. Include the child in the demonstration, if possible.

Cognitive and/or Developmental Delays—Demonstrate the activity in a step-by-step process. Teach the child (and all of the children) safety rules for using glitter and make a connection as to why the rules apply. For example: "We keep glitter on the paper. If glitter goes in our mouths, we can become sick." Keep the rules simple, but stress safety.

Emotional Disturbance—Rephrase safety rules in a positive way. For example, "Don't put glitter in your mouths or on the floor" can be phrased as "Keep glitter on the paper." Reinforce positive behaviors throughout the lesson.

Other Health Impairments/Attention Deficit Hyperactive Disorder—The child may become excited and impulsive when playing with glitter. Stand near her to serve as a reminder to stay on task. Have the child participate in the demonstration. This will allow her to move throughout the lesson.

Orthopedic Impairments—The child may need help to squeeze the glue bottle. Ask a peer or a family volunteer to use a hand-over-hand motion to assist the child. You still want the glue to be placed on the paper where the child wants it to go. Doing it for the child will make the picture less valuable to the child. Make sure the glitter, glue, and paper are accessible to the child.

Curriculum Connections

- **Art**—Provide paper, glitter, sequins, and glue so children can produce an artistic creation. Let their creations dry so they can take them home at the end of the day. Ask them to share their products during a sharing time before the end of the day.

- **Math**—Prepare patterns on paper using glitter and sequins. Buttons, stars, or other materials are useful, too. Let children try to match the pattern or create their own patterns.

- **Manipulatives**—Prepare up to eight bottles of glitter. Encourage the children to match bottles that have the same color of glitter. For a more challenging experience, ask the children to match the bottles by shaking each one and matching it to one that makes the same or similar sounds.

Flubber

Time

10–15 minutes

Materials

- Measuring cups and spoons
- Mixing bowls
- Mixing spoons
- Hot water
- School glue
- Borax
- Food coloring (optional)

Objectives

Children will:

1. Experiment with flubber.
2. Talk about their experiences with flubber.

Preparation

Before the children arrive (or on the previous day), prepare flubber using the following recipe.

Recipe

Mix 1 cup hot water and 1 cup school glue in a bowl. Mix 2 tablespoons Borax in ⅓ cup hot water and pour this mixture into the glue and water mixture. Stir right away. Let the mixture sit for two or three hours. Drain excess water before using the flubber. **Note:** Flubber will be white unless food coloring is added. If desired, add food coloring to the hot water as a first step to making the mixture.

Lesson

- Begin stretching flubber as children come to the lesson.
- Tell children that flubber is a special substance designed for play and just for fun.
- Show them that the substance stretches but does not hold its shape. Ask one or two children to stretch it apart and talk about its properties, which might include: "It's wet," "It stretches," "It smells good (clean)," "It's rubbery," and "It starts going back together when you let it go." Let the children offer as many comments as they can.
- Tell the class that you will be making more flubber in the Art Center today and they can help you, if they wish.
- Ask them to play with the flubber sometime during the day.

Accommodations/Modifications

Autism—The child might be tactilely defensive and may not want to touch or manipulate the flubber. Flubber may be placed in a resealable plastic bag for the child to squeeze.

Speech or Language Impairments—When asking the child about the properties of flubber, offer choices about its texture. For example, ask, "Is the flubber hard or soft, wet or dry, or smooth or rough?"

Review

Ask children to tell you what they know about flubber. Ask, "Why won't the flubber stay together?"

Assessment Strategy

Ask children to identify the flubber from among a group of art products.

Hearing Impairments—Place the child close to you. Speak clearly and avoid placing your hands over your mouth as some children with hearing impairments read lips.

Visual Impairments—Allow the child extended opportunities to manipulate the flubber. This will enable him to better understand the its characteristics.

Cognitive and/or Developmental Delays—When reviewing the lesson, offer the child choices as to why flubber will not separate. Allow other children in the class to respond to the question first to give the child a model.

Emotional Disturbance—Monitor behavior around the flubber. Review rules for playing with the flubber and model the proper way to handle it.

Other Health Impairments/Attention Deficit Hyperactive Disorder—Provide the child with the opportunity to stand when pulling or stretching the flubber.

Orthopedic Impairments—Make sure all materials are accessible to the child. A child with limited use of his hands may need to manipulate flubber with his feet or use a gripping device. If these options are not available, gently rub or press flubber onto his hand and arm area.

Curriculum Connections

- **Art**—Prepare flubber in various colors to include in the classroom Art Center. Encourage the children to handle it and play with it.
- **Connecting with Home**—Make copies of the flubber recipe to send home to families.
- **Language and Literacy**—After children have played with the flubber, ask them to dictate a story about their experience to an adult, or they may try their own invented spellings for words.
- **More Language and Literacy**—Add the word *flubber* to the Word Wall, along with other words that rhyme with it, such as *blubber* and *rubber*.

Dancing

Time

20–25 minutes

Materials

- CD or cassette player
- Recording of music
- *My Mama Had a Dancing Heart* by Libba Moore Gray, or another book about dancing

Objectives

Children will:

1. Dance in a group.
2. Describe how they feel about dancing.

Lesson

- Play music that children can dance to as they come to Group or Circle Time.
- As the music plays, ask the children, "What does music make you want to do?" If necessary, lead the children to the response that music makes them want to dance. Stand up and ask the children join you as you dance. Swaying to the music may be best if you have easily distractible children.
- Continue dancing until the music stops. Ask the children to tell you how they feel about dancing.
- After the children settle back into their places, read *My Mama Had a Dancing Heart* or another book about dancing. Let the children make comments about the characters and the dances in the story. Commenting will help children pay close attention and remember the story better at a later time.
- Tell the children they are going to play a dancing game such as "London Bridge," "Lobby Loo," or "Bluebird through My Window" when they go outside later in the day.

Accommodations/Modifications

Autism—Provide hand cues to prepare the child for transitions. For example, when going from dancing to sitting on the ground you might lower your hands, palms down, from your chest down to your waist. This will serve as a signal that the children will all sit down soon. Praise the child for participating in the lesson.

Speech or Language Impairments—Modify the questions about music so the child can respond with a "yes" or "no" answer. For example, "Does music make you want to dance?"

Hearing Impairments—Allow the child to sit close to the CD or tape player. Allow her to place her hand on or near the player. Feeling the vibrations of the music will support the auditory intake of the music. Provide a visual cue when the music stops.

Visual Impairments—Use a big book when reading about dancing. Place the child closer to the book as it is being read. Provide props that correspond to the characters or objects discussed in the book. Allow the child to hold the objects.

Cognitive and/or Developmental Delays—Model how to play the outdoor dancing game selected. If playing you are "London Bridge," have the child walk through each step as you discuss what will unfold: two children holding hands in the air, children walking under the bridge, and the bridge "falling down."

Review

Ask the children as a group to review the book you read to them.

Assessment Strategy

Observe children on the playground to measure their success at participating in the group dancing experience. Questions to consider are:

- Did every child participate?
- Did the children know the movements?
- Did the children move easily during the game?

Emotional Disturbance—Stand near the child. Review rules of how to sit during story time. Reinforce positive behavior during dance and story times.

Other Health Impairments/Attention Deficit Hyperactive Disorder—The child may become excited when moving and dancing around the room. Remind the child of the rules and designate a specific area where dancing is allowed.

Orthopedic Impairments—If the child cannot use her lower body when dancing, encourage her to dance by moving her hands and swaying her upper body to the rhythm of the music.

Curriculum Connections

- **Dramatic Play**—Entice boys and girls to dress up as dancers by adding attractive costumes to the Dramatic Play Center. Have recordings of Strauss waltzes available for the children.
- **More Dramatic Play**—Provide satin ribbons, sequined belts, jewelry, and net for children to use to make costumes for the dolls in the Home Living Center.
- **Language and Literacy**—Work with small groups of interested children to talk about words that rhyme with dance, such as *prance, lance, glance,* and *stance.*

GAMES AND SPORTS

What Are Sports?

Time

20–25 minutes

Materials

- Pictures of various individuals playing sports, including children
- Sports equipment (or pictures, if items are unavailable)
- Chart paper and markers or chalkboard and chalk

Objectives

Children will:

1. Name at least one sport.
2. Name a sports figure.

Preparation

Before the children arrive in the morning, place pictures of adults and children playing various sports on a bulletin board. Place the bulletin board near the Group or Circle Time area. **Note:** Ask families ahead of time for photographs of their children playing sports.

Lesson

- As children arrive for Group or Circle Time, ask them to talk about what they see. Focus their attention on the bulletin board. Tell them the pictures they see are photographs of people who are playing sports.
- Hold up a picture of a well-known sports hero, for example, Michael Jordan, Derek Jeter, Tiger Woods, Jennifer Capriati, or Tara Lipinski. Choose photos of sports figures the children will recognize. Select a photograph that is familiar to many children in the classroom.
- Ask the children if they know who the sports figure is and what he or she does. If the children do not know, identify the sports figure and offer information about the sport the person plays.
- Display the sports equipment you brought to class. Ask the children to identify the items.
- Ask the children to name as many sports as they can. Write the sports they name on chart paper or on a chalkboard.
- Tell the children sports can be classified many ways. One way is to identify whether the sport is an individual or team sport. Look at the children's list again and mark those that are team sports and those that are individual sports.
- Talk about scoring in a positive light. Tell the children that a team or an individual might lose one time and win the next time. Tell them that people who participate in sports practice in order to become better at their sport. **Note:** Talk with the children about Olympic sports if they are interested, especially if it is around the time of a Summer or Winter Olympics. Be sure to talk about the Special Olympics, whether or not you have a child with special needs in your classroom.

Review

Ask the children to stand and pretend that they are batting a ball, throwing a ball, hitting a golf ball, shooting a basket, swinging a tennis racket, running in place, or kicking a soccer ball. Talk about which movements are for a team sport and which are for an individual sport.

Assessment Strategies

Have photographs of people playing various sports. Ask each child to name the sports he knows (at least one).

Accommodations/Modifications

Autism—Display picture icons as children begin to name sports they can play. Provide several cues when each part of the lesson is ending. This will help the child transition from one part of the lesson to another.

Speech or Language Impairments—Allow other children to respond to the question, "What other sports are there?" before asking the child to respond. This will provide a model as to how to respond.

Hearing Impairments—Bring the child close to the person speaking. Use clear, articulate language and be sure to face the child when discussing sports and sports figures. The child may read lips to support his auditory intake.

Visual Impairments—Use props when presenting photos of sports figures. For example, when showing Michael Jordan, have a basketball available. If possible, use poster-size photos.

Cognitive and/or Developmental Delays—Break the lesson into clear tasks. Present instructions with simplified language and use concrete objects to make abstract ideas such as shooting a basket more concrete.

Emotional Disturbance—Provide positive reinforcement when the child useappropriate behavior and participates in the lesson.

Other Health Impairments/Attention Deficit Hyperactive Disorder—Use proximity control when you ask the child to pretend to participate in a sport. Children with ADHD often become impulsive when allowed to move about and pretend.

Orthopedic Impairments—When reviewing the lesson with the child, be sure to use a sports action that he can do. A child with limited or no use of his legs could not pretend to run in place or kick a ball but can pretend to shoot a hoop or throw a ball. Be sure the bulletin board is at a level where the child can see it.

Curriculum Connections

- **Art**—Golf balls make wonderful painting tools. Roll a golf ball in a bowl of paint and then roll it onto a piece of paper for artistic results. Use more than one color for creative effect.
- **More Art**—Ask children to make a sports mural by cutting out sports pictures from magazines and gluing them onto a large piece of butcher paper. Place this mural in the hall so other people in the school will know what your class is studying.
- **Outdoors**—Set up sports-related activities to extend the children's learning about sports. Possibilities include child-sized bowling sets, miniature golf sets, Nerf balls, and other soft balls, basketballs, and hoops.
- **More Outdoors**—Teach children about the responsibility of retrieving all of the equipment used during outdoor play. Remind children that leaving equipment on the playground means it may get broken or lost.

Games We Play

Time

30–35 minute

Materials

Ready access to materials or equipment needed for games children might ask to play

Objectives

Children will:

1. Name one game played in the classroom or on the playground.
2. Demonstrate a skill used in games, such as hopping, jumping, shaking, and so on.

Lesson

- As soon as a few children arrive at Group or Circle Time, tell them they are going to play a game called Freeze. Explain how it is played: At a signal from you (such as, "Go!"), the children begin to move. They move until you say, "Freeze!"
- Ask the children to move around the classroom. After a few moments, call, "Freeze." When everyone is frozen, tap a child to start the game again.
- When all the children have arrived at Group or Circle Time area, ask them to sit down and tell them that the topic of discussion is "Games We Play."
- Ask them, "What are some games you know how to play?" After the children respond, ask them, "Which of these games is your favorite?"
- Ask one child to name a game she wants to play. If the child names Drop the Handkerchief, find a handkerchief or scarf and play the game a few times.
- Play two or three games the children know.
- When seated, tell children that games and sports each have rules and require the players to be active. Tell the children that they will use many of the skills they use in games later on if they play sports.
- Introduce the word *athlete*. Show the children that throwing a ball is similar to an athlete's skill in throwing balls.
- Finish Group or Circle Time by asking the children to name skills they use in games. They can stand and imitate these skills, such as hitting a ball, shooting a basketball, throwing a ball, running (best to run in place), jumping, leaping, and so on. Remind children that singing games, such as "Hokey Pokey" or "Looby Loo," are games, too.

Accommodations/Modifications

Autism—Avoid games that involve touching or multiple steps. Give clear, specific directions on how to play each game and provide the child with a transition cue before changing activities. Transition cues can be a hand signal, ringing a bell, or pointing to an object.

Speech or Language Impairments—Preteach words, such as *team*, *players*, *skills*, and *actions*.

Hearing Impairments—During group discussions about games and players, position the child so she can clearly see facial expressions and read the lips of other children as they are speaking. Games involving "whispering" may be difficult for the child.

Review

Review

As children leave Group or Circle Time, ask them to jump to the next activity. Remind them that jumping is a skill that some athletes use, especially track stars.

Assessment Strategy

This might be a good time of the year to summarize the skills children have acquired. Because of the time required to do individual assessments, you may need to enlist families' assistance to finalize all of the checklists. Modify the checklist on page 290 to match the needs of the individual children involved in your classroom.

Visual Impairments—Allow the child to touch objects that relate to games and activities. She may need help when moving to participate in games. Avoid games that involve reading from cards or that focus on looking for specific items throughout the room.

Cognitive and/or Developmental Delays—Provide picture choices of various games for children to choose from when asked, "What are the names of games you know how to play?" Model how to play a game before playing it. During the review, allow other children to perform an action first before asking the child to do it. This will serve as a model of what to do.

Emotional Disturbance—Stand near the child if you feel she may become aggressive during the games. Model acceptable behaviors and review game rules frequently.

Other Health Impairments/Attention Deficit Hyperactive Disorder—Offer clear rules on how to play the games. Be sure the child understands how to play the games, and model acceptable behavior during games.

Orthopedic Impairments—If other children in the class suggest a game that this child cannot play (for example, Drop the Handkerchief would be difficult for a child in a wheelchair), the child may need assistance or you can select a different game to play.

Curriculum Connections

- **Center Time**—When you observe children playing a made-up game during Center Time, ask them to tell you the rules they are using either later on. For example, if one child is leading another around with a leash she has fashioned from string or ribbon, the rule might be "Roxie has to follow me, because she's the dog."

- **Connecting with Home**—Take photographs of the children playing their favorite games to share with families. If you use a digital camera, you can download the pictures into your class newsletter.

- **Math**—Develop a chart showing the children's favorite games. Ask each child to place a tally mark under her favorite, and then add the marks to determine the group's favorite game.

- **Outdoors**—Interact individually with children who want to practice hitting golf balls. Use child-sized golf clubs, if possible. Talk about their stance and follow-through, as if they were professional athletes. **Note:** Be sure the rest of the children stay a safe distance away from the child who is swinging the club.

Games Older Children Play

Time

30–60 minutes, depending on the playground equipment available

Materials

- Sports equipment used by older children, such as baseballs and bats, footballs, jump ropes, and basketballs
- An older child or children (Invite fourth or fifth graders who are willing to talk about their experiences with a team sport)
- Balls
- Family volunteers
- An assortment of outdoor sports equipment, such as jump ropes, roller skates, tricycles, and other equipment that is appropriate for the skills of the children

Objectives

Children will:

1. Name one game older children often play.
2. Participate in a sporting event of their choice (with supervision).

Lesson

- As children begin arriving for Group or Circle Time, remind them that the topic of the day will be the same as the previous day: games.
- Ask the children, "What are games that older children like to play?" After the children have finished responding, introduce them to the invited guests. Ask the guests to talk about the games they like to play. If possible, go outside with the guests so they can demonstrate their sport (batting a ball or kicking a soccer ball, for example).
- Encourage the children to throw balls to one another, and invite the guests to join in the activity.
- This is a good time to introduce Hopscotch to children who are interested and to teach other children how to jump rope. Ask family volunteers to assist in supervising small groups of children participating in these activities.
- Some children may want to try roller skates or bikes. Have plenty of supervision and assistance on hand! **Note:** This lesson should provide children with opportunities to experiment with pieces of equipment that are usually available only to older children in a secure environment. Consider going to a nearby school or park playground where children can play on seesaws, swings, and climbing devices. Supervise closely.

Accommodations/Modifications

Autism—When asking the question regarding which games children like to play, make sure you have the child's attention. If his social interactions are limited, rephrase the question as a yes-or-no question. For example, ask, "Is kicking a soccer ball a game that children like to play?"

Speech or Language Impairments—When talking about games older children like to play, provide pictures so the child has a visual frame of reference during the discussion. Provide pictures or verbal clues about games older children play if the child does not respond to the assessment activity.

Hearing Impairments—Outdoor environments tend to have more external noise, which can reduce a child's ability to understand clearly what is being spoken. Speak clearly, facing the child, and be sure he understands what is said.

Review

When children return to the classroom, ask each child to name one game he tried.

Assessment Strategy

Ask each child to name a game that he has observed an older child play on a regular basis.

Visual Impairments—Some equipment, such as roller skates and bikes, will require more careful supervision than other equipment. Remember that the child may have difficulty judging distance. Clearly define parameters in which the activity will occur.

Cognitive and/or Developmental Delays—Repeat instructions on how to use the equipment and safety rules frequently. The child may not comprehend the concept of playing safely. Assign a peer buddy or an adult to help him use the sports equipment properly and safely.

Emotional Disturbance—Provide appropriate supervision when the child is outside or on playground equipment. When introducing and allowing children to play with the sports equipment, define the rules clearly and model appropriate behavior.

Other Health Impairments/Attention Deficit Hyperactive Disorder—Minimize distractions outside. Model safe ways to use the sports equipment.

Orthopedic Impairments—Make sure materials are accessible to the child. During outside games, encourage his full or partial participation. Adapt outdoor equipment to increase participation in games. For example, Velcro can be used to stabilize a ball.

Curriculum Connections

- **Music**—Make sure exercise CDs are available for children. Purchase one for your classroom and use it during Center Time or at the end of the day.
- **Dramatic Play**—Find child-sized uniforms from favorite sports to put in the Dramatic Play Center to foster the children's dramatic play.
- **Connecting with Home**—Ask the children to ask their older siblings or family members about their favoritegame. When children return to school, gather the results of this informal survey to share during Group or Circle Time.

Staying Fit

Time

25–30 minutes

Materials

- Photographs of the children flexing their muscles
- Poster board
- Glue or tape
- *My First Book of the Body* by Chuck Murphy or another book about bodies
- Scale
- Measuring tape

Objectives

Children will:

1. Name one way they can keep their bodies fit.
2. Perform one simple exercise.

Preparation

A day or two ahead of this Group or Circle Time, take photographs of each child flexing her muscles. Put these on a poster board. On the day of this lesson, place the poster in the middle of the Group or Circle Time area. As children arrive, ask them to find their individual photographs.

Lesson

- Ask the children if they remember when the class talked about their bodies during the fall. Tell them that every person has the responsibility of keeping their own bodies healthy and fit.
- Ask, "What does it mean to be healthy and fit?" Engage the children in a discussion about being healthy and fit. Direct the conversation so that it covers the following statements:

  Exercise every day.
  Eat healthy food.
  Drink plenty of water.
  Get enough sleep every night.

- Read *My First Book of the Body* by Chuck Murphy or another book about bodies to reinforce what one must do to be healthy and fit.
- As the lesson is winding down, ask the children to stand up and do a series of simple exercises: touching their toes, reaching up high, jumping jacks, dancing to music, or moving creatively, such as walking like a crab, walking like a camel, slithering like a snake, or rolling like a log.

Accommodations/Modifications

Autism—Give the child transition cues before moving from one simple exercise to another. Ask the child to ring a bell or to clap her hands to let others know it is time to change exercises. This lets her prepare for the transition.

Review

Ask the children to move in a particular way, such as walking like a duck or galloping like a horse as they go to Center Time or to the next activity in the schedule.

Assessment Strategy

Weigh and measure each child and, if possible, compare the results to measurement taken at the beginning of the school year or earlier in the year. Talk to each child about the differences in the measurements. Ask each child to tell you one way they try to stay fit. **Note:** Be aware of and sensitive children who might be concerned about their weight or height.

Speech or Language Impairments—When asking children what it means to be fit, allow other children to respond first. This will serve as a model for the child with a language impairment.

Hearing Impairments—Provide simple signs that correspond to the exercises being taught. Directional signs will help when asking children to move in various positions. Speak clearly, face the child, and keep your hands away from your mouth when giving directions for each exercise.

Visual Impairments—Enlarge the children's photo that you intend to display. If a child has limited mobility due to a visual impairment, select exercises appropriately. For example, she should be able to touch her toes, but may not be able to run across a field around cones.

Cognitive and/or Developmental Delays—When asking children to respond to the question, "What does it mean to be fit?" provide two choices as answers. For example, "Does it mean to exercise or does it mean to eat a lot of candy?"

Emotional Disturbance—Review all classroom rules for active play. Praise the child for exercising appropriately and for remaining focused on the lesson.

Other Health Impairments/Attention Deficit Hyperactive Disorder—If the child becomes impulsive, stand closer to her and remind her of how to keep her hands to herself.

Orthopedic Impairments—When doing a series of exercises with the children, be sure to include exercises she can perform. For example, a child with limited use of her legs will not be able to do the Crab Walk. However, she may be able to roll like a log or slither like a snake.

Curriculum Connections

- **Art**—Give each child a paper plate. Ask them to cut out pictures of healthy food items to paste on the plate. Display their creations on a bulletin board display titled, "Keeping Fit with Food."
- **More Outdoors**—Organize an obstacle course for children. Remind them that exercise of this sort can help keep them healthy because they are using their muscles when they attempt the many maneuvers an obstacle course requires. An obstacle course can be organized inside the classroom as well.
- **Still More Outdoors**—If you live near a college or university, ask physical education students to host a stunts day for your classroom or center. Often, university students need professional hours with children to acquire specific certifications. Contact the school's physical education or athletic department to inquire about this type of assistance.

Movement Skills Checklist

Name of Child_____ Date _____

SKILL	YES	NO	COMMENTS
Is able to hop in place			
Is able to jump forward/backward			
Is able to throw a ball			
Is able to catch a ball			
Is able to catch a rolling ball			
Is able to do a somersault			
Is able to skip			
Knows how to march			
Is able to walk forward/backward			

Signature of Evaluator _____ Date _____

INTRODUCTION TO

Let's Pretend

Time

30 minutes

Materials

Chart paper and markers, chalkboard and chalk, or an overhead projector, transparencies, and markers

Note from the authors: Classroom teachers must decide if they want to teach this theme as presented or modify it, because there is some controversy about the topic. Young children have active imaginations; their play often includes make-believe characters. Children also learn about pretend characters from books, from conversations, from playing with other children, and from television programs. Some families object to this theme, so you may want to talk with other teachers or with the children's families prior to teaching it.

The authors of this book believe that children enjoy pretend activities. From a developmental perspective, their participation with make-believe is a form of play that allows them to suspend reality and offers them rich opportunities for creativity. The Let's Pretend theme adds another dimension to children's well-being as they grow into adulthood.

Objectives

Children will:

1. Describe one way to pretend.
2. Learn about the difference between make-believe and reality.

Lesson

- Begin the lesson by saying, "In your play, you have pretended to be dogs, turtles, birds, airplanes, clowns, and even Mother Goose characters. Tell me about other characters that you can pretend to be."
- Record their answers on chart paper, on a chalkboard, or on an overhead transparency.
- Ask the children what it means to pretend. As they attempt to define the word *pretend*, clarify any misconceptions they have.

Let's Pretend

- Ask them to suggest characters they would like to learn about. This is a good time to do a webbing activity with children. Begin a web by drawing a large circle on chart paper, a chalkboard, or a transparency. Write *Let's Pretend* in the middle of the circle. As the children suggest characters, draw lines away from the circle and add the names as suggested. The following is an example of a web showing possible responses by children:

- After the brainstorming is finished, tell the children that they are going to learn about pretend characters. Then guide them to recall some of the characters they have imitated in the past.
- Ask all of the children to stand and move around pretending to be airplanes, birds, turtles, dogs, sheep, and other characters suggested by the children.

Accommodations/Modifications

Autism—The concept of *pretend* may be difficult for the child to comprehend. Activities should be as concrete as possible with limited distractions. For example, instead of drawing a web, place related objects onto a web that is drawn on large paper and placed on the floor.

Speech or Language Impairments—The child may have a difficult time verbalizing the definition of *pretend.* Allow additional time for his responses and/or accept an example of pretending instead of the definition of *pretend.*

Review

As children leave the lesson area for other activities, ask them to whisper in your ear the animal or character they most enjoyed being that day.

Assessment Strategy

At a later time in the day, ask individual children to tell you what it means to pretend.

Hearing Impairments—Modifications may not be necessary. However, take into consideration the severity of the hearing impairment and be sure to use clear speech. It might be necessary to move the child closer to the activity to enhance his auditory intake.

Visual Impairments—It may be best to write the children's responses on large chart paper in large letters.

Cognitive and/or Developmental Delays—When creating a web of characters or animals, draw a picture to correspond to the printed word. Depending on the child's abilities, he may not be able to relate to the printed text.

Emotional Disturbance—Encourage and affirm the child's participation. Provide close supervision and reminders to be gentle as the children pretend to be animals. Be sure to emphasize that play is fun, and that it is important to play safely so no one is hurt.

Other Health Impairments/Attention Deficit Hyperactive Disorder—The child may become overly excited while pretending to be an animal or a character. You may need to set limits on specific areas where pretending can occur. For example, let the child act out his animal in the middle of the circle. This will prevent him from running through the room.

Orthopedic Impairments—If the pretend character and animals the children suggest are difficult for the child to pretend to be, you may need to offer additional suggestions. For example, a child in a wheelchair could not gallop like a horse, but could use his arms and facial expressions to pretend to be a fish.

Curriculum Connections

■ **Book Center**—Add appropriate books that focus on pretend experiences such as *Where the Wild Things Are* by Maurice Sendak, *The Little Old Lady Who Was Not Afraid of Anything* by Linda Williams, or one of the *Monster Mama* titles by Liz Rosenberg.

■ **Dramatic Play**—Place costumes, capes, top hats, crowns, and other props in the Dramatic Play Center to allow children to participate in make-believe experiences.

■ **Manipulatives**—Place pictures showing real animals, real people, and pretend characters in the Manipulatives Center for children to sort into two categories: Real and Pretend.

Princes and Princesses

Time

20 minutes

Materials

- Book about a prince and princess, such as the story of "Cinderella" or "Sleeping Beauty" (many versions are available)
- Photograph of a modern prince and/or princess, such as Prince Charles (England), Princess Kiko (Japan), or Princess Caroline (Monaco)
- Crown(s) and scepters (from party stores or teacher-made), one for each child
- Royal cape (use a pillowcase or a large piece of paper)
- Red carpet (use a long piece of red paper or red towels)

Objectives

Children will:

1. Demonstrate being a prince or princess.
2. Name one responsibility of modern royal families.

Preparation

Make a royal cape from a pillowcase or large piece of paper. If necessary, make a crown and scepter.

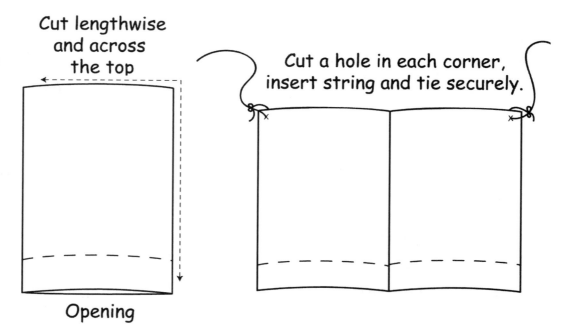

Cut lengthwise and across the top

Opening

Cut a hole in each corner, insert string and tie securely.

Lesson

- At Group or Circle Time, read a book to the children about a prince or princess.
- Tell the children there are princes and princesses in some countries and that they are people who may become kings and queens later in life.
- Show the children a photograph of a modern day prince or princess, such as Princess Anne, and tell children that she lives in England.
- Ask the children why they think princes and princesses are special. Accept all of their responses. Tell them in modern times royal families visit hospitals, orphanages, animal shelters, museums, and other countries.

As children leave the lesson area for other activities, provide a crown for each child to wear down the red carpet. Announce the departure of each child— "Prince Hagan," "Princess Margarita,"— addressing ach child by name as a prince or princess.

Assessment Strategy

Later in the day, ask each child if she would like to be a member of a royal family. Why or why not?

■ When members of a royalty family visit other countries, they often walk on a red carpet and sometimes wear glamorous clothes and crowns. Show the children the capes and crowns.

Accommodations/Modifications

Autism—This abstract lesson may be a problem for the child. Photos of hospitals, museums, and orphanages may make the concept of the work modern royal families do more concrete and understandable.

Speech or Language Impairments—The child may need additional time to respond to why they think princes and princesses are special. Often a child with articulation disorders has a difficult time with words ending in /es/ or /s/. Use caution when asking a child with a specific articulation disorder to pronounce a word such as *princesses* in front of peers.

Hearing Impairments—Move the child close to you. Decreasing the distance between the speaker and the child will increase the amount of auditory information received.

Visual Impairments—Enlarge a photograph of a prince or princess so details are more clearly seen, or invite the child to place a tripod lens over the photo.

Cognitive and/or Developmental Delays—A prince or princess doll may make the concept more concrete.

Emotional Disturbance—Use proximity control to monitor the child's behavior. Provide positive praise for contributing responses or uesses to the discussion.

Other Health Impairments/Attention Deficit Hyperactive Disorder—The child may become impulsive when acting out characters or when discussing what princes and princesses do with other children. Using carpet squares to designate spaces for the children is a proactive approach to prevent pushing each other.

Orthopedic Impairments—If the child is unable to walk down the red carpet, allow her to use her wheelchair to move down the carpet. Make sure to use adhesive double-sided tape to prevent the carpet from pulling up when a wheelchair moves across it.

Curriculum Connections

■ **Art**—Suggest that children make scepters out of straws or dowel rods and silver streamers.

■ **Dramatic Play**—Place prince and princess costumes in the Dramatic Play Center for children to use for their play.

■ **Writing**—Write each child's prince or princess name ("Prince Juan," "Princess Alicia") on a chart in the Writing Center. Some children may want to write their royal names on sentence strips.

LET'S PRETEND
Castles

Lookout Tower

Turret

Moat

Time
20 minutes

Materials
- Photographs or pictures of castles
- Pictures of homes that are not castles

Objectives
Children will:
1. Identify a castle from among a choice of pictures.
2. Describe what they think living in a castle would be like.

Lesson
- Remind the children about the lesson about princes and princesses earlier in the week. Ask them to talk about what they remember from that lesson. Say, "Today, we are going to talk about where a prince or princess might live. Their homes are called *castles*."
- Show a photograph of a castle and describe its appearance. Say, "Castles are large buildings with many, many rooms in them." Compare castle to their homes by saying that a castle might have 50 rooms while most homes have six or seven).
- Tell the children that castles have rooms where the royal family lives and rooms where their servants live. That is the reason so many rooms are in castles. Royal families entertain large numbers of people, another reason they need large homes. Point out that most castles have large, heavy doors for protection.
- Introduce terms that relate to castles, such as:
    - sentinel (someone who guards the front door of the castle)
    - lookout tower
    - guards
    - turret (an ornamental tower on top of a castle)
    - moat
    - dungeon
    - summer castle
    - winter castle
- Show pictures of each as the words are introduced to the children. **Note:** School supply stores and catalogs and toy stores and catalogs offer many props that will enhance this lesson and the discussion of Let's Pretend. You can use a large refrigerator or oven box to create a Classroom Castle. Show it to the children and tell them that you will work with them to create a castle during Center Time with this box. This project could take several days to complete.

Review

Review

While children are still in the group, point to a specific part of a castle in a photograph or picture and ask them to identify each component.

Assessment Strategy

Have several photographs or pictures of homes including a castle available. Ask each child to pick out the picture of a castle. Ask the child what makes it a castle.

Accommodations/Modifications

Autism—Use as many concrete items as possible when explaining *castle* words. For example, let the child hold the sentinel or guard from a set of castle figures. For a more concrete experience, have the child dress up like a guard and guard the classroom castle. This will make an abstract concept more concrete and easier to understand.

Speech or Language Impairments—Reduce the number of words relating to castles and focus on one or two key concepts.

Hearing Impairments—Use sign language for a few castle-related words. Speak clearly and keep your hands away from your face (for children who read lips). Placing the child closer to the person speaking will help him take in more auditory information.

Visual Impairments—Enlarge photographs of castles or add texture to the photographs, or give the child a castle-related object to hold and explore.

Cognitive and/or Developmental Delays—When introducing words that relate to castles, use a model of a castle, pointing to the areas of the castle that correspond to the word introduced. Allow the child to repeat newly identified words frequently.

Emotional Disturbance—Provide positive reinforcement to the child for appropriate behaviors and responses. Praise his attempts at identifying parts of a castle. For example, say, "That was a very good guess! What else might be found in a castle?"

Other Health Impairments/Attention Deficit Hyperactive Disorder—Model how to play in the Classroom Castle, emphasizing not to jump, run, or climb on other children.

Orthopedic Impairments—Make sure the Classroom Castle will accommodate a child using assistive devices, such as crutches or a wheelchair. If openings are not large enough, the child may need assistance getting in and out of the Classroom Castle.

Curriculum Connections

- **Art**—Children can create castles with paint, markers, shoeboxes, and construction paper. Or you can encourage a small group of the children to build a castle from the refrigerator box; contact a local furniture or appliance store for their discards. Use some of the terminology mentioned in the lesson as you help the children plan their construction. Ask, "Will the castle have any turrets? How can we add the heavy door? Is it possible to make a moat?"
- **Games**—Play Who's Guarding the Castle? Have children close their eyes, and appoint one child to hide in the room. Ask the rest of the children to open their eyes and name the person who is guarding the castle (the child who is missing from the group).
- **Outdoors**—Take the refrigerator box castle (Classroom Castle) to the playground where the children can continue their pretend play. If possible, look for a spot in the play area that could represent a moat around the castle.

Wild Things

Time

15 minutes

Materials

Where the *Wild Things Are* by Maurice Sendak

Objectives

Children will:

1. Retell the story of *Where the Wild Things Are*.
2. Describe one thing they liked about the story.

Lesson

- As children arrive for the lesson, tell them that today the class will talk about a boy named Max who had a dream.
- Read Maurice Sendak's book, *Where the Wild Things Are*. Give children an opportunity to comment about the wild things in the book.
- Ask the children why you think this book is about a dream Max had. Comment about the wild things roaring and gnashing their teeth in order to strengthen the language of the book.
- Ask the children what they think about Max's mother sending Max to his room without supper.
- While the children are still in a group, ask them to answer the following questions:
  - What was Max doing that made his mother angry?
  - What did she do to punish him?
  - Who were the wild things?
  - What did the wild things do?
  - What does it mean to say, "Roar their terrible roars"?
  - What does it mean to say, "Show their terrible teeth"?
  - What happened at the end of the story that made Max happy?

Accommodations/Modifications

Autism—Instead of asking the child why she thinks the book is about a dream Max had, offer two choices, one correct and one incorrect. Allow the child to choose "why" out of the two choices. You may want to review the concept of "dreams" briefly.

Speech or Language Impairments—Allow additional time for the child to respond to why they think this book is about a dream Max had. Use a prompt, such as, "This book is about a dream Max had because…"

Hearing Impairments—Keep the book well below your mouth as you read because the child may use lip reading when listening to stories or engaging in conversations with others.

Visual Impairments—*Where the Wild Things Are* comes in the big book format, the preferred format for a child with visual impairments. Seat the child close to the book as you read it.

Review

As children leave Group or Circle Time, ask them to tell the group their favorite part of the story.

Assessment Strategy

In small groups, ask the children to retell the story. You can assist them with prompts by showing pictures from the book.

Cognitive and/or Developmental Delays—Offer choices for responses as to why this book is about a dream Max had. When reading the book, provide opportunities to discuss why something is not real. Use a prompt, such as, "On this page there is a scary monster with claws: Is this real or make-believe?"

Emotional Disturbance—When discussing the concept of dreams, place an emphasis on whether the story in the book is real or make-believe.

Other Health Impairments/Attention Deficit Hyperactive Disorder—Use proximity control to reduce the child's impulsive behaviors. Using carpet squares or lap pads during story time helps children to sit in one area and to stay seated during the reading.

Orthopedic Impairments—If the child is immobile, be sure to position her so she has a clear view of the book being read.

Curriculum Connections

- **Art**—Provide small brown paper bags for children to stuff with newspaper and then decorate to make their own "wild things." Markers, construction paper, paint, pieces of fabric, and googly eyes will nurture children's creativity. Display the children's "wild things" on a classroom table with a sign that reads, "Our Wild Things Zoo."
- **Language and Literacy**—Encourage the children to make Wild Things out of socks. After children have fashioned their own Wild Thing puppet, they can use them to retell the story of the book.
- **More Language and Literacy**—In small groups, ask children to say words that rhyme with *Max* or *thing*. Write these words on a chart so children can observe the similarities and differences among the words (*ax, tax, fax, wax, lax, sacks, backs, whacks*, as examples of words that rhyme with *Max*).

Monsters and Dragons

Time

35 minutes

Materials

- Red hot candies
- *The Dragons Are Singing Tonight* by Jack Prelutsky or *Go Away, Big Green Monster!* by Ed Emberley

Objectives

Children will:

1. Describe monsters and dragons.
2. Pretend to be a monster or dragon.

Preparation

Before beginning the lesson, eat a handful of cinnamon red hot candies or another red candy to make your tongue red.

Lesson

- When children come to the Group or Circle Time area, show the children your tongue and ask them if they know why your tongue is red. Tell them your tongue is red because you ate red candy.
- Talk about the myths that dragons existed and that they breathed fire from their mouths and nostrils. Remind children that dragons and monsters never existed, but it is fun to pretend that they did.
- Read a book or books about dragons or monsters, such as *The Paper Bag Princess* by Robert N. Munsch; *St. George and the Dragon* by Margaret Hodges; *The Knight and the Dragon* by Tomie dePaola; *Where the Wild Things Are* by Maurice Sendak; *Go Away, Big Green Monster!* by Ed Emberley; and *There's a Nightmare in My Closet* by Mercer Mayer.
- When you are finished reading the story, ask some of the children to act out the story line. The rest of the children will be the audience. Then switch the groups so the audience can take a turn pretending to be monsters and dragons.
- Tell children that later in the day the class will have a Monster Parade. Before that time, they need to go to the Art Center to make a Monster Mask.

Accommodations/Modifications

Autism—Use pictures and line drawings to represent the sequence of events in the lesson. This creates a predictable and structured activity.

Speech or Language Impairments—Allow the child to point to pictures in the story rather than retelling a specific story line. For example, if a child is demonstrating how the monster crawls over a hill, he can point to this place in the book and then act it out without having to use oral language.

Review

While the children are still in the group, ask them to pretend to be monsters or dragons.

Assessment Strategy

Evaluate the children's behavior during the Monster Parade to determine what each child has learned about dragons and monsters. Notice the children who have difficulty creating or saying the class poem (see Curriculum Connections). Follow up with individual reviews.

Hearing Impairments—Bring the child closer to the story as it is being read. Attempt to include props and simple sign language when reading the story. Using a flannel board reinforces the story through visual representation.

Visual Impairments—Let the child touch props that relate to the lesson, such as large plastic dragon figures (sold in toy stores or toy sections of retail stores).

Cognitive and/or Developmental Delays—Rephrase explanations using short, simple sentences. Use gestures and modeling as you present the lesson. Modeling is especially important when children are making their monster masks.

Emotional Disturbance—If a child does not want to participate in retelling or acting the story, provide him with a quiet area where he can observe the other children. Provide consistent reinforcement for participation and appropriate behavior.

Other Health Impairments/Attention Deficit Hyperactive Disorder—Have the child get the materials to be used in the later steps of the lesson. This enables her to move about more frequently. When acting out a monster, designate a specific space where the child should remain. For example, mark an area on the carpet with masking tape to represent a stage where the children will act out the story. This will prevent children from running through the room as they pretend to be a monster.

Orthopedic Impairments—When selecting children to act out the story, be sure to select a part the child is able act out.

Curriculum Connections

■ **Art**—Provide children with paper bags that are large enough to fit over their heads. Precut large eyeholes in the bags before you give them to the children. Children can use any of the materials in the Art Center to create their Monster Mask. Be sure to have red construction paper available so children can make "tongues of fire" to attach to their dragon masks.

■ **Dramatic Play**—Plan with your school or center to have a Monster Parade at a designated time during the day's schedule. Ask the children to put on their masks and parade through all of the rooms in the building. Be aware that some children may not want to participate in the Monster Parade. They can walk in the parade without their masks.

■ **Writing**—Children grasp the concept of poems when you provide support for them to write class poetry. Working with a small group of children, give them an example (suggestions follow). The results will be fascinating. Children might suggest:

We're monsters and we're big and mean;
Sometimes we're green.

We're monsters and we're big and ugly;
Sometimes we're buggy.

LET'S PRETEND

Fairies and Elves

Time

20 minutes

Materials

- Recording of "Danse Macabre" (Saint-Saens) or "The Sorcerer's Apprentice" (Dukas)
- Tape recorder or CD player
- Fairy wand (purchased or teacher-made)
- Pictures of fairies, elves, or gnomes
- Poems about fairies or elves; suggestions include Rose Fyleman's "The Best Game the Fairies Play" or Eleanor Farjeon's "For a Mocking Voice" (optional)
- *The Elves and the Shoemaker* (many versions available)

Objectives

Children will:

1. Learn about fairies, elves, or gnomes.
2. Demonstrate through dance how to be a fairy or an elf.

Preparation

Have music playing as children arrive for the lesson (see suggestions in the Materials section).

Lesson

- As the children enter the Group or Circle Time area, wave the fairy wand and tell them that you are changing them into fairies, elves, or gnomes. Ask children how the music makes them feel.
- Show the children pictures of fairies, elves, and gnomes. Ask if they know what fairies, elves, and gnomes do. If possible, read one of the selected poems to the children. Ask them if they have ever heard the name Tinker Bell. Tell the children she was the fairy who helped Peter Pan learn to fly.
- Ask the children to say what they know about the story of Peter Pan. Discuss fairy dust. Tell the children that elves and gnomes are so small they can hide under mushrooms. Remind children that these creatures are make-believe characters.
- If the children are interested, continue the lesson by reading one version of *The Elves and the Shoemaker* by The Brothers Grimm.
- When you are finished reading the story, wave the magic wand and invite the fairies, elves, and gnomes to dance to the recorded music. Encourage them to be *very quiet*, because fairies, elves, and gnomes move so quickly and quietly that no one can see or hear them.

Accommodations/Modifications

Autism—During the assessment part of this lesson, let the child choose from Picture Communication Symbols of feelings. Some good choices of symbols might include *angry, happy, excited, scared,* and *sad.*

Speech or Language Impairments—Use gestures or sign language to help the child participate in the lesson. If she has an expressive language problem, let her point to pictures that represent feelings rather than respond verbally when you ask her what she knows about Peter Pan and how music makes her feel.

Review

Ask the children to talk about how they feel when they pretend to be fairies, elves, or gnomes.

Assessment Strategy

Play the selected music again later in the day. Evaluate each child's behavior as she dances to determine her understanding of elves, fairies, and gnomes.

Hearing Impairments—Provide an opportunity for the child to place her hand on the tape player. Often the vibrations from the tape will enable the child to feel the music. If her hearing impairment is mild, increase the volume. Seat the child near you when you read the story.

Visual Impairments—Use concrete objects when reading the poems and the story. For example, give the child a fairy doll as a prop when reading the poem about a fairy. Allow the child to touch the various props.

Cognitive and/or Developmental Delays—Use simplified language when giving directions for the activity. Using objects will help the child better understand the concepts of fairies, elves, and gnomes.

Emotional Disturbance—Provide opportunities for the child to dance alongside you. This will help her stay on task.

Other Health Impairments/Attention Deficit Hyperactive Disorder—Ensure that you have the child's attention before introducing the activity. Use a predictable strategy to get the child's attention, such as holding up your hand before introducing the story. Seat the child near you when reading the story.

Orthopedic Impairments—Recognize that a child with specific orthopedic impairments may not be able to dance to the music and encourage her to use other parts of her body to dance. For example, she can wave her hands or tap her feet to the beat of the music.

Curriculum Connections

- **Art**—Add silver glitter to the materials in the Art Center. Encourage the children to draw a fairy, cover it with glue, and then sprinkle glitter on top of their creation.
- **Book Center**—Add different versions of *The Elves and the Shoemaker* to the Book Center.
- **Language and Literacy**—Purchase fairy, elf, or gnome puppets to add to the Puppet Center.

Dreams

Time

30 minutes

Materials

- Chalk and chalkboard or marker and chart paper
- A book that reads as if it were a dream (*Where the Wild Things Are* is a good choice)
- *Ira Sleeps Over* by Bernard Waber, or another appropriate book

Objectives

Children will:

1. Describe what dreams are.
2. Retell a recent dream they have had.

Note: A series of multicultural books written by Idries Shah would enhance this lesson on dreams (and the Let's Pretend theme). The books include *The Man with Bad Manners; The Old Woman and the Eagle; The Boy Without a Name; The Clever Boy and the Terrible, Dangerous Animal; The Silly Chicken; The Farmer's Wife; Neem the Half-Boy; The Lion Who Saw Himself in the Water;* and *The Magic Horse*. These books are modern-day fables, which can be framed as dreams.

Lesson

- Pretend to sleep as the children gather for the lesson. You might even snore!
- Pretend to wake up and continue the lesson by asking the children what people do every night. Ask them, "Do you ever dream?"
- Ask two or three children to share one of their recent dreams. If no one can think of a dream, be prepared to share one of your own.
- Use a chalkboard or chart paper to draw images related to your dream. Ask the children, "Are these pictures real?"
- Ask children if dreams seem real to them. Tell them that dreams are just images or pictures they store in their brains while they are sleeping. Sometimes dreams are memories from the day. If, for example, they had had an ice cream cone during the day, they might dream about ice cream that night.
- Ask if anyone has ever had a nightmare. Tell the children that nightmares are dreams that are frightening. Tell them that they are going to learn about a boy named Max who had a nightmare.
- Read the book that can be framed as a dream. If available, read *Ira Sleeps Over* by Bernard Waber. Ask the children to lie down on the floor as if they are sleeping while you read the book.

Accommodations/Modifications

Autism—Dreams are an abstract and often confusing concept for the child to understand. If possible, act out having a dream. Have the child lie down, close his eyes, and picture himself running across the playground. Now have them open his eyes. Did he "see" himself running across the playground? Then ask, "Were you really on the playground or were you in the class lying down?" (Give the child two choices.) Now, once the

Review

While children are still in the group, ask them to talk about dreams and nightmares. Ask what they liked about the book(s) you read.

Assessment Strategy

Ask each child to share a recent dream.

child confirms that he was in class and not on the playground, link this experience to the concept of a dream, except that dreams happen when you are sleeping. A child with severe autism may not be able to grasp this concept at a young age.

Speech or Language Impairments—Allow additional time for the child to share one of his dreams.

Hearing Impairments—Read the story clearly. Be sure to face the child because he may be reading your lips as a way to help him gain auditory information.

Visual Impairments—Use high contrast colors when drawing images on a chalkboard or chart paper. Allow the child to sit closer to the chalkboard as well as to the book being read. If possible, select a big book as it has larger images, which are much easier for the child to see.

Cognitive and/or Developmental Delays—A dream is an abstract concept that may be difficult for the child to understand. Use simple vocabulary to represent the word *pretend*. Some children may have prior knowledge of the words *not real* or *fake*.

Emotional Disturbance—Use caution when asking the child to talk about one of his dreams. Often a child with emotional disturbances has experienced an unsettling situation that may cause him to feel uncomfortable, become withdrawn, become violent, or perhaps cry. Do not require the child to close his eyes while listening to the story or pretending to sleep.

Other Health Impairments/Attention Deficit Hyperactive Disorder—Designate a specific area where the child can pretend to sleep. Perhaps small blankets can be laid out for children when you ask them to pretend to sleep.

Orthopedic Impairments—If the child is in a wheelchair and the other children are lying on the floor to listen to the story or pretending to sleep, consider moving the child from the wheelchair to the floor. Always check with medical provider or a family member for proper positioning when moving a child out of the wheelchair and onto the floor.

Curriculum Connections

- **Art**—Ask the children to draw pictures of their dreams or nightmares. Remind the children that these are just images or pictures in our minds. They are not real!
- **Dramatic Play**—Add pillows and blankets to the Home Living Center so the children can pretend to sleep and dream.
- **Writing**—Encourage the children to use invented writing to tell about a dream they have had. Family volunteers can take dictation from children who want someone to record their dreams.

Trolls

Time

20 minutes

Materials

- *The Three Billy Goats Gruff* by Ellen Appleby, Janet Stevens, Paul Galdone, or others
- Copier
- Scissors
- Markers, crayons
- Tongue depressors
- Glue or tape

Objectives

Children will:

1. Name one character in the "The Three Billy Goats Gruff."
2. Describe trolls.

Preparation

Make puppets of the characters in the story, copying the illustrations of the characters in the book. Cut them out, color them, and laminate each one. Glue each to a tongue depressor.

Lesson

- Tell the children that you are going to read them a story about a troll. Ask, "Does anyone know what a troll is?"
- Show the children the picture of the troll in the book. Introduce the title of the book and tell the children the name of the person who drew the pictures. Read the book to the children.
- Select a few children to hold the tongue depressor puppets. Ask all the children to help remember the story as you help them retell the story with the puppets.
- Ask the children some of these questions (or think of your own):
  - Where did the troll live?
  - Why did the billy goats want to cross the bridge?
  - Was the smallest billy goat using his head? Why do you think so?
  - Do you think the troll and the goats could ever live together peacefully?
  - What would need to change to make this a peaceful story?

Accommodations/Modifications

Autism—Praise the child for participating in the lesson (holding the puppets).

Speech or Language Impairments—Allow other children to model responses to "What is a troll?" before asking the child to respond. Provide choices for responding to this question or ask a specific question about a troll. For example, ask, "Is a troll a large animal or is a troll a make-believe character?"

Review

Ask the children to name the four characters in the story.

Assessment Strategy

During the day, ask each child to tell you which one of the characters in the story was her favorite and ask why.

Hearing Impairments—When you read a story about trolls, move the child close to you and use expressive facial movements such as looks of surprise, anger, and happiness. Be sure to face the child when reading the book. She may be reading your lips as you read the book.

Visual Impairments—When reading the book, use expressive vocal intonations for each character. If possible, select a big book to use for this lesson and place the child near the book.

Cognitive and/or Developmental Delays—Retell the story for the child and allow her to select the appropriate puppet to demonstrate one part of the retelling.

Emotional Disturbance—Seat the child near you when you read the book and when the children act out the story. Model or role-play how to hold the tongue depressor puppets.

Other Health Impairments/Attention Deficit Hyperactive Disorder—Define the space on the floor with carpet squares or pillowcases where the child is to sit during story time.

Orthopedic Impairments—If the child is unable to hold the puppets, attach them to a gripping device such as a Velcro glove.

Curriculum Connections

- **Block Center**—Encourage the children to build a bridge like the one the troll was hiding under and to reenact the story.
- **Language and Literacy**—Cut out flannel pieces of the four characters in the story so children can retell the story. Use the book to sketch the characters onto felt and cut them out, or copy the characters and add Velcro to the back of each piece. Remember to laminate the paper pieces to make them last.
- **Listening Center**—Have a taped copy of the story for children to listen to as they look at the printed pages of the book.

Superheroes

Time

25 minutes

Materials

- Pictures of heroes (firefighters, police officers, disaster relief workers)
- Pictures of superheroes
- Chart paper and maker or chalkboard and chalk
- *Stories for Heroes* CD by Marc Brown and other celebrity readers (optional)

Objectives

Children will:

1. Name one superhero.
2. Describe how it feels to pretend to be a superhero.

Preparation

Post pictures of firefighters, police officers, nurses, and EMT personnel on a bulletin board near the Group or Circle Time area.

Lesson

- As children come for the lesson, ask them why the people in the photographs are important. Tell them that they are sometimes called *heroes*. You can also have pictures of rescue animals.
- Define the word *heroes* for children or ask them to define it. Ask children if they know any heroes. Tell them that many make-believe characters are superheroes because they can do extraordinary activities. Ask the children to name superheroes; record their responses.
- Ask, "What extraordinary activities can these superheroes do?"
- As they suggest characteristics, write the words the children say (*fly, save people, pick up heavy things, save the world*, and so on) on chart paper or a chalkboard. Remind them that these superheroes are not real characters; they are make-believe.
- Talk with the children about Paul Bunyan, Johnny Appleseed, and Pecos Bill if you have not already discussed them. Remind children that these mythical figures are often called *heroes*. If children appear to be interested and the *Stories for Heroes* CD is available, play portions of it for the children.

Accommodations/Modifications

Autism—When introducing heroes, add concrete items such as community helper dolls, a firefighter's hat, police badges, or stethoscopes. Break the lesson down into smaller tasks and use a picture chart to represent the series of events occurring in the lesson. For example, one card may show children sitting in a circle, the next a picture of a firefighter, the next a teacher writing on the board, and finally a picture of a CD player.

Speech or Language Impairments—If the child has an expressive language disorder, use a lead-in statement when asking him to tell you what extraordinary things superheroes do. For example, say, "Batman is a superhero. Batman can…"

Hearing Impairments—When introducing the photos, seat the child near the front of the group. Use gestures, pictures, and objects to support the activity.

Review

Ask children as a group to name a hero or superhero.

Assessment Strategy

During the day, ask each child to name the hero or superhero he likes best. Ask, "Why do you like this hero best?"

Visual Impairments—Use props that support the photos. Allow the child to touch and hold the various props during the discussion. Community helper dolls and figures and action are available in school supply stores and catalogs, as well as in some toy stores. Community helper clothing and superhero capes will also provide a more tactile experience for the child.

Cognitive and/or Developmental Delays—Use Picture Communication Symbols or clip art to provide pictorial cues for the child during the group discussion. Provide choices for the child when asked why a specific superhero is extraordinary. For instance, ask the child, "Is The Hulk special because he is a good swimmer or because he is very strong?"

Emotional Disturbance—When you introduce the photos of heroes, seat the child near you.

Other Health Impairments/Attention Deficit Hyperactive Disorder—Allow the child to play with hero or superhero figures if they are available. Handling the props will help the child focus his attention on an object representing the concepts presented and allow appropriate "fidgeting."

Orthopedic Impairments—Make sure all props and books read are presented at the child's level and all materials are within his reach.

Curriculum Connections

- **Dramatic Play**—Have superhero costumes available in the Dramatic Play Center to promote the children's dramatic play.
- **Games**—If appropriate, play a riddle game with small groups of children. Make up riddles about heroes and superheroes for children to guess. Here are a few suggestions:

  I wear a black costume and my headwear has ears on it. I drive a fancy car called a Batmobile. Who am I? (Batman)

  My costume is red with black stripes on it to look like a web. Who am I? (Spiderman)

  I wear a blue costume with a red cape. I can fly through the air. Who am I? (Superman)

  I wear a blue and red costume that has stars on it. The costume looks like a swimsuit, and I also wear gold-colored boots. I have long black hair. Who am I? (Wonder Woman)

  I'm a person who puts out fires. I come to your house in a red truck. Who am I? (firefighter)

  I work in hospitals and in doctors' offices. I usually wear a white uniform. I take your temperature. Who am I? (nurse)

- **Listening Center**—Place the *Stories for Heroes* CD in the Listening Center for children to listen to at their leisure.

Vacations

Time

15–20 minutes

Materials

- Items to pack for a vacation
- Paper bag
- Calendar
- Marker
- Small suitcase
- Paper
- Paint
- Paintbrushes

Objectives

Children will:

1. Describe a vacation as a time when people stop working and spend time relaxing and playing together.
2. Describe things people do on vacations.

Preparation

Place items to pack for a vacation in a large paper bag.

Lesson

- During Group or Circle Time, draw a star on the next date that is a holiday for most of the families in your classroom. Show the children the date of the holiday. When you review the calendar each morning, count the number of days until the next vacation time.
- Talk about vacations as a time when people take time away from work and spend time together relaxing. Show the children pictures of typical vacation activities, such as visiting grandparents, camping, or picnicking. Explain that families have fun together on vacation. Sometimes families spend vacation time together at home; the parents do not go to work and the children do not go to school.
- Show the children a small suitcase and talk about the fact that some of them may be going on vacation soon.
- Ask the children questions, such as:
    - Who is going to visit their grandparents?
    - What will you pack in your suitcase for your trip?
    - Will the weather on your vacation be hot or cold?
    - What kind of clothes will you need to take on your vacation?
    - What will you do on your vacation?
- Have each child tell one thing that she might need to pack in a suitcase.
- Sing the song below and give each child a turn to add something to pack. When it is each child's turn, have her pull an item out of a paper bag, say what it is, and pack it in the suitcase.

    I'm Going on Vacation by Sharon Lynch
    (Tune: "Have You Ever Seen a Lassie?")
    I'm going on vacation, vacation, vacation.
    I'm going on vacation,
    And I'm packing my _____.

Review

Review the fact that vacation time is a time when families take time away from work and spend time together relaxing. Ask the children to identify the next vacation time, how many days it is until vacation time, and what they want to do during their next vacation.

Assessment Strategy

Suggest that the children paint pictures of what they would like to do on vacation. Have each child tell you about her picture. Write what she says on the back of her picture.

Accommodations/Modifications

Autism—Provide clip art or Picture Communication Symbols for the suitcase, items in the suitcase, and the items in the song.

Speech or Language Impairments—Scaffold the child's language by providing verbal models or sentences for the child to complete during the lesson.

Hearing Impairments—Use sign language, gestures, and/or pictures during the group activity and song.

Visual Impairments—Describe your actions and the objects the children remove from the bag. Let the child sit near the suitcase so she can feel the items placed inside.

Cognitive and/or Developmental Delays—Provide physical assistance if needed during the assessment activity. Provide the names of the objects in the suitcase, if needed.

Emotional Disturbance—Seat the child near you during the lesson.

Other Health Impairments/Attention Deficit Hyperactive Disorder—Make sure you have the child's attention before giving her instructions for the song and the assessment activity.

Orthopedic Impairments—Provide a paintbrush holder and physical assistance for the child during the assessment.

Curriculum Connections

- **Language and Literacy**—Display books about travel and about places the children are going to visit in the Book Center. When children return from vacations, help each child write a story about her vacation on chart paper, and review the stories from time to time. Encourage families to share pictures, artifacts, and stories from family vacations.

- **Math**—During morning calendar time, count the number of days until vacation time.

- **Science**—Show the children a large weather thermometer. Talk about upcoming vacations. Show them the thermometer, explaining that the temperature goes up in the summer when it is hot and goes down in the winter when it is cold. In the fall and spring, the temperature is in the middle. Ask the children if they think it will be hot or cold on their next vacation.

- **Social Studies**—Talk about where children in the class will go on their next vacation. Mark the locations on a map.

Going on a Car Ride

Time
15–20 minutes

Materials
- Paint paper
- Scissors
- Toy car and people that fit inside the toy car
- Chairs
- Paint
- Paintbrushes

Objectives

Children will:
1. Describe the things that they like to do on long car rides.
2. Describe where they go on long car rides.

Preparation

Cut paint paper into car shapes.

Lesson

- When the children come to Group or Circle Time, show them a toy car. Place the toy people inside the toy car. Explain that today the topic will be long car rides.
- Ask the children, "When do you go on long car rides?" Talk about going to visit grandparents, to the park, or to a friend's house.
- Ask them, "Where do you like to go on long car rides?" Push the toy car and tell the children where you like to go on long car rides. Let each child have a turn pushing the car and telling where he likes to go on long car rides.
- Say, "Now that we have talked about where we can go on long car rides, what else can we talk about that is part of a long car ride?" Encourage the children to respond to the following questions:
  - Who do you go to see on long car rides?
  - What do you do on long car rides?
  - Who drives the car?
  - What do you do in the car?
- If the children are slow to respond, provide suggestions or choices to get the conversation started.

Review

Ask the children to tell you about their long car rides. Summarize their responses.

Assessment Strategy

Cut out car shapes from paper. Ask each child to paint his car with his favorite colors, and then tell you what he likes best about long car rides. Write what he says on the back of his car.

Accommodations/Modifications

Autism—Use Picture Communication Symbols or clip art to promote the child's participation so he will know the sequence of upcoming events.

Speech or Language Impairments—Scaffold language by providing the child with a phrase he can complete verbally. Provide verbal choices for children who have limited verbal expression.

Hearing Impairments—Use sign language, gestures, pictures, and objects during the lesson.

Visual Impairments—Verbally describe what you are doing as you introduce the lesson.

Cognitive and/or Developmental Delays—Call on the child after other children model appropriate responses.

Emotional Disturbance—Seat the child near you during the discussion.

Other Health Impairments/Attention Deficit Hyperactive Disorder—Seat the child near you during the discussion.

Orthopedic Impairments—For a child with severe fine motor problems, provide an adapted holder for paintbrushes during the assessment activity.

Curriculum Connections

- **Blocks**—Create a Car Center by providing cars and a road map rug or butcher paper road map. If you use butcher paper, the children can help by adding trees, houses, road signs, and other things to the road map.
- **Book Center**—Place books about cars in the Book Center. Some suggestions include *The Wheels on the Race Car* by Alexander Zane; *You Can Name 100 Cars, Trains, Boats and Planes* by Jim Becker; *Richard Scarry's Books on the Go* by Richard Scarry; *Beep Beep* by Kay Widdowson; and *Miss Spider's New Car* by David Kirk.
- **Dramatic Play**—Set up a set of chairs with a front seat, a back seat, and a play steering wheel set to create a Driver's Center.
- **Math**—Provide a set of small cars. Sort them by color and count them. Line them up by color to make a graph with the cars.
- **Science**—Play "What would happen if…" On cards write the phrase "What would happen if…" on one side and a situation on the other. Some examples are "cars could fly" or "cars did not have wheels" or "we did not have stop signs." Have one child draw a card from the pile. Read the card and ask the child to tell you what would happen if…. Scaffold the children's responses.
- **Social Studies**—Show the children a road map of your town. Use a pointer to show how you get from place to place in your town or city.

A Visit to Grandparents' House

Time

15–20 minutes

Materials

- Photographs of grandparents or other special family members or family friends
- Pictures of car, train, plane, boat, bus
- Beanbag
- Paper
- Markers or paint and paintbrushes

Objectives

Children will:

1. Describe the things they can do when they visit their grandparents or other relatives or family members.
2. Describe their grandparents or other relatives or family members. **Note:** To include all the children in this lesson plan, including those who do not have grandparents, let them talk about another family member or a family friend whom they visit.

Preparation

Ask families to send photographs of the children with their grandparents, a special family member, or a family friend.

Lesson

- At Group or Circle Time, tell the children they will be talking about grandparents, other special family members, or family friends today.
- Tell them you are going to show them some pictures and you want them to identify the child whose grandparents or family members or friends are in each picture.
- Show the pictures one at a time. After a few guesses from the children, identify the people in the picture. Talk about grandparents as special people. They are our mother's and father's parents.
- Talk about how special it is to visit grandparents. Ask the children where their grandparents live and how they get to their grandparents' home: by car, bus, train, boat, or plane. Show pictures of the various forms of transportation.
- Ask the children to tell what they do at their grandparents' home (or the home of another special family member or family friend) and when it is that they go to see their grandparents or family member or friend.
- Play My Favorite Thing, a game that focuses on grandparents: Hold a beanbag and tell the class your favorite thing about going to visit your grandparents, other special family members, or family friends. Toss the beanbag to one child who tells the class what she likes about going visiting her grandparents, special family members, or family friends. This child tosses the beanbag to another child who then tells the class what he likes about going to see his grandparents, special family members, or family friends. If necessary, scaffold the children's responses by asking leading questions.

Accommodations/Modifications

Autism—Use clip art or Picture Communication Symbols to list the sequence of events for the lesson. Encourage the child to respond during the discussion by pointing to picture choices.

Review

Summarize what you have talked about:

- Who are our grandparents? (our parents' parents)
- Where do your grandparents live?
- How do you get to your grandparents' house?
- What do you do when you get there?

Assessment Strategy

Ask the children to use paint or markers to draw a picture of their grandparents' home. Ask each child to tell you about visiting her grandparents. Write what she says on the back of her picture.

Speech or Language Impairments—Scaffold the child's responses during the discussion by asking leading questions and by providing sentences the child can complete. Call on the child to respond after other children provide model responses.

Hearing Impairments—Use sign language, gestures, and pictures when introducing the lesson and talking about grandparents as special people.

Visual Impairments—Describe your actions during the game with the beanbag. Tell the child when you are going to toss

Cognitive and/or Developmental Delays—Allow the child to participate in the discussion by providing object and picture choices. Use hand-over-hand guidance, if needed, for the assessment strategy.

Emotional Disturbance—Seat the child near you during the discussion and introduction.

Other Health Impairments/Attention Deficit Hyperactive Disorder—Ensure that you have the child's attention before beginning the discussion and giving directions.

Orthopedic Impairments—Provide an adaptive holder for the markers during the assessment activity. Use a piece of nonskid shelf liner under the child's paper to stabilize it as she works.

Curriculum Connections

- **Language and Literacy**—Read the story of "Little Red Riding Hood." Talk about how Little Red Riding Hood got to her grandmother's house and where her grandmother lived.
- **Math**—Count the number of grandparents and siblings on the family tree.
- **Science**—Make a family tree for each child with parents, grandparents, and siblings. Write the names of each family member on the family tree.
- **Social Studies**—Show where the children's grandparents live on a map of the state, country, or world.

Amusement Parks

Time

15–20 minutes

Materials

- Ferris wheel picture
- Picture of an amusement park
- Chart paper and marker

Objectives

Children will:

1. Describe at least two activities associated with amusement parks.
2. Learn that amusement parks are places where we go to have fun.

Lesson

- At Group or Circle Time, show the children a toy Ferris wheel or a picture of a Ferris wheel. Ask if anyone has seen a real Ferris wheel.
- Explain that amusement parks often have a Ferris wheel.
- Sing the song below several times. Encourage the children to imitate and sing.

    Here We Go Up on the Ferris Wheel by Sharon Lynch
    (Tune: "Here We Go 'Round the Mulberry Bush")
    Now we go up on the Ferris wheel, Ferris wheel, Ferris wheel.
        (hold hand on "rail" and rock)
    Now we go up on the Ferris wheel, way above the tree tops. (hands up in the air)

- Explain that amusement parks are places where people go to have fun. They go on rides or play games at amusement parks.
- Show the children pictures of an amusement park and engage them in a discussion about the Ferris wheel, the roller coaster, pony rides, boats, bumper cars, or other amusement park rides the children might know about and enjoy. Ask if anyone has been on any of these rides.
- Suggest that the children pretend to be on a Ferris wheel while they repeat each line of the following chant after you say it and imitate your actions as you pantomime the actions in each line. (The chant is similar to "Going on a Bear Hunt.")

    Going on the Ferris Wheel by Sharon Lynch
    Going on the Ferris wheel.
    Okay. Okay.
    Let's go.
    Climb in the swing.
    Put on the seat belt.
    Lock the seat belt.
    Let's go.
    Now we're going up.
    Now we're going higher.
    Now we've stopped.
    It's very high up here.

Review

Show the children a picture of an amusement park and ask them which ride or rides they like best.

Assessment Strategy

Have the children tell a group story about going to an amusement park. Write their group story on a chart tablet. Tape a picture of an amusement park beneath the story. Provide each child with an opportunity to tell you about the amusement park and to "read" the story.

We're swinging in the wind.
Everyone looks so little down there on the ground.
I'm scared.
Now we're going down.
Now we're going up.
Now we're going fast.
Now we're slowing down.
Now we've stopped.
Unlock the swing.
Take off the seat belt.
Get on the ground.
Okay! Let's do it again!

■ If appropriate, repeat with other amusement park rides.

Accommodations/Modifications

Autism—Provide the child with pictures and objects to refer to as you talk about them.

Speech or Language Impairments—During the review and assessment strategy, provide picture cues. Invite the child to make picture choices. Scaffold the child's language by giving verbal choices and modeling appropriate responses.

Hearing Impairments—Use pictures and objects for the child to refer to as you conduct the lesson.

Visual Impairments—Let the child hold a toy Ferris wheel as you talk about it.

Cognitive and/or Developmental Delays—Allow the child to use objects and pictures to make choices during the review and assessment strategy.

Emotional Disturbance—Seat the child next to you during the lesson.

Other Health Impairments/Attention Deficit Hyperactive Disorder—Ensure that you have the child's attention before giving the instructions during the review and assessment activity.

Orthopedic Impairments—The child may need help to perform the actions associated with "Going on the Ferris Wheel."

Curriculum Connections

■ **Art**— Provide paper, tissue paper, rickrack, markers, and crayons so the children can decorate a mural for the wall with a Ferris wheel on it.

■ **Language and Literacy**—With the children, practice reading the group story that the class developed. Send home a copy for the children to read with their families.

■ **Math**—Count the number of swings on the Ferris wheel using a toy Ferris wheel or a picture of one.

Beach Fun

Time

15–20 minutes

Materials

- Beach ball, sunglasses, sunscreen, beach hat, pail and shovel, beach towel, mask and flippers
- Picnic basket
- Pictures of things found at a beach and pictures of things found elsewhere

Objectives

Children will:

1. Describe activities associated with a beach.
2. Learn about things you find at the beach.

Lesson

- During Group or Circle Time, show the children a beach ball and see if they can guess the topic of the day. Introduce additional items associated with the beach until someone guesses that you are going to talk about the beach.
- Explain that you are going to take a pretend trip to the beach. Take out the picnic basket and ask the children what they want to take in the basket for dinner. Pretend to pack each item as the children name it, and encourage them to imitate you as you pack the basket.
- Then say the following chant. Ask the children to repeat each line after you say it and to pretend to drive to the beach. The chant is similar to "Going on a Bear Hunt."

Going to the Beach by Sharon Lynch
Let's get in the car.
Put in the picnic basket.
Start the car.
Drive down the highway.
I smell the ocean. (or lake, if that is more appropriate for your area)
I see the birds.
I see the beach.
Let's stop the car.
Let's get out.
Yeah! We're at the beach!

Review

Lie down and say, "I am tired. We had fun at the beach. What did we do at the beach?" After the children describe things you did at the beach, affirm them and ask the class what else we did at the beach. Finally, say, "It was fun at the beach, but I am tired. Now I am going to sleep." (Pretend to sleep.)

Assessment Strategy

Using pictures of things found at a beach and things found elsewhere, ask each child to find the things she might see at the beach. Encourage her to tell you about each item.

- Ask the children what they would like to do at the beach.
- Pantomime each suggested activity. Suggestions include building a sandcastle, swimming, digging in the sand, catching fish, and going for a walk.

Accommodations/Modifications

Autism—Provide clip art or Picture Communication Symbols to refer to items during the lesson and to let the child know the sequence of events during the lesson.

Speech or Language Impairments—Call on the child after other children have modeled appropriate responses. Provide verbal choices when asking the child to respond during the discussion.

Hearing Impairments—Use gestures, pictures, and objects for the child to refer to during the discussion.

Visual Impairments—Describe objects found at the beach as you present them. Allow the child to hold the objects you refer to.

Cognitive and/or Developmental Delays—Provide objects and pictures to allow the child to make a choice during the lesson. During the assessment activity, invite the child to select the objects found at the beach from groups of two to three cards.

Emotional Disturbance—Seat the child near you during the discussion.

Other Health Impairments/Attention Deficit Hyperactive Disorder—Be sure that you have the child's attention before beginning the discussion, giving instructions, and asking questions.

Orthopedic Impairments—Some children may need physical assistance to imitate your motions during the picnic basket portion of the lesson.

Curriculum Connections

- **Art**—Provide sponges cut into star shapes. Encourage the children to dip the star shapes into school glue to make star stamps on blue paper. Dust with playground sand to make starfish.
- **Language and Literacy**—Read the story *Just Grandma and Me* by Mercer Mayer or *Five Little Sharks Swimming in the Sea* by Steve Metzger. Provide copies of the books in the Book Center.
- **Math**—Provide shells for sorting and counting in the Math Center.
- **Science**—Place a magnifying glass or a stationary microscope in the Science Center with things from the beach, such as sand, shells, and other objects.
- **Social Studies**—Provide a map of your area highlighting a path to the nearest beach.

Swimming Pools

Time
15–20 minutes

Materials
- Tote bag with swimsuit, towel, sandals
- Swimming pool pictures
- Crayons, markers, chalk
- Paper

Objectives
Children will:
1. Describe a swimming pool.
2. Describe what they can do in a swimming pool.

Lesson
- If possible, plan a trip to a swimming pool. If you are not able to take a trip to a pool, set up a small wading pool for the children to take turns in. Introduce the idea of a swimming pool by showing a tote bag with a bathing suit, sandals, and a towel in it.
- If you are going to a pool, ask the children to guess where you are going. If they guess that you are going swimming, tell them you are going to a pool. If you are using a small wading pool, tell the children that there is a wading pool set up outside.
- Show the children pictures of different kinds of swimming pools. Be sure to include small backyard pools as well as large swimming pools. Ask them to tell you how the pools are the same and how they are different.
- Sing the following song several times, encouraging the children to sing along.

    We're Going to the Swimming Pool by Sharon Lynch
    (Tune: "London Bridge")
    We're going to the swimming pool, swimming pool, swimming pool.
    We're going to the swimming pool, swimming pool, swimming pool.
    When it's hot and sunny.

- Show the children pictures of activities at a swimming pool, such as diving, swimming, jumping, splashing, and so on. Talk about each activity.
- Ask the children what they like to do at a swimming pool. Examples of activities include swimming, sliding, jumping, splashing, and diving.

Accommodations/Modifications
Autism—Provide picture choices for the child to refer to during the discussion.

Speech or Language Impairments—Scaffold language by providing verbal choices or allowing the child to complete sentences during discussion. Call on the child after others have modeled responses.

Review

Show the tote bag with the swim suit and pictures of activities at a swimming pool. Ask the children their favorite thing about a swimming pool.

Assessment Strategy

Have the children use crayons, markers, or chalk to draw pictures of swimming. Write their descriptions on the back of their pictures.

Hearing Impairments—Use gestures, pictures, and objects as you present the lesson.

Visual Impairments—Provide verbal descriptions of activities at a swimming pool.

Cognitive and/or Developmental Delays—Provide hand-over-hand assistance with drawing, if needed.

Emotional Disturbance—Seat the child near you during the discussion of swimming pools.

Other Health Impairments/Attention Deficit Hyperactive Disorder—Ensure that you have the child's attention before giving instructions for the assessment activity. Have the child repeat the instructions to you.

Orthopedic Impairments—Use a crayon holder and nonskid matting under the paper during the assessment activity.

Curriculum Connections

- **Art**—Encourage the children to crumble small pieces of blue tissue paper and glue them on paper to make a swimming pool.
- **Language and Literacy**—Write a group story on chart paper to tell about your trip to the swimming pool. Write each child's description of the trip on lined paper. Copy the story and each child's description and send them home for each child to read with his family.
- **Math**—Count the steps leading in the swimming pool or the number of steps you take before you jump into the water.
- **Science**—Remind the children not to drink the water in a swimming pool. It smells the way it does because it has a chemical called *chlorine* in it. Chlorine prevents germs from growing in the water, but it is not good for us to drink.

A Trip to the Lake

Time
15–20 minutes

Materials
- Lake-related object, such as a towel, a fishing pole, water mask or goggles, a toy boat
- Large paper bag
- Pictures of a lake
- Chart tablet and marker
- Blue paper
- Markers, crayons, and other art materials

Objectives
Children will:
1. Describe a lake.
2. Learn several things to do and see at a lake.

Preparation
Before the children arrive, place the lake-related objects in a large paper bag.

Lesson
- Tell the children you will be talking about a place people like to go when they are on vacation.
- One at a time, take the lake-related objects out of a bag, such as a towel, a fishing pole, water mask or goggles, and a toy boat. Ask the children to guess the topic of the day. Remind them that it is a someplace people might go for a vacation.
- Give clues and continue presenting objects until someone guesses that you will be talking about going to a lake. If no one can guess, then say the word *lake*, one sound at a time (*l-a-k*), and ask them to say the sounds quickly to see what word you get.
- Show the children a picture or pictures of a lake and ask the children to describe what they see in the pictures.
- Talk about the things you can do at a lake: fish, swim, wade, ride in a boat, or watch the sun go down.
- Ask if any of the children has visited a lake. Invite them to tell about it.

Let's All Go to the Lake Today by Sharon Lynch
(Tune: "Here We Go 'Round the Mulberry Bush")
Let's all go to the lake today, lake today, lake today.
Let's all go to the lake today
Where we can swim in the water. (pretend to swim)

Let's all go to the lake today, lake today, lake today.
Let's all go to the lake today
Where we can go on a boat ride. (pretend to drive a boat)

Let's all go to the lake today, lake today, lake today.
Let's all go to the lake today
Where we can all go fishing. (pretend to fish)

Review

Ask the children to describe the things to see and do at a lake. Write their responses on a chart tablet.

Assessment Strategy

Give each child a piece of blue paper to use as a lake. Provide markers, chalk, and objects, such as toothpicks and straws. Invite each child to draw or put what she likes in the lake. Ask each child to tell about her lake, as well as the things she put in her lake. Display the lake pictures in the classroom.

Accommodations/Modifications

Autism—Provide pictures, objects, clip art, or gestures during the lesson to give the child a visual reference to your discussion. After the review, go over the responses that you have written on the chart tablet multiple times.

Speech or Language Impairments—Say the words to the song several times to give the child practice saying the words before you sing it. During the review, provide a carrier phrase to get the child started. For example, "At the lake I can …"

Hearing Impairments—Seat the child across from you where she can see your face and mouth. Refer to pictures and objects as you offer verbal explanations.

Visual Impairments—Let the child feel the items as you present them to introduce the lesson. Describe the picture of the lake. Describe your actions as you sing the song.

Cognitive and/or Developmental Delays—Use simple sentences and vocabulary in your explanations during the lesson. When asking the child to draw or put objects in the lake, make suggestions using a forced-choice format: "Should you put a cow or a fish in the lake?" "Should you put a boat or a train in the lake?" Be aware that some children will answer with the last item you name, so alternate the position of the correct response.

Emotional Disturbance—Have the child sit next to you during the lesson. Affirm her for participating. Have the child place the items in a "finished" box after you display them.

Other Health Impairments/Attention Deficit Hyperactive Disorder—Make sure you have the child's attention before you speak. Have the group stand to sing the song "Let's All Go to the Lake Today."

Orthopedic Impairments—This child may need assistance in making the motions to the verses in the song "Let's All Go to the Lake Today." For the art activity in the assessment, physically help the child make the items that go in a lake.

Curriculum Connections

- **Art**—Make a classroom mural with a lake. Have the children make pictures of things they find at a lake for the mural.
- **Language and Literacy**—Provide books that include pictures and topics that involve lakes. Suggested books include *Swine Lake* by James Marshall, *We're Going on a Lion Hunt* by David Axtell, *Cazaremos un Leon* by David Axtell (Spanish version), and *All Night Near the Water* by sky.
- **Math**—Provide a set of ducks for the children to use in the water table. Count the ducks and line them up from biggest to smallest if they are varied in size; sort the ducks by color if they are varied in color.
- **Social Studies**—Provide a map of your area; point out the lakes that are in blue on the map.

A Trip to the Country

Time

15–20 minutes

Materials

- Pictures of things found in the country and in the city
- *Night in the Country* by Cynthia Rylant

Objectives

Children will:

1. Describe things or activities associated with the country.
2. Identify activities associated with the country.

Lesson

- Show the children pictures of things found in a city, such as tall buildings, apartments, and city buses. Talk about the fact that most people live in cities. In the city there are tall buildings, many stores, and apartments and neighborhoods where people live.
- Show a picture of country scenes, such as a farm, fields, forests, as well as pictures of animals found in the country, such as deer, bear, and cattle. Talk about the fact that some people live outside of the city; we often say that they live out in the country.
- Tell the children that sometimes people who live in the city visit the country when they are on vacation, or on the weekend. Some people visit family members who live in the country.
- Show the pictures of the country scenes again and ask if anyone has visited the country. If so, ask what they did in the country.
- Read *Night in the Country* by Cynthia Rylant. Talk about the sounds that can be heard in the country.

Accommodations/Modifications

Autism—If the child is not able to answer questions during the lesson and review, provide verbal cues and pictures to help him respond.

Speech or Language Impairments—During the review, call on the child after others have modeled responses. During the assessment, leave pictures in sight when you ask the child to tell you about the country.

Hearing Impairments—Refer to the pictures to demonstrate the concepts of city and country. Have the child sit across from you during the lesson so he can see your face and mouth.

Visual Impairments—Describe the pictures as you show them to the class, as well as when you read the book, *Night in the Country*. Describe your actions as you perform them. For the assessment, describe for the child which picture you are holding, and ask him if it goes with the city or with the country.

Review

Show the children a variety of pictures, some of city scenes and some of country scenes. Examples include pictures of shopping malls, tall buildings, highways with many cars, apartments, fields of cattle, fields with crops, narrow roads with no cars, a pond with frogs and snakes. Ask the children to tell you about the pictures. If they do not state that the item is found in the country or city, ask them whether the picture is a country scene or a city scene.

Assessment Strategy

Ask each child to sort the pictures you used in the review into city and country pictures. Ask each child to tell you about the country.

Cognitive and/or Developmental Delays—For the assessment, present the pictures one at a time and model several responses. Then ask the child to sort the pictures into city and country pictures, presenting them one at a time.

Emotional Disturbance—Seat the child near you to monitor his activities. Affirm him for being helpful and attentive.

Other Health Impairments/Attention Deficit Hyperactive Disorder—Be sure that the child is looking at you before giving him instructions. Establish a signal for "look" such as a raised finger.

Orthopedic Impairments—The child may need help sorting the pictures into piles during the assessment activity.

Curriculum Connections

- **Language and Literacy**—Place books about the country in the Book center. Suggestions include *Lucy Goes to the Country* by Joseph Kennedy; *The Country Mouse and the City Mouse* by Patricia Scarry; *Town Mouse, Country Mouse* by Jan Brett; and *Night in the Country* by Cynthia Rylant.
- **Math**—Count sets of small plastic frogs, snakes, and insects. Talk about which group has the most or the least. Make a graph by lining up the items on lined poster board.
- **Science**—Provide small plastic frogs, snakes, and insects in the Science Center for the children to sort into piles.
- **Social Studies**—Provide a map of your area of your state. Talk about the locations of cities and where the country is in your state.

Camping

Time

15–20 minutes

Materials

- Sticks
- Red tissue paper
- Pictures of different places people camp, such as the woods, a lake, the beach, the mountains

Objectives

Children will:

1. Describe activities associated with camping.
2. Describe places where they would like to camp.

Preparation

In the Group or Circle Time area, build a "campfire" made of sticks and pieces of red tissue paper.

Lesson

- Explain to the children that you will be talking about camping today, and that one thing that people do when they camp is to build a campfire.
- Talk about things people do when they sit around a campfire, such as sing songs, get warm, roast marshmallows. Sing a few campfire songs around the campfire. Suggestions include "I Love the Mountains," "The Ants Go Marching," "The Bear Went over the Mountain," "Boom, Boom, Ain't It Great to Be Crazy?" and "Shoo, Fly."
- Ask if anyone in the class has gone camping. Ask what they did when they went camping.
- Explain that when people camp, they stay outside for a few days or even weeks so they can enjoy the outdoors. Where do people camp? Some places include in the woods, at a park, at the beach, at the lake, and in the mountains. If possible, show the children pictures of different places where people camp.
- If appropriate, ask the children other questions about camping:
  - Where do people sleep when they camp? (They sleep in a tent, camper, or cabin; most sleep in a sleeping bag.)
  - How do people cook when they camp? (They cook over a fire or over a camp stove.)
  - What do people do when they camp? (They go hiking, fishing, or swimming.)
- Sit around the pretend campfire. Sing the children's favorite songs, and then chant the following with them. Ask the children to repeat each line after you say it.

We're Going Camping Now by Sharon Lynch

We're going camping now.
We're going to the _____ (lake).
We're going camping now.
We'll sleep in a _____ (tent).

We're going camping now.
We're going to the _____ (lake).
What will we do at the _____ (lake)?

Review

Show the children pictures of different places to camp and have the children say what they would do at each place.

Assessment Strategy

Provide pictures that can be answers to the following questions: Where do you want to camp? What will you do there? Where will you sleep? Ask each child to select a picture that would answer each question and then line up the pictures to tell a story about camping.

- At the end of the chant, children say what they will do at the lake.
- Repeat with other places, such as the mountains, the woods, the beach, or a park.

Accommodations/Modifications

Autism—Let the child participate in the discussion using clip art or Picture Communication Symbols depicting places where people camp and things they do there.

Speech or Language Impairments—Call on the child after other children have modeled appropriate responses. Provide verbal models if the child needs them.

Hearing Impairments—Use gestures, pictures, and/or objects to enable the child to follow the sequence of the lesson.

Visual Impairments—Provide objects for the child to touch as you talk about camping. Describe your actions during the activity. Use objects during the assessment activity.

Cognitive and/or Developmental Delays—Provide objects for the child to relate to rather than pictures. During the assessment activity, provide choices for the child to respond to rather than telling the story.

Emotional Disturbance—Seat the child next to you during the lesson.

Other Health Impairments/Attention Deficit Hyperactive Disorder—Make sure you have the child's attention before asking questions and giving instructions during the lesson and assessment activity.

Orthopedic Impairments—The child may need help lining up the pictures during the assessment activity.

Curriculum Connections

- **Art**—Suggest that the children decorate a paper tent. Provide tent-shaped cutouts and have the children decorate them with markers, braid, rickrack, buttons, and other art materials.
- **Dramatic Play**—Place a tent, sleeping bag, "campfire" materials, a mess kit, and a fishing pole to create a Camping Center.
- **Science**—Explain that when you camp outdoors you can see the moon and stars at night. Explain that the moon looks different at different times of the month. Show the children pictures of a full moon, a half moon, and a crescent moon.
- **Social Studies**—Display a state map marked with state parks that allow camping. point out the state parks closest to the school.

Going on a Boat Ride

Time
15–20 minutes

Materials
- Toy boat
- Pictures of a rowboat, a motorboat, ship, and a canoe
- Paper cut into a boat shape
- Markers, crayons, and art materials

Objectives
Children will:
1. Describe three things about going on a boat ride.
2. Describe forms of transportation used in the water.

Lesson
- Show the children a toy boat.
- Explain that boats come in many different sizes. Some are small boats for just a few people and others are large boats for many people. Ask if anyone has ridden in a boat. Some children may have ridden in small boats at amusement parks. Large boats are called ships and they carry many people. On vacations, some people go on a boat ride at a lake, on a river, or at the beach.
- Ask if any of the children have ridden on a boat or a ship.
- Teach the following song to the children.

> **Boat Ride** by Sharon Lynch
> (Tune: "My Bonnie Lies over the Ocean")
> *I want to ride over the ocean.*
> *I want to ride over the sea.*
> *I want to ride down a wide river.*
> *A boat ride is just right for me!*
> *Boat ride! Boat ride!*
> *The water is where I should be, should be.*
> *Boat ride! Boat ride!*
> *A boat ride is just right for me!*

- Show the children pictures of different kinds of boats, including a rowboat, a motorboat, and a canoe.
- Talk about what it is like to go on a boat ride. Explain that people ride on boats in a river, on the sea, or on the ocean. Boats can be used to go from one place to another. Sometimes people stay on a boat for many days.

Accommodations/Modifications

Autism—Provide clip art or Picture Communication Symbols to show the sequence of activities during the lesson.

Speech or Language Impairments—Recite partial sentences that the child can complete during the discussions. During the chant, provide pictures to help the child. If needed, model verbal responses.

Review

Show the children pictures of a rowboat, a motorboat, a canoe, and a ship. Ask them to show you a boat. Ask them, "What is the difference between a ship and a boat?" Talk about going on a boat ride. Ask them, "Where will we go?" or "What will we take with us?"

Assessment Strategy

Provide each child with a cutout of a boat. Ask him to decorate the boat with markers, buttons, rickrack, cut straws, and other art materials. Ask the child to tell you about going on a boat ride. Write his responses on his picture.

Hearing Impairments—Use gestures, pictures, and objects during the lesson activity. Seat the child so he can see your face and mouth.

Visual Impairments—Describe your actions during the lesson and the assessment. Let the child hold and touch objects associated with the pictures throughout the lesson. Describe pictures as you show them. Provide hand-over-hand assistance during the assessment activity.

Cognitive and/or Developmental Delays—Provide hand-over-hand assistance during the assessment activity. You can also provide a boat in a tub of water to make the activity more concrete.

Emotional Disturbance—Seat the child next to you during the lesson.

Other Health Impairments/Attention Deficit Hyperactive Disorder—Let the child touch objects as you talk about them. Make sure you have the child's attention before you give directions for the assessment.

Orthopedic Impairments—Provide hand-over-hand assistance during the assessment activity.

Curriculum Connections

- **Language and Literacy**—Provide books about boats for the book center. Some books might include *Boats on the River* by Peter Mandel; *You Can Name 100 Cars, Trains, Boats and Planes* by Jim Becker; *This Is the Way We Go to School: A Book About Children Around the World* by Edith Baer; *Around the World: Who's Been Here* by Lindsay Barrett George; and *Tattered Sails* by Verla Kay.

- **Math**—Place different types of boats in a water table or tub. Count the number of boats and categorize them as boats or ships.

- **Science**—Explain that the ocean is made of saltwater, and that lakes and rivers are made of fresh water. Dissolve 1 teaspoon of salt in 8 ounces of warm water. Explain that saltwater is not good to drink. Let the children taste a spoon of water and say whether it is saltwater or fresh water.

- **Social Studies**—Show a map of your state or country and point out rivers, lakes, and oceans.

Glossary of Terms

Accommodations—Changing instruction to provide an appropriate way for children with disabilities to access information and demonstrate mastery of skills.

Adaptive Holder/Gripping Device—Any device used to assist a child in gripping or holding a specific object. An example of a gripping device would be the use of Velcro taped to an object and also attached to a child's glove to assist in picking up the object.

ASL—American Sign Language.

Bolsters and Wedges—Devices (similar to pillows and pads) used to support a child in a specific position.

Bubble Wrap Gloves—A technique used to assist children who have tactile defensiveness towards specific objects (often objects that are sticky or gooey). Bubble wrap is cut into two hand shapes that are slightly larger than the child's hands. The two pieces of bubble wrap are taped together on the outer edge, creating loosely fitting mittens to be placed on the child's hands while he is exploring the object. Use caution with bubble wrap gloves as many children who have tactile defensiveness may also resist placement of any object over their hands.

Developmentally Appropriate Practices (DAP)—An orientation toward teaching children that considers their age, individual abilities, needs and interests, and culture when determining what classroom activities should be used with them (often referred to as "best practices").

FM System—An amplification system worn around the neck of a child with a hearing impairment. The teacher wears a microphone that broadcasts to the child's FM receiver.

Forced-Choice Questions—Questions with answers such as true/false or yes/no, or questions in which the teacher offers two or three possible answers, allowing the child to select from a reduced range of options.

Hand-Over-Hand Assistance—The placement of the teacher's hands directly over the child's hands as he or she assists the child with a specific task.

Inclusion Classrooms—Classrooms that include all children, both with and without disabilities.

Impulsive Behaviors—Specific behaviors that occur without direct intention or thought from the child and are often difficult for a child to control.

Lap Pad—Term used to define a weighted pad, such as a bean-filled stocking, that is placed on a child's lap to remind him or her to remain seated.

Modifications—Necessary changes to expected criteria on assessment activities for children with disabilities.

Object Cues—An object, such as a toy or household material, predetermined by the child and teacher, that is used as a prompt to elicit a response from a child.

Peer Assistant—Assigning one child to another to assist the first child, as needed, to complete a specified task or activity.

Peer Modeling—Requesting some children to demonstrate acceptable or appropriate behaviors to other children in the room.

Phonemic Awareness Activities—Classroom activities designed to facilitate children's understanding that letters make sounds.

Picture Communication Symbols—An alternative communication system composed of icons or pictures to assist a child in communicating his or her wants or needs.

Picture Cues—Photograph or picture representations that elicit responses from a child.

Picture Schedule—A representation of the daily schedule through pictures, such as icons or photographs, displayed in the classroom.

Preteach—Teaching a specific skill or concept to an individual child prior to the time when the skill or concept is formally introduced to the class.

Proximity Control—Placing a child within a certain distance from the teacher so the teacher is close enough to intervene as necessary. This distance serves as a reminder to the child of the teacher's presence to help the child maintain appropriate behaviors.

Reinforcement—Use of extrinsic or intrinsic means, such as verbal praise or stickers, to encourage a specific behavior.

Self-Stimulation—Repetitive behavior by a child that causes sensory gratification (sometimes called "stimming").

Scaffold—Method in which someone with more knowledge helps a person with limited knowledge understand a given concept or response by providing a series of cues in order to ensure a correct response.

Sequence Activities—Instruction that helps a child understand the concept of putting objects or events in order.

Tactile Defensiveness—Children with an inability to tolerate touch certain objects or materials, either due to over- or under-reactivity to sensations.

Transition Cues—Any form of cuing (verbal, object, or visual) to prepare a child to move from one activity to another.

Verbal Cue—A spoken prompt that elicits a response from a child.

Visual Cue—An easily identified symbol or physical object that visually prompts a child to respond.

Visual Proximity—Keeping a child within the visual range of the teacher.

Wait Time—The amount of time given to a child for a response. Ample wait time would be based on the child's cognitive ability to plan and make a response.

"Wikki Sticks"—Long pipe cleaner-like manipulatives that have a sticky wax outer coating.

Appendix

Resources

Aigner-Clark, Julie. 2004. *Baby Einstein: The World Around Me, Sky.* New York: Hyperion Books.

Aigner-Clark, Julie. 2003. *Baby Einstein: Who Lives in the Pond?* New York: Disney Press.

Aliki. 1997. *Manners.* New York: HarperCollins.

Aliki. 1989. *My Five Senses.* New York: HarperCollins.

Anholt, Catherine and Laurence Anholt. 2000. *Harry's Home.* New York: Farrar Strauss Giroux.

Asch, Frank. 1994. *The Earth and I.* New York: Macmillan/McGraw Hill.

Baylor, Byrd. 1985. *Everybody Needs a Rock.* Riverside, NJ: Simon & Schuster.

Bedford, David. 2002. *Ella's Games.* Hauppage, NY: Barron's Educational Series.

Berenstain, Stan and Jan Berenstain. 1985. *The Berenstain Bears Forget Their Manners.* New York: Random House.

Berger, Melvin. 1995. *Germs Make Me Sick.* New York: HarperCollins.

Berger, Melvin, G. Berger and J. Rice. 2001. *What Makes an Ocean Wave? Questions and Answers about Oceans and Ocean Life.* New York: Scholastic, Inc.

Brainard, Beth. 1990. *Soup Should Be Seen, Not Heard.* New York: Dell.

Brett, Jan. 1996. *Goldilocks and the Three Bears.* New York: Putnam Publishing Company.

Bryant-Mole, Karen. 1998. *You're a Sports Pro.* Portsmouth, NH: Heinemann Library.

Carle, Eric. 2001. *The Tiny Seed.* Riverside, NJ: Simon & Schuster.

Carle, Eric. 1971. *The Very Hungry Caterpillar.* New York: Penguin.

Cauley, Lorinda Bryan. 1992. *Clap Your Hands.* New York: Scholastic, Inc.

Cole, Joanna. 1991. *This Is the Place for Me.* Scranton PA: Scholastic, Inc.

Coy, John. 2000. *Vroomaloom Zoom.* New York: Crown Books.

Cherrington, Janelle. 1999. *Dirt Is Delightful.* Riverside, NJ: Simon and Schuster.

Curry, Don L., N. Vargas and J. Waddell. 2004. *How Do Your Lungs Work?* New York: Scholastic, Inc.

Curry, Don L., J. Waddell and J. Clidas. 2004. *How Does Your Heart Work?* New York: Scholastic, Inc.

Curtis, Jamie Lee. 1998. *Today I Feel Silly: And Other Moods That Make My Day.* New York: Joanna Cotler.

Dadey, Debbie. 1999. *Goblins Don't Play Video Games.* New York: Scholastic, Inc.

Day, Alexandra. 2000. *Teddy Bears' Picnic.* Riverside, NJ: Simon & Schuster.

dePaola, Tomie. 1982. *Charlie Needs a Cloak.* Riverside, NJ: Simon and Schuster.

Demi, Hitz. 1999. *Kites.* New York: Knopf.

Douglas, Lloyd. G. 2004. *My Hands.* New York: Children's Press.

Emberly, Ed. 1993. *Go Away, Big Green Monster!* Boston: Little Brown & Co.

Ernst, Lisa Campbell. 1995. *Miss Penny and Mr. Grubbs.* New York: Aladdin.

Fleming, Denise. 1993. *In the Small, Small Pond* New York: Henry Holt & Company.

French, Vivian. 1992. *It's a Go-To-The-Park Day.* New York: Simon & Schuster.

Frasier, Debra. 2002. *Out of the Ocean.* New York: Harcourt Brace.

Gans, Roma. 1997. *Let's Go Rock Collecting.* New York: HarperCollins.

George, Lindsay Barrett. 1999. *Around the World: Who's Been Here?* New York: Greenwillow.

Gerth, Melanie. 2001. *Ten Little Ladybugs*. Intervisual Books Inc.

Gomi, Taro. 1997. *My Friends*. New York: Macmillan.

Grace, Will. 2004. *Caterpillar Dance*. New York: Scholastic, Inc.

Gray, Libba Moore. 1999. *My Mama Had a Dancing Heart*. New York: Orchard Books.

Gibbons, Gail. 1999. *Deserts*. New York: Holiday House.

Harrison, Troon. 2001. *The Memory Horse*. Plattsburgh, NY: Tundra Books.

Hall, Kirsten. 2004. *Zoom Zoom Zoom* New York: Scholastic, Inc.

Hall, Zoe. 1996. *The Apple Pie Tree*. New York: Scholastic, Inc.

Havill, Juanita. 1994. *Jennifer, Too*. New York: Hyperion Books.

Hest, Amy. 2003. *You Can Do It, Sam*. New York: Candlewick.

Hoban, Tana. 1987. *I Read Signs*. New York: HarperCollins.

Hoban, Tana. *Look Again*. 1971. New York: Simon & Schuster.

Hoban, Tana. 1997. *Look Book*. New York: HarperCollins.

Hoberman, Mary Ann. 1982. *A House Is a House for Me*. New York: Puffin.

Hodgson, Mona Gansberg. 1999. *I Wonder Who Stretched the Giraffe's Neck*. St. Louis, MO: Concordia Publishing.

Hutchins, Pat. 1995. *What Game Shall We Play?* New York: William Morrow & Company, Inc.

Johnson, Crockett. 1981. *Harold's Trip to the Sky*. New York: HarperCollins.

Kalman, Bobbie. 1997. *Community Helpers A to Z*. New York: Crabtree Publishing Company.

Kalman, Bobbie and Kate Calder. 1999. *Sports from A to Z*. New York: Crabtree Publishing Company.

Kay, Verla. 2001. *Tattered Sails*. New York: Putnam Publishing.

Kirk, David. 1997. *Miss Spider's New Car*. New York: Scholastic, Inc.

Krensky, Stephen. 1999. *Bones*. New York: Random House Children's Books.

Leedy, Loreen. 1999. *Who's Who in My Family*. New York: Holiday House.

Liu, Jae-Soo. 2002. *Yellow Umbrella*. La Jolla, CA: Kane/Miller Publishers.

Marsh, T. J., and Jennifer Ward. 1998. *Way Out in the Desert*. Flagstaff, AZ: Northland Publishing AZ.

Martin, Bill, Jr. 2000. *Here Are My Hands*. New York: Henry Holt & Company.

Martin, Bill, Jr. and John Archambault. 1989. *Chicka Chicka Boom Boom*. New York: Simon and Schuster Books for Young Readers.

McGuire, Leslie. 1993. *Brush Your Teeth, Please*. Pleasantville, NY: Reader's Digest Publishing.

Mora, Pat. 1994. *Listen to the Desert*. New York: Scholastic, Inc.

Murphy, Chuck. 1995. *My First Book of the Body*. New York: Scholastic, Inc.

Parr, Todd. 1999. *This Is My Hair*. Boston: Megan Tingley.

Pfeffer, Wendy. 2002. *Thunder and Lightning*. New York: Scholastic, Inc.

Pfister, Marcus. 1992. *The Rainbow Fish*. New York: North-South Books.

Pledger, Maurice. 1998. *In the Forest*. Berkeley, CA: Silver Dolphin Books.

Prelutsky, Jack. 1998. *The Dragons Are Singing Tonight*. New York: Greenwillow Books.

Raskin, Ellen. *Spectacles*. 1972. New York: Macmillan.

Ripley, Catherine. 2001. *Why? The Best Ever Question and Answer Book About Nature, Science, and the World Around You.* Toronto, Canada: Maple Tree Press.

Rosenberg, Liz. 1993. *Monster Mama.* New York: Philomel.

Ruffins, Reynold. 1979. *My Brother Never Feeds the Cat.* New York: Scribner Book Company.

Schaefer, Lola. 2003. *Arms, Elbows, Hands, and Fingers.* Portsmouth, NH: Heinemann.

Sendak, Maurice. 1964. *Where the Wild Things Are.* New York: HarperCollins.

Shah, Idries. 2003. *The Man with Bad Manners.* Los Altos, CA: ISHK.

Shaw, Charles. G. 1988. *It Looked Like Spilt Milk.* New York: HarperCollins.

Showers, Paul. 2001. *What Happens to a Hamburger?* New York: HarperCollins.

Shulevitz, Uri. 1998. *Snow.* New York: Farrar, Straus, & Girous.

Silverstein, Shel. 1964. *The Giving Tree.* New York: HarperCollins.

Simon, Seymour. 1997. *Mountains.* New York: William Morrow & Company, Inc.

Tafuri, Nancy. 1997. *What the Sun Sees, What the Moon Sees.* New York: Scholastic, Inc.

The Arbuthnot Anthology of Children's Literature. 1976. Glenview, IL. Scott, Foresman and Company.

Thomas, Patricia. 1990. *"Stand Back," Said the Elephant, "I'm Going to Sneeze!"* New York: William Morrow & Company, Inc.

Thompson, Kay. 2000. *Eloise's Guide to Life: Or, How to Eat, Dress, Travel, Behave, and Stay Six Forever.* Riverside, NJ: Simon & Schuster Children's Publishing.

Traditional. *The Elves and the Shoemaker.* 1997. New York: North-South Books.

Traditional. 1998. *The Three Billy Goats Gruff.* New York: HarperCollins.

Twinem, Neecy. 1999. *Peek at a Pond.* New York: Grosset & Dunlap.

Viorst, Judith. 1972. *Alexander and the Terrible, Horrible, No Good, Very Bad Day.* New York: Aladdin Books.

Waber, Bernard. 1975. *Ira Sleeps Over.* New York: Houghton Mifflin.

Wells, Rosemary. 2001. *World Around Us.* New York: Puffin Books.

Williams, Linda. 1988. *The Little Old Lady Who Was not Afraid of Anything.* New York: HarperCollins.

Wilson, Mark. 2003. *Mark Wilson's Complete Course in Magic.* Philadelphia, PA: Running Press.

Yagyu, Genichiro. 1994. *The Holes in Your Nose.* La Jolla, CA: Kane/Miller Book Publishers.

Zepol, Mik. 1992. *Splash in the Ocean!* New York: Harcourt.

Ziefert, Harriet. 1988. *A Clean House for Mole and Mouse.* New York: Scholastic, Inc.

Ziefert, Harriet. 2004. *Noisy Forest!* Brooklyn, NY: Handprint Books.

Zoehfeld, Kathleen Weidner. 1995. *How Mountains Are Made.* New York: HarperCollins.

Big Book Selections

Asch, Frank. 1994. *The Earth and I.* New York: Macmillan/McGraw-Hill.

Bowie, C. W. 1998. *Busy Toes.* Dallas, TX: Whispering Coyote Press.

Carle, Eric. 1987. *The Tiny Seed.* New York: Scholastic, Inc.

Cauley, Lorinda Bryan. 1992. *Clap Your Hands.* New York: Scholastic, Inc.

Ehlert, Lois. 1987. *Growing Vegetable Soup.* San Diego, CA: Harcourt Brace & Company.

Gomi, Taro. 1989. *My Friends.* New York: Scholastic, Inc.

Mora, Pat. 1994. *Listen to the Desert—Oye al desierto.* New York: Scholastic, Inc.

Pellegrini, Nina. 2000. *Families Are Different.* New York: Scholastic, Inc.

Rotner, Shelley and Sheila M. Kelly. 2000. *Lots of Dads.* Glenview, IL: Scott Foresman.

Scholastic. 2000. *Kindergarten Place-High Frequency Reader, Can You See It?* New York: Scholastic, Inc.

Scholastic. 2000. *Kindergarten Place-High Frequency Reader, I Can See.* New York: Scholastic, Inc.

SRA Open Court Reading. 2000. *Machines in Our Garden.* Columbus, OH: McGraw-Hill.

SRA Open Court Reading. 2000. *The Wind.* Columbus, OH: McGraw-Hill.

Tafuri, Nancy. 1997. *What the Sun Sees. What the Moon Sees.* New York: Scholastic, Inc.

Wildsmith, Brian and Rebecca Wildsmith. 1993. *Look Closer.* Orlando, FL: Harcourt.

Zepol, Mik. 2002. *Splash in the Ocean!* Orlando, FL: Harcourt.

List of States by Order of Entry into the Union

1	Delaware	12-07-1787
2	Pennsylvania	12-12-1787
3	New Jersey	12-18-1787
4	Georgia	1- 2-1788
5	Connecticut	1-9-1788
6	Massachusetts	2-6-1788
7	Maryland	4-28-1788
8	South Carolina	5-23-1788
9	New Hampshire	6-21-1788
10	Virginia	6-25=1788
11	New York	7-26-1788
12	North Carolina	11-21-1789
13	Rhode Island	5-29-1790
14	Vermont	3-4-1791
15	Kentucky	6-1-1792
16	Tennessee	6-1-1796
17	Ohio	3-1-1803
18	Louisiana	4-30-1812
19	Indiana	12-11-1816
20	Mississippi	12-10-1817
21	Illinois	12-3-1818
22	Alabama	12-14-1819
23	Maine	3-15-1820
24	Missouri	8-10-1821
25	Arkansas	6-15-1836
26	Michigan	1-26-1837
27	Florida	3-3-1845
28	Texas	12-29-1845
29	Iowa	12-28-1846
30	Wisconsin	5-29-1848
31	California	9-9-1850
32	Minnesota	5-11-1858
33	Oregon	2-14-1859
34	Kansas	1-29-1861
35	West Virginia	6-20-1863
36	Nevada	10-31-1864
37	Nebraska	3-1-1867
	District of Columbia	2-21-1871
38	Colorado	8-1-1876
39	North Dakota	11-2-1889
40	South Dakota	11-2-1889
41	Montana	11-8-1889
42	Washington	11-11-1889
43	Idaho	7-3-1890
44	Wyoming	7-10-1890
45	Utah	1-4-1896
46	Oklahoma	11-6-1907
47	New Mexico	1-6-1912
48	Arizona	2-14-1912
49	Alaska	1-3-1959
50	Hawaii	8-21-1959

Indexes

Index of Children's Books

Index

C

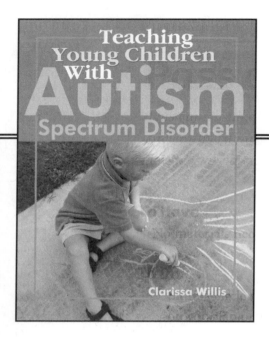

Teaching Young Children With Autism Spectrum Disorder

Clarissa Willis

This book discusses autism in straightforward language. The first two chapters discuss the major characteristics associated with autism, decipher the jargon related to this disability, and help teachers understand the ways children with autism relate to the world. Other chapters focus on setting up a proactive preschool environment, helping children learn life skills, managing behavior, helping children with autism communicate, encouraging children with autism to play, helping children with autism to get along with others, and working with families. Each chapter contains specific strategies for the teacher to use in the classroom. 224 pages. 2006.

Gryphon House / ISBN 978-0-87659-000-0 / 13115

Sensory Integration
A Guide for Preschool Teachers

Christy Isbell and Rebecca Isbell

Do you have a child in your preschool classroom who:

- Climbs on top of furniture and jumps off?
- Covers his ears when children are singing?
- Refuses to touch clay, paint, or sand?

If so, it is possible the child is having sensory processing problems. How can you help children with these problems so they can enjoy learning and grow in positive ways? *Sensory Integration* helps identify children who have difficulties with their sensory processing, and offers teachers simple, easy-to-use solutions to support the sensory needs of young children in the preschool classroom. Easy-to-implement solutions include adaptations and activities for children with different types of Sensory Processing Disorder. 160 pages. 2007.

Gryphon House / ISBN: 978-0-87659-060-7 / 16561

The Inclusive Early Childhood Classroom

Easy Ways to Adapt Learning Centers for All Children

Patti Gould and Joyce Sullivan

Each chapter focuses on adapting either a learning center, such as art or science, or a time of the day, such as snack time or dismissal, with particular attention to the needs of children who are developmentally delayed, orthopedically impaired, have Autism/Pervasive Developmental Disorder, Attention Deficit Hyperactivity Disorder, behavioral issues, motor planning problems, or visual impairments. 208 pages. 1999.

Gryphon House / ISBN 978-0-87659-000-0 / 19652

The Inclusive Learning Center Book

For Preschool Children with Special Needs

Christy Isbell and Rebecca Isbell

The Inclusive Learning Center Book is designed for teachers and directors who work with all young children, both those with special needs and those who are developing typically. The activities in each learning center have suggested adaptations that will help these activities be effective for children with special needs. The last two chapters of the book focus on assessment and evaluation tools and building and creating items for centers that will be especially useful for children with special needs. 320 pages. 2005.

Gryphon House / ISBN 978-0-87659-000-0 / 19357